Barrio Harmonics

Barrio Harmonics
Essays on Chicano/Latino Music

Steven Loza

UCLA Chicano Studies Research Center Press
Los Angeles
2019

CSRC Director: Chon A. Noriega
Senior Editor: Rebecca Frazier
Business Manager: Darling Sianez
Design and Production: William Morosi

Cover image: Detail of a temporary mural painted by Gronk at the Fowler Museum at UCLA in 2010. Photography by Michael Stone. Image copyright 2010 by the Regents of the University of California.

Library of Congress Cataloging-in-Publication Data

Names: Loza, Steven Joseph, author.
Title: Barrio harmonics : essays on Chicano/Latino music / Steven Loza.
Description: Los Angeles : UCLA Chicano Studies Research Center Press, 2019.
    | Includes index.
Identifiers: LCCN 2018047754 | ISBN 9780895511676 (pbk.)
Subjects: LCSH: Popular music--Latin America--History and criticism. |
    Mexican Americans--Music--History and criticism. | Popular music--United
    States--History and criticism.
Classification: LCC ML3475 .L69 2019 | DDC 781.64089/68--dc23
LC record available at https://lccn.loc.gov/2018047754

☒ This book is printed on acid-free paper.

 UCLA Chicano Studies
Research Center
193 Haines Hall
Los Angeles, California
90095-1544
www.chicano.ucla.edu

 Distributed by the University
of Washington Press
PO Box 50096
Seattle, Washington
98145-5096
www.washington.edu/uwpress

CONTENTS

Preface

This collection of essays represents a good amount of my thoughts and writings from 1982 through 2011. The essays deal with the diversity of musical expression of Chicana/os, Mexicans, Cubans, and Latina/os and the intersection of these identities, not to mention their interface with those of other diverse communities. I have titled the volume Barrio Harmonics for, in many ways, it is a sequel to my 1993 book Barrio Rhythm.

The meditations and analyses here thus touch on a variety of topics, ranging from the origins and development of Chicano/Latino forms or styles and their transformations in the United States to observations of these areas through sociocultural analyses of issues such as marginality, identity, intercultural conflict and aesthetics, reinterpretation, postnationalism, resistance, and mestizaje, the mixing of race and culture. In assessing Chicana/o musical expression, I also critique a variety of contexts that represent the music industry, major representative musical artists, the African diaspora, and globalization.

I have selected "Chicano/Latino Music, from the Southwest to the Northeast" as the introductory piece for a practical reason: it sums up much of my work on the musical culture of, generally speaking, the Chicana/o sector in the US Southwest and, in similar terms, that of Latina/os of Caribbean heritage, especially Cuban and Puerto Rican, in the US Northeast. I do recognize that much of the other Latino sectors in the United States are not included in this essay.

Subsequent essays explore the origins of the Cuban *son* (chapter 2), the Mexican *son jarocho* and its transformation in the Southwest (chapter 3), sociocultural issues associated with the diverse musical styles of Chicana/o musicians in Los Angeles (chapter 5), and Latin American styles, specifically salsa, mariachi, and *trio romantico*, as interpreted in Japan (chapter 6). Three of the essays focus specifically on the musical life of individual artists: Lalo Guerrero (chapter 4), Tito Puente (chapter 7, which is from my book on him), and Poncho Sanchez (chapter 8). In chapter 9 I present a historically constructed model incorporating three generational processes that I use to theorize the development of Chicana/o music. The next essay is similar in some sense, but it incorporates a larger global perspective with some specific reference to the music industry. In chapter 11

I examine a theme that has gained speed in recent decades, that of the African legacy in Mexican and thus Chicana/o music, as well as the prolific presence of African American culture in Chicano/Latino life and expression. I end the collection with a relatively recent essay published in the journal *Ethnomusicology* that assesses the daily scholastic grind of living the academic canon and its relationship to intellectual capitalism.

My first published article appeared in 1982 in the Chicano studies journal *Aztlán*. It feels fitting that this retrospective of my work is now published through the same press, that of the UCLA Chicano Studies Research Center, which has continued in a socially significant manner the publication of *Aztlán* to this day. I must thank Juan Gómez-Quiñones, who seemed to see something in the early work of a graduate student in music and accepted his work for publication.

Finally, I would like to give thanks here to those who have been so instrumental in helping me put together this collection. To Chon A. Noriega, director of the UCLA Chicano Studies Research Center, and to Rebecca Frazier, managing editor of the center's publication unit, I am indebted for their interest and loyalty to the project. I also owe much credit to my research assistants for their passionate work on the many details the volume has demanded. These individuals include Dr. Francisco Crespo, Dr. Kathleen Hood, and Galstyan Varazdat.

¡A los musicos!

CHAPTER 1

Chicano/Latino Music, from the Southwest to the Northeast

As statistics of the population of people of Latin American descent in the United States continue to hover in the range of 14 percent or more as of 2006, with 90 percent in urban areas, the musical culture of this sector continues to be as diverse as Latin American culture in general. In order to control the immense possibilities for review and discussion of the rapidly growing identity of this US-based musical culture and its related scholarship, I will structure this essay on the following general categories: I) sectors of Mexican derivation; II) centers of Spanish-speaking Latin Caribbean development; III) contemporary international styles; and IV) the music industry and LARAS (Latin Academy of Recording Arts and Sciences). It should be noted that this very limited framework assumes much diversity within each of its categories and that it cannot, in this limited space of one essay, possibly be comprehensive. I will, however, attempt to portray what I have seen as some of the dominant musical styles, movements, and traditions that are encompassed by the general topic.

Sectors of Mexican Derivation

EARLY HISTORICAL CONTEXTS

Music of Mexican and Spanish origin has existed since the turn of the seventeenth century in the area presently known as the US Southwest and has developed in a diversity of contexts in the states of New Mexico, Texas, Arizona, and California. James K. Leger observes that New Mexicans "possess the longest historical presence of any nonnative people in the United States" (2001, 754). It should also be pointed out that the terms *Mexican* and *Spanish* are somewhat ambiguous, as much of the music must be described as mestizo music, signifying the mixture of race and culture

1

involving four continents—Native America (comprising North and South America), Europe, and Africa—with diverse musical genres that are reflective of specific origins.

With the appointment of Santa Fe as the capital of "Nueva Mejico" in 1610 by colonists who had arrived in 1598 from Mexico, then known as Nueva España and under the dominion of Spain, music in the northern region reflected contemporary practices brought by the mestizo culture from the south in addition to a diversity of ecclesiastic music. The situations in Texas, Arizona, and California were similar to that of New Mexico, although not generally as early. Social institutions of music and dance that developed extensively included the populist eighteenth- and nineteenth-century fandango and the more formal baile. In his book on the Mexican American *orquesta*, Manuel Peña (1999a) presents extensive analysis on the class dichotomy of these two social dance contexts. Whereas the baile was organized by formal invitation, the informal and more class-free fandango gatherings featured a *tecolero*, or master of ceremonies of the dance, who called out each woman for her turn. Improvised song verses were also a feature at fandangos (see Bryant 1936, 409; Loza 1993, 7; Swan 1952, 92).

The mission system in the Southwest is an area in which to observe the musical interaction of the various native Indian cultures of the area. In New Mexico plainchant was sung in the early mission churches and liturgical missals were being printed by the early seventeenth century (Leger 2001). In California the Beneme and Genigucchi Indians sang *alabados* (praise songs) and *benditos* (grace) at the San Gabriel Mission, where "until 1834 the singing of the mass was always accompanied by instruments (such as flutes, violins, and trumpets) that local Indians had been taught to play by missionaries" (Stevenson 1986, 107). Active in the teaching of Western music to the Indian neophytes of the California missions was the Franciscan Narciso Durán (1776–1846), who developed a basic pedagogy to teach church music. Mission choirs composed largely of Indians were developed throughout New Mexico, California, Arizona, and Texas. The mission choirs developed an extensive repertoire, performing an abundance of the plainchant for several masses in addition to the chant of the Proper of the Mass for Sundays and feast days.

A rich Spanish Mexican tradition that continued into the second half of the nineteenth century throughout the Southwest was that of the *pastores* and *pastorelas*. Based on the birth of Christ, these musical dramas depicted the journey of the shepherds to the nativity manger. Pastorelas were often enacted at churches or private homes in conjunction with the *posada*, a social, religious gathering where songs celebrating the Christmas season were sung. The traditions of the pastorela and posada continue to the present, although sometimes in a more formal context. Another intensely rich tradition based on religious belief is that of *los matachines*, which Romero (2003, 81) describes as "a ritual morality dance drama brought by the Spanish, which survives in the southwestern United States and Mexico among Indo-Hispanos and indigenous populations." Romero notes that there are two versions of the matachines dance in New Mexico, the "Spanish" version, accompanied by violin and guitar and performed in both Indo-Hispano and Pueblo Indian contexts, and a version performed in the Jemez and Santa Clara Pueblos, referred to by outsiders as the "drum" version, which features a male chorus accompanied by a drum. Romero has also observed that

> while the dance originates in the Old World and was brought by way of the Spanish, perhaps as early as the sixteenth century, in the New World it has merged with traditional indigenous dances and ideologies in many settings, sometimes so much that it can equally be described as an indigenous dance with only a superficial underlay of the Old World Matachines. (1993, 1)

In New Mexico a rich history of musical expression and dance dating from the seventeenth century has been documented by various scholars, including, among others, Aurelio Espinoza (1985), Arthur Campa (1979), John Donald Robb (1980), Ruben Cobos (1956), Vicente Mendoza and Virginia R. R. de Mendoza (1986), Jack Loeffler (1999), Enrique Lamadrid (1994, 2003), Sylvia Rodriguez (1996), Brenda Romero (1997, 2003), James K. Leger (2001), and Peter J. García (1996).

Romero makes the following observation concerning the Mexican tradition in New Mexico:

> Much of the folk music of the Mejicanos was already old when the Spaniards settled New Mexico in the early seventeenth century. Some of the songs collected here from 1930 to 1960 date back to the twelfth century and some are still older. They represent many different genres, including narrative ballads (*romances*), topical songs (*canciones*), and children's game songs. For centuries, folk singers took out their *cancioneros* (song books) in the evening hours, after the day's farmwork. They entertained themselves and taught songs to their children and relatives in extended family structures. Among those who continue to perform the old music today, this style of musical transmission is much the same as it used to

be. It is not unusual to find similar transmission, from parent to offspring or sibling to sibling, of such nontraditional music as rock and roll, and many local bands reflect kinship ties among members. While the prevalence of older Spanish/Mejicano music has declined since the advent of electricity and the availability of radio and television, traditional Spanish/ Mejicano music is still the musical foundation for many contemporary styles. (1997, 166)

One of the unique elements to have occurred in New Mexico has been the interrelationships between the Mejicano culture and various Native American groups. Native American captives who assimilated the Mexican culture became known as *genízaros*, creating an eventual legacy of mixed and often conflictual identity. With Mexican independence from Spain in 1821, Native Americans were granted full citizenship. Nevertheless, on the level of musical culture, unique hybrid expressions and rituals began to take form, including the phenomenon of the Los Comanches ritual tradition shared by Pueblo and Mejicano groups in New Mexico. The Comanche, a Native American group of the southern plains traditionally called the *numunuh*, had contact, much of it conflictual, with Pueblo Native Americans and the Mexicans in the area of New Mexico. These conflicts and other relationships are enacted in the Comanche ritual dramas that incorporate substantial musical expression (see Lamadrid 2003). Another form that represents the juxtaposition of Mexican and Native American culture is that of the *indita*, which developed significantly during the nineteenth century in Mexico, including New Mexico. The form is based on a *son* type of rhythm, alternating 2/4 and 3/4 meters and melodically imitating what Mexican musicians perceived as indigenous-sounding songs. The texts also often referred to themes based on the indigenous population. The transcription below (example 1) is a fragment of an indita, "La jeyana," sung for the San Luis Gonzaga dancers of San Acacio, originally a Spanish settlement on the Rio Grande in central New Mexico. San Luis Gonzaga was a young seventeenth-century Italian Jesuit saint and patron of devotional and social dance. The indita is characterized by sung "vocables" common among Native American music and chant and devotional dances reminiscent of those of the Pueblo Indians (Lamadrid 2003, 88–89). Noting the contemporary stylization of the traditional melody, Lamadrid notes that "although there are many more lyrics sung for San Luis, the most poignant for this young singer is the verse 'Dicen que las golondrinas de un volido pasan el mar' (They say the swallows cross the ocean in one flight), a symbolic reference to the Iberian diaspora" (137–38).

4

Example 1: "La jeyana"

Ana jeyana
Ana jeyana
Ana jeyana
Yo jeyana
Yo jeyana yo
Ana jeyana, jeyana
Ana jeyana, je yo
Ana jeyana, jeyana
Ana jeyana, je yo.
Dicen que las golondrinas de un volido
Pasan el mar.
Dicen que las golondrinas de un volido
Pasan el mar.

On yet another regional front in the Southwest, it was during the early twentieth century, between 1904 and 1912, that writer and photographer Charles F. Lummis produced a collection of sound recordings of Mexican folksongs. They were originally recorded on 340 wax cylinders but have been rerecorded on magnetic tape and are cataloged and housed at the Southwest Museum in Los Angeles. These may be the first sound recordings of Mexican American folksongs in California. Although most of the collection was not widely disseminated, Lummis did publish fourteen of the songs in 1923 (transcribed by Arthur Farwell) in *Spanish Songs of Old California*.

THE BORDER CONTEXT AND INTERCULTURAL CONFLICT

Perhaps the musical forms that took strongest root throughout the Southwest, especially during the late nineteenth and early twentieth centuries, were the *canción mexicana* (eventually evolving as the ranchera) and the corrido. Numerous studies have been done on these genres, but the work of Américo Paredes (1958, 1995) stands out, especially in terms of his lucid observations of the issues of identity and conflict embodied in the song or ballad repertoire. His reference to this corpus of music as the "Greater Mexican folksong" is especially significant in that it ties contemporary Mexican culture to the former Mexican territory taken by the United States in the Mexican-American War of 1846–48 (1995, xiv). Paredes determined that the most salient theme of the corridos that he studied was that of intercultural conflict, a theory that he nurtured throughout his analyses of the ballads of the Texas-Mexico border, the Southwest, and other sectors of the United States. In Texas, he perceived the consistent theme of conflict between the two dominant groups, the Anglo-Americans and the Chicanos, and he describes sixty-six folksongs of the lower Texas-Mexico border (Paredes 1995).

Manuel Peña, a student of Paredes who has perhaps written more on Chicano music than any other scholar, wrote seminal studies of the music of Texas Mexicans, specifically that of the conjunto and orquesta ensemble styles (1985a, 1985b). Adapting a Marxist framework, Peña observed not only the class divisions between the Mexicans and Anglos but also the conflicts at work within the Texas-Mexican, or Tejano, community itself. Among his many significant conclusions is that "the symbolic structure(s) of conjunto and orquesta reflect the state of flux in which Chicano society is maintained" (1982, 284–85).

Paredes and Peña both provide lucid musical examples and analysis in their various bodies of work. Paredes, in fact, wrote a complete book, *"With His Pistol in His Hand,"* based on a ballad that is based on the experience of a Texas-Mexican, Gregorio Cortez, whose experience with the Texas legal system became a legendary epic among Mexicans in the United States and was also made into a corrido. In his *A Texas-Mexican Cancionero*, Paredes notes that "Gregorio Cortez" (example 2) is without a doubt the epitome of the border corrido, with the hero "betrayed into the hands of his enemies" (1995, 31). Paredes comments on the origin of the Mexican corrido, which in part evolved from the Spanish *romance*, speculating that the earliest corridos could have emerged in the northern border area of Mexico and the United States. He cites the "El corrido de Kiansis" (Kansas) as the "oldest Texas-Mexican corrido that we have in complete form" (25) and as having been sung since the 1860s. Paredes notes that there is intercultural conflict in "Kiansis" even at this early date, but it is expressed in professional rivalries rather than in violence between men (see example 3).

Example 2: "Gregorio Cortez"

En el condado de El Carmen
miren lo que ha sucedido,
murió el Cherife Mayor,
quedando Román herido.

En el condado de El Carmen
tal desgracia sucedió
murió el Cherife Mayor,
no saben quién lo mató.

Se anduvieron informando
como media hora despúes
supieron que el malhechor
era Gregorio Cortez.

Ya insortaron a Cortez
por toditio el estado,
que vivo o muerto se aprehenda
porque a varios ha matado.

Decía Gregorio Cortez
con su pistola en la mano:
"No siento haberlo matado,
lo que siento es a mi hermano."

Decía Gregorio Cortez
con su alma muy encendida:
"No siento haberlo matado,
la defensa es permitida."

Venían los americanos
más blancos que una amapola,
de miedo que le tenían
a Cortez con su pistola.

Decían los americanos,
decían con timidez:
"Vamos a seguir la huella
que el malhechor es Cortez."

Soltaron los perros jaunes
pa' que siguieran la huella,
pero alcanzar a Cortez
era seguir a una estrella.

Tiró con rumbo a Gonzales
sin ninguna timidez:
"Síganme, rinches cobardes,
yo soy Gregorio Cortez."

Se fue de Belmont al rancho,
lo alcanzaron a rodear,
poquitos más de trescientos,
y alli les brincó el corral.

Cuando les brincó el corral,
según lo que aquí se dice,
se agarraron a balazos
y les mató otro cherife.

Decía Gregorio Cortez
con su pistola en la mano:
"No corran, rinches cobardes,
con un solo mexicano."

Salió Gregorio Cortez,
salió con rumbo a Laredo,
no lo quisieron seguir
porque le tuvieron miedo.

Decía Gregorio Cortez:
"¡Pa' qué se valen de planes?
No me pueden agarrar
ni con esos perros jaunes."

Decían los americanos:
"Si lo alcanzaos ¿qué hacemos?
Si le entramos por derecho
muy poquitos volveremos."

Allá por El Encinal,
según lo que aquí se dice,
le formaron un corral
y les mató otro cherife.

Decía Gregorio Cortez
echando muchos balazos:
"Me he escapado de aguaceros,
contimás de nublinazos."

Ya se encontró a un mexicano,
le dice con altivez:
"Platícame qué hay de nuevo,
yo soy Gregorio Cortez."

Dicen que por culpa mía
han matado mucha gente,
pues ya me voy a entregar
porque eso no es conveniete.

Cortez le dice a Jesús:
"Ora sí lo vas a ver,
anda diles a los rinches
que me vengan a aprehender."

Venían todos los rinches,
venían que hasta volaban,
porque se iban a ganar
diez mil pesos que les daban.

Cuando rodearon la casa
Cortez se les presentó:
"Por la buena sí me llevan
porque de otro modo no."

Decía el Cherife Mayor
como queriendo llorar:
"Cortez, entrega tus armas,
no te vamos a matar."

Decía Gregorio Cortez,
les gritaba en alta voz:
"Mis armas no las entrago
hasta estar en calaboz'."

Decía Gregorio Cortez,
decía en su voz divina:
"Mis armas no las entrego
hasta estar en bartolina."

Ya agarraron a Cortez,
ya terminó la cuestión,
la pobre de su familia
lo lleva en el corazón.

Ya con ésta me despido
a la sombra de un ciprés,
aquí se acaba el corrido
de don Gregorio Cortez.

"Gregorio Cortez" (English)

In the county of El Carmen, look what has happened;
The Major Sheriff is dead, leaving Roman badly wounded.

In the county of El Carmen such a tragedy took place:
The Major Sheriff is dead; no one knows who killed him.

They went around asking questions about half an hour afterward;
They found out that the wrongdoer had been Gregorio Cortez.

Now they have outlawed Cortez throughout the whole of the sate;
Let him be taken, dead or alive, he has killed several men.

Then said Gregorio Cortez, with his pistol in his hand,
"I don't regret having killed him; what I regret is my brother's death."

Then said Gregorio Cortez, with his soul aflame,
"I don't regret having killed him; self-defense is permitted."

The Americans were coming; they were whiter than a poppy
From the fear that they had of Cortez and his pistol.

Then the Americans said, and they said it fearfully,
"Come, let us follow the trail, for the wrongdoer is Cortez."

They let loose the bloodhounds so they could follow the trail,
But trying to overtake Cortez was like following a star.

He struck out for Gonzales, without showing fear;
"Follow me, cowardly *rinches*; I am Gregorio Cortez."

From Belmont he went to the ranch, where they succeeded in surrounding him,
Quite a few more than three hundred, but he jumped out of their corral.

When he jumped out of their corral, according to what is said here,
They got into a gunfight, and he killed them another Sheriff.

Then said Gregorio Cortez, with his pistol in his hand,
"Don't run, you cowardly *rinches*, from a single Mexican."

Gregorio Cortez went out towards Laredo;
They would not follow him because they were afraid of him.

Then said Gregorio Cortez, "What is the use of your scheming?
You cannot catch me, even with those bloodhounds."

Then said the Americans, "If we catch up with him, what shall we do?
If we fight him man to man, very few of us will return."

Way over near El Encinal, according to what is said here,
they made him a corral, and he killed them another sheriff.

Then said Gregorio Cortez, shooting out a lot of bullets,
"I have weathered thunderstorms; this little mist doesn't bother me."

Now he has met a Mexican; he says to him haughtily.
"Tell me the news; I am Gregorio Cortez."

"They say this because of me many people have been killed;
so now I will surrender, because such things are not right."

Cortez says to Jesus, "At last you are going to see it;
Go and tell the *rinches* that they can come and arrest me,"

All of the *rinches* were coming, so fast that they almost flew,
Because they were going to get the ten thousand dollars that was offered.

When they surrounded the house, Cortez appeared before them:
"You will take me if I'm willing but not any other way."

Then said the Major Sheriff, as if he was going to cry,
"Cortez, hand over your weapons; we do not want to kill you."

Then said Gregorio Cortez, shouting to them in a loud voice,
"I won't surrender my weapons until I am in a cell."

Then said Gregorio Cortez, speaking in his godlike voice,
"I won't surrender my weapons until I'm inside a jail."

Now they have taken Cortez, and now the matter is ended;
His poor family are keeping him in their hearts.

Now with this I say farewell in the shades of a cypress;
This is the end of the ballad of Don Gregorio Cortez.

Example 3: "El corrido de Kiansis"

Cuando salimos pa' Kiansis
con una grande partida,
¡ah, qué camino tan largo!
no contaba con mi vida.

Nos decía el caporal,
como queriendo llorar:

"Allá va la novillada,
no me la dejen pasar."

¡Ah, qué caballo tan bueno!
todo se le iba correr,
¡y, ah, qué fuerte aguacerazo!
no contaba yo en volver.

Unos pedían cigarro,
otros pedían que comer,
y el caporal nos decía:
"Sea por Dios, qué hemos de hacer."

En el charco de Palomas
se cortó un novillo bragado,
y el caporal lo lazó
en su caballo melado.

Avísenle al caporal
que un vaquero se mató,
en las trances del corral
nomás la cuera dejó.

Llegamos al Río Salado
y nos tiramos a nado,
decía un americano:
"Esos hombres ya se ahogaron."

Pues qué pensaría ese hombre
que venimos a esp'rimentar,
si somos del Río Grande,
de los buenos pa' nadar.

Y le dimos vista a Kiansis,
y nos dice el caporal:
"Ora sí somos de vida,
ya vamos a hacer corral."

Y de vuelta en San Antonio
compramos buenos sombreros,
y aquí se acaban cantando
versos de los aventureros.

Kansas (English)

When we left for Kansas with a great herd of cattle,
Ah, what a long trail it was! I was not sure I would survive.

The Caporal would tell us, as if he was going to cry,
"Watch out for that bunch of steers; don't let them get past you."

Ah, what a good horse I had! He did nothing but gallop.
And, Ah, what a violent cloudburst! I was not sure I would come back.

Some of us asked for cigarettes, others wanted something to eat;
And the caporal would tell us, "So be it, it can't be helped."

By the pond at Palomas a vicious steer left the heard,
And the caporal lassoed it on his honey-colored horse.

Go tell the caporal that a vaquero has been killed;
All he left was his leather jacket hanging on the rails of the corral.

We got to the Salado River, and we swam our horses across;
An American was saying, "Those men are as good as drowned."

I wonder what the man thought, that we came to learn, perhaps;
Why, we're for the Rio Grande, where the good swimmers are from.

And then Kansas came in sight, and the caporal tells us,
"We have finally made it, we'll soon have them in the corral."

Back again in San Antonio, we all bought ourselves good hats,
And this is the end of the singing of the stanzas about the trail drivers.

In his book *Música Tejana*, Peña presents diverse examples of both conjunto and orquesta contexts and artists. The instrumentation of the traditional Tejano conjunto is largely characterized by the use of accordion and *bajo-sexto* (a double stringed guitar with both bass and upper register strings). Early conjunto innovators of South Texas included Narciso Martínez, Pedro Ayala, and Santiago Jiménez. Martínez, born in 1911, became known as "el huracán del valle" (the valley hurricane), and many consider him the "father" of conjunto music. Conjuntos of later generations would include those of Valerio Longoria, Tony de la Rosa, Paulino and Eloy Bernal, Mingo Saldívar, Steve Jordan, and Flaco Jiménez. A corrido representing a good portion of conjunto repertoire reflecting the theme of intercultural conflict is "Los rinches de Texas" (The Texas Rangers), composed in response to a series of strikes organized by melon workers and the United Farm Workers in Starr County in South Texas during the summer of 1967.

The *orquesta tejana*, as defined by Peña (1999b), can be traced to origins in the late nineteenth century and evolved having "ready made" models ranging from full symphonic groups to brass bands to minimal string groups both in the United States and Mexico. Thus, the orquesta style was not tied to any particular indigenous innovation, as with the conjunto. Peña notes a particular *bimusical* identity in the orquesta and remarks that "this identity mirrored, at the level of musical expression, the ideological structures underpinning the *bicultural* identity of middle-class Texas Mexicans who forged the orquesta tejana" (119).

Beto Villa, considered by many as the "father" of the orquesta tejana, first recorded in 1947. His style inaugurated what Peña refers to as the "Tex-Mex ranchero" variant of the *polca-ranchera*, becoming "by far the most important stage in the evolution of a Texas-Mexican orquesta. More important, Villa exerted enormous influence over countless epigones, not only in Texas but throughout the Hispanic Southwest" (Peña 1999b, 119). Peña cites the final stage in the orquesta tejana evolution and its political aesthetic to be the style launched during the late 1960s by Little Joe and the Latinaires, renamed Little Joe y La Familia in 1970. A bimusical style was forged thereafter, known as La Onda Chicana, and was imitated by musical groups throughout the Southwest. The style was also often referred to as Tex-Mex.

The conflict of the Mexican experience, as presented above in the case of the Texas-Mexico border area, was also being expressed in other regions of the United States. One example of many relating to Southern California is the classic corrido "El lavaplatos" (The Dishwasher), composed by Jesús Osorio, who recorded the song with Manuel "El Perro" Camacho on the Victor label in 1930. It was later recorded by Los Hermanos Bañuelos during the same year on the Brunswick/Vocalion label and again by Chávez y Lugo on Columbia. Incorporating satire into the expression of an immigrant's illusion and disillusion with the dreams and myths of Hollywood, the song is a tragicomic sociocultural commentary critiquing contemporary life of the era (Loza 1993). Peña cites this particular corrido as a thematically significant one because of its reference to "political and economic issues that were at the heart of the Mexican's subordination in the capitalist Anglo order that reigned over the Southwest by this time" (1989, 67).

Urban Contexts of Tradition and Innovation

In the 1920s and 1930s, musical activity among Mexicans in the Southwest was largely diffused through Spanish-language radio broadcasts. During the mid-1920s recording companies such as Victor, Brunswick, Okeh, and Columbia "began to exploit for commercial gain the musical traditions of Mexicans in California and in the Southwest" (Peña 1989, 67). Genres recorded and marketed included the cancíon mexicana, the corrido, boleros, and huapangos, among others. Instrumentation was frequently based on ensembles such as the trio and the mariachi. The latter had evolved from its rural identity into a larger and more commercialized instrumental format in Mexico, incorporating, by the 1930s, violin, vihuela, guitar, and *guitarrón*, and later the trumpet.

It is the mariachi ensemble that has come to be more associated with Mexican music than any other type of musical group, and it has been extremely popular in the United States since it became the vogue of Mexican radio during the 1930s. As immigration from Mexico to the United States has continuously increased, so has the growth of mariachis. As the most international symbol of Mexican music, thousands of mariachis based in the United States perform at restaurants, clubs, weddings, civil functions, holiday celebrations, and a variety of other occasions. Because of the constant popularity of rancheras and the singers who interpret them, mariachis have been a mainstay of musical accompaniment for that genre in addition to performing the traditional Mexican son, a musical form associated with the origin of the mariachi in the Mexican regions of Jalisco and Michoacán. Artists from Mexico have constantly toured cities in the United States, catering especially to inhabitants of Mexican origin and performing in spectacular shows and venues. Mexican artists accompanied by mariachis and appearing since the 1930s throughout the United States have included such notables as Jorge Negrete, Lucha Reyes, Pedro Infante, José Alfredo Jiménez, Lola Beltrán, Miguel Aceves Mejía, Luís Aguilar, Lucha Villa, Vicente Fernández, Chelo Silva, Juan Gabriel, Rocío Dúrcal, Aida Cuevas, Pepe Aguilar, Alejandro Fernández, and Luís Miguel, among many others.

Highly successful mariachis in the Southwest attaining international recognition have included Mariachi Cobre of Tucson, Arizona; Los Reyes de Albuquerque of New Mexico; Mariachi Campanas de America of San Antonio, Texas; and three based in Los Angeles, California: Mariachi Los Camperos de Nati Cano, Mariachi Sol de México de José Hernández, and Mariachi Los Galleros de Pedro Rey. The latter three mariachis, along with

15

the internationally renowned Mexico City–based Mariachi Vargas de Teca-litlán, recorded and performed extensively with Linda Ronstadt during the period when she was awarded two Grammy awards for her mariachi albums *Canciones de mi padre* (1988) and *Mas canciones* (1991). Ronstadt, born and raised in Tucson and the daughter of a Mexican American, recorded not only mariachi music in Spanish but also other popular and tropical styles. Her involvement in mariachi sparked new interest in the style beginning in the late 1980s, especially among young Mexican American musicians and especially among women musicians, although it must be said that women were already entering the realm of mariachi music in the 1960s. Exclusively female mariachis have especially emerged since the 1990s, exemplified by groups such as Mariachi Las Reynas de Los Angeles, Mariachi Adelita, and Mariachi Feminil 2000. Another highly popular phenomenon has been the great success of mariachi festivals, highlighted by both concerts and mariachi performance classes, in cities including San Antonio, Tucson, Fresno, Los Angeles, and Albuquerque, among numerous others, and school programs throughout the Southwest and other parts of the country have incorporated mariachi classes into their curricula. Daniel Sheehy (1997, 1999) and Candida Jáquez (2003) have conducted extensive fieldwork and published on the mariachi context in the United States.

There have been numerous individual artists who became musical lead-ers and symbolic beacons of hope for the Mexican population throughout the United States. In Texas, Lydia Mendoza attained immense popularity not only in the context of *música tejana* but also throughout the United States and Mexico. Born in Houston in 1916, Mendoza would at times during her youth also live in Monterrey, Mexico, San Antonio, and other Texas locales, and she learned from an early age within her family to sing and perform the guitar. Mendoza would eventually become a major innova-tor in the interpretation and extensive recording of the canción, corrido, bolero, huapango, and other musical forms. Her first solo hit, "Mal hombre," was recorded in 1933 on RCA Victor's Bluebird label, and she eventually recorded on the Falcón, Ideal, RCA Victor, Columbia, and DLB labels, and had great success with the recordings of "Celosa," "Amor de madre," "Joaquin Murrieta," among many others. She is featured in the documen-taries *Chulas fronteras* by Les Blank and *Songs of the Homeland* by Hector Galán. In 1982 she received the National Endowment for the Arts National Heritage Award, and in 1999 she was awarded the National Medal of Arts by President Bill Clinton. A bilingual book, *Lydia Mendoza's Life in Music/La historia de Lydia Mendoza*, was written by Yolanda Broyles-González (2001).

Another individual artist who demands mention is Lalo Guerrero. Born in Tucson in 1916 and raised there in the Mexican neighborhood known as Barrio Libre, he based himself in Los Angeles during his early twenties and established a dynamic musical career as a songwriter, singer, and guitarist, a recording artist, and a music club owner. During World War II he performed for troops as part of a USO tour through different parts of the United States, and he composed songs that became standards in the Mexican repertoire, including "Canción mexicana," recorded by Lucha Reyes in 1940, and "Nunca jamás," recorded by both Trío Los Panchos and Javier Solís. His orchestra recorded extensively and toured throughout the Southwest, performing popular music forms such as boleros, danzones, mambos, and *cumbias,* and he also recorded his own material as a singer with trios, mariachis, and conjuntos norteños. During the 1940s he composed a number of songs related to the pachuco culture of young Chicanos in Los Angeles, adapting the caló slang of Spanish that was popular among them. A number of these songs, including "Vamos a bailar," "Chucos suaves," and "Marijuana Boogie," were adapted by playwright and director Luis Valdez in his musical play *Zoot Suit,* which was made into a major film by Universal Studios in 1982, starring Edward James Olmos and musician and actor Daniel Valdez. Guerrero became highly recognized as a musical satirist who composed songs related to the United Farm Workers movement, immigration, and Chicano culture. Humor is an essential component of his music (e.g., "Pancho López," "There's No Tortillas," "No Chicanos on TV," "No Way José"), and he inspired many younger artists, including Los Lobos, who in 1995 recorded with Guerrero a children's music album, *Papa's Dream,* which was later nominated for a Grammy award. In 1991 Guerrero was awarded a National Heritage Award by the National Endowment for the Arts, and in 1997 he was awarded the National Medal of Arts by President Bill Clinton. Lalo Guerrero is extensively profiled in *Barrio Rhythm: Mexican American Music in Los Angeles* (Loza 1993), and he wrote, with Sherilyn Meece Mentes, his autobiography *Lalo: My Life and Music* (2002).

In the numerous and diverse urban settings of cities throughout the United States, musicians and their followers of Mexican descent have nurtured musical forms reflecting the contradictions of tradition, nationalism, assimilation, innovation, reinterpretation, and hybridization, the latter term reminiscent of the Mexican–Latin American notion of mestizaje, the mixing of race and culture, and the evolutionary process that emerges from such interaction. By the 1950s and 1960s, Chicanos had begun to both assimilate and change "mainstream American" styles, including R&B (rhythm and blues), rock and roll, jazz, disco, punk, and hip-hop.

In an article titled "The View from the Sixth Street Bridge: The History of Chicano Rock," Rubén Guevara, an important contemporary figure in the "Eastside renaissance" of music in East Los Angeles, formulates various theories concerning the development and adaptation of different musical styles and preferences among Mexican Americans in Los Angeles. Guevara's historical perspective traces his own musical life and enculturation in Los Angeles beginning in the 1940s: "In East L.A., as in so many other places, the link between swing and early R&B and rock 'n' roll was jump blues. Jump evolved in the thirties from Harlem bands like those of Cab Calloway and the Kansas City groups of Count Basie and Louis Jordan. In Los Angeles the leading early practitioners were Roy Milton and the Solid Senders" (Guevara 1985, 115). By the end of World War II, Roy Milton had achieved national prominence with his hit "R.M. Blues," recorded on Specialty Records. He was among the many swing artists who became popular among Mexicans in Los Angeles.

The zoot suit era of the 1940s was characterized not only by the popularization of swing but also by an assortment of Latin styles, including the mambo, rumba, and danzón, all Cuban imports, often via Mexico, and Mexican music was also popular among zoot-suiters. Swing and tropical rhythms were more popular among the zoot suit "cult," which adopted particular styles of dress, language (the caló dialect of Spanish previously cited in the music of Lalo Guerrero), music, and dance. Zoot-suiters patronized particular entertainment spots and formed social groups that eventually became known as gangs. Many speculate that the pachuco gang evolved as a defense mechanism in response to the zoot suit riots, confrontations between pachucos and enlisted military men during the period of World War II.

A growing number of blacks were settling in Los Angeles in search of better-paying war industry jobs. The availability of low-rent housing in the Mexican neighborhoods of east and south-central Los Angeles prompted many blacks to settle there. Conversely, as Anglos became economically mobile, they moved away from those neighborhoods. "Blacks and Chicanos, isolated together, began to interact and, in large numbers, they listened to the same radio stations. For instance, there was Hunter Hancock ('Ol' H.H.') on KFVD. He had a show on Sundays called 'Harlem Matinee' that featured records by Louis Jordan, Lionel Hampton, and locals Roy Milton, Joe and Jimmy Liggins, and Johnny Otis," the latter who, as also noted by Guevara, introduced jump blues to Chicanos at Angeles Hall, a club in the eastside Boyle Heights neighborhood of Los Angeles, in 1948 (Guevara 1985, 116).

One of the Chicano bands to emulate the jump blues style was the Pachuco Boogie Boys, led by Don Tosti and featuring Raúl Díaz on vocals and drums, Eddie Cano on piano, and Bob Hernández on saxophone and flute. A local hit emerged from the group's various recordings titled "Pachuco Boogie," which Guevara describes as a "jump style shuffle with either Raul or Don rapping in Caló [pachuco street slang: half Spanish, half English] about getting ready to go out on a date. Very funny stuff" (Guevara 1985, 117). Tosti, whose real name was Edmundo Martínez Tostado and who was originally from El Paso, Texas, came to Los Angeles as a young boy. He performed with the bands of Tommy Dorsey, Charlie Barnett, Les Brown, and Jack Teagarden. He also worked extensively as an arranger for the popular Los Angeles–based Mexican singer Rubén Reyes. Eddie Cano would emerge as a leading exponent of Latin jazz, performing with Miguelito Valdés in New York and eventually leading and recording with his own Latin jazz groups in Los Angeles (profiled in Loza 1993). In the same vein of Latin jazz, another Chicano based in Los Angeles, Poncho Sánchez, who often worked with Cano, would eventually emerge as an internationally acclaimed artist.

In 1952 Hunter Hancock aired an instrumental single titled "Pachuco Hop" by African American saxophonist Chuck Higgins. Hancock later became a disc jockey at KGFJ, the first station to broadcast the music of black artists exclusively, seven days a week. "A massive audience in East L.A. tuned in on each and every one of those days. At about the same time DJs like Art Laboe and Dick 'Huggy Boy' Hugg started playing jump and doo-wop on the radio" (Guevara 1985, 118). Chicano saxophonists Li'l Bobby Rey and Chuck Rio (Danny Flores) emulated the styles of the black saxophonists (in addition to Higgins, Joe Houston and Big Jay McNeely), but also added their own particular Mexican- and Latin-based stylistic idioms. Rio, as a member of the Champs, achieved international attention with his own composition and instrumental hit "Tequila" in 1958. The record rose to the number one spot on the national rating charts and since then has become a world classic.

In his book *The Mexican American Orquesta* (1999a), Peña conceptualizes the orquesta as a musical ensemble much like the orquesta tejana, but as a phenomenon throughout the Chicano Southwest. It should be noted that this conceptualization, especially in regard to the use of the term *orquesta*, is not necessarily universal among Mexican American musicians. Recognizing the influences of the big swing band styles of Duke Ellington and Stan Kenton, in addition to the heavy influx of Afro-Cuban styles of dance music by way of the mambo and cha-cha-cha, in addition to the constant demand for typical Mexican dance music, it is safe to say that there did exist a proliferation of such orquestas throughout the Mexican American Southwest. Peña offers some cross-regional analysis in observing the historical routes of ensembles in Texas, California, and Arizona. In addition to critiquing the orquesta tejana's evolution and its various artists, he offers an ethnographic portrayal of bandleaders in California and Arizona, specifically Don Tosti, Lalo Guerrero, Chico Sesma, and Pedro Bugarín. Of interest are the issues of class and musical aesthetics as related to Tosti and Sesma and their experience with ranchera music. Tosti and Sesma, both formally trained musicians, gravitated much more to the tropical styles of Afro-Cuban music in addition to jazz, while Guerrero represented a diversity that swung from ranchera to boogie to mambo. Other important musicians emerging from East Los Angeles and associated with big band or Latin jazz styles included Andy Russell (Andrés Rabago), Eddie Cano, Paul López, Johnny Martínez, and Rudy Macías (see Loza 1993; Peña 1999a). Another, although younger, artist who emerged from this context is 1999 Grammy-award-winning Poncho Sánchez, who performed as the *conguero* for Cal Tjader (1925–1982) and his Latin jazz ensemble for seven years until Tjader's death. Sánchez was contracted to Discovery Records, for which he recorded his first album as a leader in 1979, and to Concord Records in 1983, for which he continues to record. Sánchez has also experimented with the blend of Afro-Cuban jazz and R&B music, recording various interpretations of the music of one of his early idols, James Brown, and has invited artists such as Tito Puente, Mongo Santamaría, Freddie Hubbard, Dianne Reeves, Chick Corea, and Ray Charles to record on his albums. (For in-depth studies on Sánchez, refer to Loza 1993, 1999, 2001a, 2001b.)

Much attention has been given to what has been referred to as the "Eastside Sound" of Los Angeles (Loza 1993; Reyes and Waldman 1998; L. Rodriguez 1980a, 1980b), produced by the multitude of bands that emerged in East Los Angeles from the early 1960s through the early 1980s, and the dynamic ambience and impact that these groups nurtured during a period of Chicano awakening. Although these R&B, rock-influenced bands largely emulated the pop music of the day, ranging from James Brown to the Beatles and from the Supremes to disco music, it has been argued that there did exist a specific style in their music, and that the sound and experience reflected the bimusical, bicultural context of Mexican Americans, especially those living in large urban areas. Thus, the sound was not limited to Los Angeles, but resonated in San Francisco, San Diego, Phoenix, Tucson, Albuquerque, San Antonio, Houston, and Dallas.

Although not from the Eastside of Los Angeles, Ritchie Valens (Richard Valenzuela), who was raised in the Pacoima barrio of the San Fernando Valley, on the north side of Los Angeles, achieved major stardom in the rock-and-roll music industry. He was promoted by producer Bob Keane, who recorded Valens on his own Del-Fi Records. Certainly "La bamba"—a Mexican folk son jarocho, recorded in Spanish by the seventeen-year-old Valens and an international hit—represented a radical change in the Top 40 music industry. What would have been an even more sensational impact—a Chicano entering the mainstream recording industry—was precluded by the death of Valens in a 1959 plane crash along with rock-and-roll stars Buddy Holly and J. P. "Big Bopper" Richardson. Other hits by Valens included "Donna," "Come On, Let's Go," "That's My Little Suzie," and "Little Girl" (the last two posthumously). Besides Valens, for many years the only other Chicana/o musical artist to achieve a comparable height of fame was Vikki Carr (Victoria Cardona), born in El Paso, Texas, and raised in the San Gabriel Valley of Los Angeles County. Carr had a string of international hits during the 1960s, including "It Must Be Him" and "With Pen in Hand." She would later emerge as a major artist throughout Latin America and Spain, recording new material in Spanish on the CBS International label and receiving Grammy Awards in 1986 and 1992. Another El Paso native who also eventually relocated to Southern California was singer-guitarist Trini López, who attained national and international attention with various recordings on major labels during the 1960s and 1970s with his folk-blues-Mexican hybrid of interpretation.

It was in San Francisco that another dynamic and innovative context nurtured the emergence of bands led by Carlos Santana in addition to others such as Malo, Azteca, Tower of Power, and Cold Blood. Santana literally led a musical revolution with his mixing of Afro-Cuban music, rock, and blues, now universally referred to as Latin rock. His recordings such as "Evil Ways," "Black Magic Woman," "Samba pa ti," "Europa," and "Oye como va" (a Tito Puente composition) transformed the world of popular music. In 1998 Santana was still at the top of pop music radio charts, characterized by his album *Supernatural,* which was awarded a record-setting eight Grammys for that year. The LP sold over 25 million copies, forming a substantial part of Santana's career 80 million. Born in Jalisco, Mexico, raised in Tijuana and San Francisco, and inspired by blues artists such as John Lee Hooker, B. B. King, and Muddy Waters, Carlos Santana represents, along with the California bands in general, the bimusical, bicultural character that epitomizes so much of the musical expression described in this essay.

In the Eastside of Los Angeles, this context was personified through groups such as the Premiers, Thee Midniters, Cannibal and the Headhunters, Li'l Ray Jiménez, El Chicano, and Tierra. Although there were hundreds more bands in the circuit during a twenty-year span, only a few such as those just cited reached popularity beyond Southern California. Cannibal and the Headhunters had a major radio hit in 1965 with "Land of a Thousand Dances," while in 1970 El Chicano recorded the now classic "Viva Tirado," composed by African American jazz bandleader Gerald Wilson, who was married to a Chicana and was highly influenced by Mexican culture. Tierra, featuring brothers guitarist Rudy Salas and lead vocalist Steve Salas, reached unprecedented success among Eastside bands in 1980 with the group's rendition of the Intruders' "Together," which became a platinum record.

An interesting regional parallel to the Eastside Sound of Los Angeles was the music of San Antonio–bred Sunny Ozuna and the Sunglows, who in 1962–63 recorded a major R&B-style ballad that became a national hit. "Talk to Me" achieved gold record status, and the group appeared on Dick Clark's Top 40 television show *American Bandstand*. Ozuna would eventually return to contemporary Tejano music and become a major figure in La Onda Chicana of the 1970s. Leading this movement was the aforementioned Little Joe (José María de León Hernández), who grew up picking cotton and who attended school only through the seventh grade. Learning guitar from friends and relatives, he joined the group David Coronado (his cousin) and the Latinaires. The group recorded its first single, a rock tune titled "Safari," parts 1 and 2. According to Peña (1999b, 153), the recording "is an important milestone in tejano music, because it may well have been the first rock-and-roll tune recorded by a tejano group." Peña adds that "it testifies to the intensive assimilation of popular American music taking place among Mexican American youth throughout the Southwest." In 1959 Little Joe assumed leadership of the Latinaires, which developed a stylistic feature—that of the polca-ranchera (a ranchera in polka tempo), with vocal duets sung in the traditional ranchera harmony of parallel thirds. Johnny Hernández, Little Joe's brother, accompanied the latter's voice and their harmonic blend began to personify the group sound and a new Tejano direction. In 1969 Little Joe change the name and concept of the band from the Latinaires to Little Joe y La Familia, and Peña notes that "by 1970, the aesthetic transformation was complete—new fashions and hairstyles (hippie/militant Chicano), a new name, a countercultural lifestyle that included drugs (principally marijuana), and for Little Joe at least a drift toward the ideology of *chicanismo* (1999b, 164). Launching La Onda Chicana to its next stage, Little Joe y La Familia recorded the LP *Para la gente* on Little Joe's own Buena Suerte Records label. The album became a hit throughout the Chicano Southwest, and one of the tracks, "Las nubes," became a virtual anthem of the Chicano generation (167). Stylistically, the arrangement of "Las nubes" included a brass section, electric guitar, electric bass, Hammond organ, trap set, and a string section. Peña notes that "the horn obbligato inserted between the vocal phrases maintain a steady barrage of jazz-oriented licks in what amounts to a constant code-switching between Mexican and an American musical 'language' (ranchero and swing-jazz)" (168). Little Joe y La Familia continued to record LPs in a similar vein throughout the 1970s. In 1985 Little Joe signed a contract with CBS Records, and in 1991 he received a Grammy Award for his album *16 de septiembre*. In 1992 he incorporated another record label of his own, Tejano Discos. His recordings, over a million sold, have been distributed throughout the United States, Latin America, Asia, and Europe.

La Onda Chicana was also represented in New Mexico through the music of Al Hurricane in a similar yet somewhat different style. Leger (2001, 765) refers to Al Hurricane (Alberto Sánchez) as "the most influential New Mexican Hispano musician of the second half of the twentieth century." Along with his brothers Tiny Morrie (Amador Sánchez) and Baby Gaby (Gabriel Sánchez), Al Hurricane began a rock-and-roll group in the 1950s, and in the 1960s he recorded the popular Mexican ranchera "La mula bronca," which became a hit in the Southwest and Mexico. His groups have since concentrated on a contemporary style of Spanish language music, especially arrangements of the ranchera and ensembles featuring guitar, electric bass, and a horn section. The style is similar to that of Little Joe y La Familia, Sunny Ozuna, and other Tejano groups of La Onda Chicana.

CONTEMPORARY CHICANO MUSICAL EXPRESSION

The short-lived story of Selena (Selena Quintanilla-Pérez) is not so different from that of the stardom-tragedy paradox of Ritchie Valens. Born in 1971, she began singing professionally at an early age and led her own group, Selena y los Dinos, with her sister Suzette at the age of eleven. Although she developed within the Tejano musical tradition, she eventually began to record a more international style of pop and became highly successful internationally, winning several Tejano Music Awards and a Grammy. She was contracted by one of the major record labels, Capitol/EMI, in 1989. Her top-selling album was *Amor prohibido*, released internationally in 1994. She also recorded extensively in English, also attaining great success, and was attempting to develop a larger crossover style and market when she was tragically murdered in 1995 by one of her business employees. A major film, *Selena* (1998), directed by Gregory Nava, was produced shortly after her death, starring actors Jennifer Lopez and Edward James Olmos. In addition to Selena, other contemporary Tejano artists representing a period that Peña (1999a) refers to as the post-Chicano era include El Grupo Mazz, La Mafia, and Emilio Navaira.

Los Lobos is a group that defies categorization, yet in many ways it fits into most of the categories overviewed in this section on the musical culture of Mexican derivation in the United States. Originally organized as high school colleagues out of Garfield High School in East Los Angeles and named Los Lobos del Este de Los Angeles, the young group began by performing Mexican and other Latin American folk music, and they developed a strong following in the Eastside of Los Angeles during the early years of the Chicano movement. Their first album, produced by Luis Torres and released in 1978, featured folk and traditional repertoire. With time, the group diversified its style, expanded into the rock and blues that members had learned even before their venture into Mexican music, and recorded a series of seven albums from 1983 to 1994 on Slash Records, a Warner Bros. affiliate. Notable among these were the first, *And a Time to Dance* (1983), which was awarded a Grammy for its track "Anselma" (a norteño-Tejano, conjunto-styled ranchera-polka), the 1988 *La pistola y el corazón*, comprised solely of Mexican folksongs, which was awarded yet another Grammy, and the highly acclaimed 1992 *Kiko*, which featured an eclectic mix of rock, blues, Mexican folk, and world music influences such as the use of Japanese taiko drums and North Indian sitar. In 1987 Los Lobos collaborated on the major portion of the commercial soundtrack of the highly successful film *La Bamba*, based on the life of Ritchie Valens and written and directed by Luis Valdez. The title track, "La bamba" (a remake of the original Valens hit of 1959), achieved the number one spot on the national charts in twenty-seven countries. In the United States it held that spot for three weeks and earned a double platinum record for selling over two million copies. It was also nominated for a Grammy in the

Song of the Year category. In 1995 the group released the aforementioned Grammy-nominated children's album *Papa's Dream* with Lalo Guerrero. Los Lobos consists of four Chicanos: Louie Pérez, César Rosas, Conrad Lozano, and David Hidalgo, and Steve Berlin, a Jewish American originally from Philadelphia. A drummer, Victor Bisetti, was added to the group in the early 1990s. They perform on a variety of musical instruments ranging from the Mexican jarana, requinto, violin, vihuela, guitarrón, *hidalgarrón* (an innovation of David Hidalgo), bajo-sexto, the Bolivian charango, and the Tejano-style Hohner accordion to electric guitars and bass, tenor and soprano saxophones, keyboards, drum set and congas. Frequently referred to as a postmodern ensemble, Los Lobos represents the hybrid, intercultural characteristics of popular music that emerged at the end of the twentieth century, and they have been recognized as innovators in this artistic movement. During the late 1990s the group switched labels to the Disney affiliate Hollywood Records.

Yet another movement that has personified much of the Chicano musical affinity is punk and, by evolution, new wave, especially in the dense urban contexts of Los Angeles, San Francisco, and even Chicago, the city with the second highest Mexican-descent population in the United States (Los Angeles has the highest such population). Groups that achieved major recognition in Los Angeles during the 1980s included The Brat, Los Illegals, the Undertakers, and Los Cruzados (also known as The Plugz). "El Lay" is an immigration-themed song recorded by Los Illegals, in which the dialectic of conflict persists in what can in some ways be construed as a corrido concept. Molded in a heterogeneous musical style incorporating nuances from punk and hard rock, reggae, Latin, and the Spanish language, the song reflects the urban diversity of a city such as Los Angeles and its various levels of urban "angst." Added to this cultural ambience is some explosive political thought directed toward the exploited urban immigrant: the undocumented worker, or the "illegal alien." The song's title, "El Lay," refers both to Los Angeles and to the slang expression for sexual intercourse, "a lay." Hopelessness and exploitation are thus conveyed through a metaphor that connotes a casual, demeaning sexual lifestyle characterized by faceless, noncommittal sexual activity and promiscuity. The song describes the illegal alien's arrival in, employment in, and deportation from Los Angeles—to the song's authors, nothing more than "a lay" (Loza 1993, 230–33).

Political and ideological undertones have characterized the music of the Chicano United States, from the previously noted corridos of South Texas and 1920s Los Angeles to the more contemporary musical movement of Los Illegals, among many others. Music utilized in direct collaboration with the Chicano movement and the farmworkers' movement has also developed. Popular songs and tunes such as El Chicano's "Viva Tirado" and Little Joe y La Familia's "Las nubes" (a traditional ranchera reset in La Onda Chicana tejana vein described earlier) received radio play and also became associated with an evolving Chicano identity. At an even more political level of musical activism was the music of Mexican farmworkers throughout the Southwest, which expressed the organizational and social issues of farmworkers, union strikes, and protests. Some of the recordings produced in California were *¡Huelga en general!*, produced by El Teatro Campesino, a collection of farmworker songs recorded by the Center for the Study of Comparative Folklore and Mythology at the University of California, Los Angeles (*Las voces de los campesinos*), and the LP *Corridos y canciones de Aztlán*. Numerous artists in California have produced music relevant to both the farmworker movement and other social issues of cultural identity. Daniel Valdez, a veteran musician-actor of El Teatro Campesino, released an important album, *Mestizo,* during the 1970s on the A&M label (later reissued by El Teatro Campesino). Another musician-composer from northern California is Agustín Lira of Fresno, who also wrote songs of the farmworker movement. Also from Fresno is singer-guitarist Al Reyes, whose album *California Corazón* featured his compositions about farmworkers, Vietnam veterans, and Chicano culture in the San Joaquin Valley. From San Diego, Los Alacranes Mojados established themselves as important troubadours of the Chicano movement, incorporating both border conflict and farmworker themes in their music. The album *Si se puede* (1976) features a collection of various Chicano musicians from Los Angeles and is dedicated to the farmworker struggle. From the San Francisco area, Los Peludos was another prolific group with a political message stemming from the Chicano movement.

During the early 1990s the emergence of a uniquely Mexican style of music and ensemble exploded onto the music scene of Mexicans and Chicanos in Los Angeles, other cities in the Southwest, and eventually the Midwest and Northeast. It was banda, and the movement became known as the "banda craze" in the English-speaking media, which gave the phenomenon much attention. This intense vogue in Los Angeles was one of a specific nationalist character—namely, a Mexican character. The banda ensemble format can be traced historically and stylistically to the traditional *banda sinaloense*, originally developed at the turn of the twentieth century in the state of Sinaloa, Mexico. It is rightfully one of the long recognized and colorful styles in the ample variety of regional music in Mexico. The distinctive instrumentation of the Sinaloa style, consisting primarily of woodwind and brass instruments, became the standard of the contemporary banda ensemble. It did, of course, undergo major innovation. A lead vocalist became a standard element in the formerly instrumental format, and electric bass often replaced the traditional tuba. A modern drum set and Cuban-style timbales also often became part of the percussion section, formerly characterized by a battery, or *tamborazo*, of marching band cymbals, bass drum, and snare drum (although timbales had already been in use in the Sinaloa style).

The dance aspect of banda, referred to as *la quebradita*, was in many ways the central focus of this socio-artistic experience. Although the quebradita and its tango-like "break" choreography, executed at many of the banda night clubs and dances throughout Los Angeles and other cities, became the symbol for discussion of banda in general, the essential dance steps conform somewhat to combinations of the genres performed by the banda ensemble, ranging from a polka beat to tropical rhythms to traditional Mexican *sones*. A dance style emerged that at times was a hybrid of cumbia, norteño, Tex-Mex, and zapateado. At many dances the actual quebradita was never executed because of space limitations.

In assessing the factors of identity, nationalism, and the emergence of a collective aesthetic in the making of the banda phenomenon, it has been useful to think in terms of both the movement's social force and its artistic representation and regeneration. One of the principal reasons for the international media exposure of this style was the ascension of radio station KLAX, with its banda-ranchera format. Known as "La X," it was spearheaded by disc jockey Juan Carlos Hidalgo. In August 1992, according to Arbitron ratings, KLAX moved into the number one spot for the city of Los Angeles, surpassing the syndicated KLSX morning talk show hosted by Howard Stern, which had previously held the number one rating. The radio industry immediately reacted in an almost bewildered manner (the phrase "shock waves" in the industry was used by *Music Connection* magazine), not only unable to explain this demographic "alarm clock" but also unable to develop immediate and competitive marketing strategies to regain top ratings. The Spanish-speaking public of Los Angeles was simply not part of the mainstream radio industry. In 2001 a historical and analytical book on banda both in Mexico and the United States was released, written by Helena Simonett (2001a) and titled *Banda: Mexican Musical Life across Borders*.

Hip-hop is a more recent context exhibited by young Chicano musicians, with artists such as Kid Frost (Arturo Molina), A Lighter Shade of Brown, Aztlan Underground, Cypress Hill (including Mexican, Cuban, and Italian Americans), ALT (Al Trivette), the Los Angeles–based Cuban American Mellow Man Ace, and Delinquent Habits. A highly successful 1990 recording by Kid Frost on his LP *Hispanic Causing Panic* sampled the musical theme of El Chicano's (and Gerald Wilson's) "Viva Tirado" on his "La raza" track. Pérez-Torres makes the following note concerning the recording:

> Kid Frost's use of the popular "Viva Tirado" evokes that moment of great political and social activism among Chicano populations in the late 1960s and early 1970s. From the affirmation of Brown Power to the Blowouts (the school walkouts in East Los Angeles), the Chicano Movement formed a high-water mark of the struggle by Chicanos for civil rights and political engagement. The musical incorporation of El Chicano suggests a recollection of subaltern resistance. (2000, 212)

Kid Frost's creative work, however, cannot be assessed solely through "La raza." On a subsequent album he collaborated with other Latino rappers in a project titled *Latin Alliance*. One track from the album, "Latinos unidos," is a mosaic of Latin R&B musical texture and rhythmic flavor; bilingual historical referents and interpretations of the Mexican southwest, Puerto Rico, and Nicaragua; and direct commentary on issues related to minority politics and intercultural conflict. Other compositions on the album include themes based on reflections on American identity, lowrider and boulevard culture, the political wars of Central America, and gangsta raps imaging violence, discrimination, incarceration, immigration, the Border Patrol, and romance.

In assessing the issues of cultural identity and ethnic nationalism, the aesthetics of rap emerge as a highly charged vehicle among a constantly growing corps of young Chicano and Latino contemporary rap artists. Although the aesthetic of rap has become webbed across the globe as a preferred expression of youth culture in a variety of languages, its relationship to Latinos in the United States as part of African American music is not simply an artistic interaction, dialectic, or experiment. Rather, it is reflective of living in neighborhoods such as South Central Los Angeles, Chicago's Southside, or the Bronx of New York, spaces almost exclusively populated by Latinos and African Americans. Rap has been a point of synthesis and inevitable value to the young members of this geographic and cultural sector.

Pérez-Torres also notes the manner in which Chicano hip-hop artists incorporate various expressive modes of mestizaje. He notes that "the multiracial rap group Delinquent Habits makes it a point to highlight the hybrid nature of their cultural and racial identities. Employing caló, English, Spanish, and street slang, the rappers Ives, Kemo, and deejay O. G. Style employ code-switching and bilingualism as both their linguistic and personal identities are foregrounded" (2000, 218).

Other musical enterprises that have developed in recent years continue the eclectic mix of musical mestizaje that has been identified as an essential factor of culture and creativity throughout this essay. Incorporating diverse styles from hip-hop to Mexican folk forms, from rock to jazz, and from Afro-Cuban forms and cumbia to R&B have been groups such as Rage Against the Machine, Goddess 13, Ozomatli, Quetzal, and A. B. Quintanilla y los Kumbia Kings, the latter from Texas and a Grammy winner. For some time the innovative, multiracial rock group Rage Against the Machine was fronted by lead singer Zak de la Rocha, who wrote prolific rap-styled lyrics with potent political and social messages.

Other Los Angeles–based groups such as Ozomatli and Quetzal also represent the musical mestizaje referred to by Pérez-Torres. The indigenous names of the groups, both of Aztec reference, are reinforced by the incorporation of a multitude of musical styles, reflecting a multicultural and multiracial world in which these multiracial group members live. Ozomatli makes use of forms including hip-hop, cumbia, salsa, Afro-Cuban son, merengue, flamenco, tango, and Mexican genres such as son and ranchera. Quetzal juxtaposes compositions ranging from Latinized R&B to "funkified" Mexican *son jarocho*. Pérez-Torres makes a significant point in noting that "the face of Chicano music continues to undergo a profound transformation as the Latino population in the U.S.—and in traditionally Chicano communities—comes to be increasingly diverse. The great continued flows and fluxes of transnational movements signal an ever-shifting musical landscape" (2000, 225).

The musical duo Goddess 13 has received much attention in both the academic press and the media, although unfortunately not the record industry, as the group has never recorded on a major label. Composed of two veteran songwriters who were formerly lead singers for the Los Angeles–based punk bands The Brat and The Bags, Teresa Covarrubias and Alicia Armendariz epitomize what George Lipsitz has conceptualized as a postmodern musical enterprise. In place of the electric, raging punk ambience of their former years, they have recently composed songs with intricate two-part vocal harmonies flavored by rock, folk, jazz, and Latin styles. They perform on acoustic guitars and are backed up by a versatile rhythm section. Their songs are in both Spanish and English, and they address contemporary issues of romantic love, domestic violence, multiculturalism, and misogyny. In the following passage, Lipsitz makes an eloquent observation concerning not only Goddess 13 but also the musical culture of the Chicano people in the United States.

> In their insistence on being Chicanas in their own way, Armendariz and Covarrubias grapple with the historical invisibility of their community in the mass media as well as with their determination to avoid being reduced to their race to the point of erasing their experiences as women, as workers, and as citizens. Chicano artists have long grappled with these problems, and they have often found solutions by taking on unexpected identities in order to make visible the hybridity and heterogeneity of their own community. (1994, 90)

Latin Caribbean Development

Since the latter part of the nineteenth century, musical styles from the Spanish-speaking Caribbean have not only migrated in great volume to the United States but also had a major impact on its music, including jazz, blues, rock, and classical. The dominant influences have come from Cuba, Puerto Rico, and the Dominican Republic. In cities such as New York, Latino barrios formed that included immigrants from the latter three countries, although it should be noted that immigrants have arrived there and in other US cities from all parts of Latin America. In New York during the 1920s through the 1950s, most of the Caribbean immigrants, driven by economic motives, were from Puerto Rico (technically not "immigrants," as Puerto Rico was and still is a US "possession") and Cuba. Interestingly, there are now more Dominicans in New York City than the other two groups. Other cities with large Caribbean-derived populations include Miami, Chicago, San Francisco, and Los Angeles.

Contemporary Afro-Cuban music has not only retained a profound and significant portion of its African tradition but has influenced music internationally, especially within the Americas. The habanera, danzón, son, rumba, guaracha, mambo, cha-cha-cha, and *songo* all emanated from Cuba, spreading throughout Latin America and the Latin quarters of the United States, and eventually throughout Europe, Asia, and Africa. The habanera was the first Cuban style to strongly influence music in the United States and was probably the most influential style throughout the Americas. Calling the habanera "perhaps the most universal of our musical genres," Cuban musicologist Emilio Grenet cites the melody "La paloma" as an example of its influence (Grenet 1939, in Roberts 1979, 5). Composed in the 1940s by a Spaniard stationed in Havana, Sebastián Yradier, it most likely came to the United States via Mexico, with which it is identified strongly. The most salient rhythmic feature of the habanera is its bass configuration.

CUBAN INFLUENCES

The music of such early pianists as Scott Joplin ("Solace: A Mexican Serenade," 1909), Jesse Pickett ("The Dream"), and Jelly Roll Morton ("New Orleans Joys," recorded in 1923) attests to the presence of the early Cuban habanera form, which many believe was first brought to New Orleans by the Eighth Cavalry Band in about 1884. Morton claimed that it was the "Spanish tinge" that differentiated jazz from the earlier ragtime style of New Orleans music. One of the most vivid examples of the impact of the habanera and other Afro-Cuban forms on music in the United States was the musical and musicological work of W. C. Handy, one of the early innovators and composers of the blues. Handy toured Cuba and absorbed many musical ideas and practices, which influenced many of his compositions. Notable was his "St. Louis Blues" (1914), which incorporated the habanera rhythm in the middle of its three sections. One of the most significant recordings of this landmark piece was made in 1929 by Louis Armstrong, and it became one of his signature vehicles. By the 1930s another vein was being established in this Latin and jazz encounter. Juan Tizol, the Puerto Rican trombonist who was a member of the Duke Ellington orchestra, co-composed with Ellington a piece that would strongly impact the concept of American jazz: "Caravan" (1936), featuring an alternation of a rumba and habanera based on *clave*—the rhythmic heartbeat of Afro-Cuban dance music.

The Cuban style that most influenced music in the United States has been the son, which was the basis of the rumba's popularity during the 1930s. The son utilized Afro-Cuban rhythmic concepts such as the anticipated bass, in which the bass line and drum *tumbao* precede the downbeat of a measure by a half-beat. Son does not refer to a specific, formal, or uniform musical structure, but describes a particular sound and instrumentation, characterized by a unique feel or, to use a jazz term, "groove." It originally emerged from the black population in the rural districts of Cuba as a vehicle for entertainment at informal gatherings. In the early 1900s, it migrated to urban centers, eventually molding the entire phenomenon of Cuban music from the dance hall to the concert hall. Although the son form was based on African concepts, son guitar (specifically, *tres*) playing also displayed a strong Spanish tradition. Most original sones incorporated the African tradition of call-response vocals and/or other instruments, accompanied by complex rhythmic patterns played on the *tumbadora* (conga drum) and bongos. During both its rural and urban development in Cuba, the son acquired distinctive musical and dance characteristics. Both the Cubans and Puerto Ricans who migrated to the United States sustained and intensified the popularity of the son, especially in New York.

Arsenio Rodríguez was a major innovator of the son and lived out his musical career in Cuba, New York, and Los Angeles. Rodríguez, who was blind and performed the guitar-type Cuban tres, expanded the son sound by returning to the African-derived elements found in the rural performances of the son that had been simplified or omitted in some of the earlier Cuban ensembles. Instrumentally, he added a *campana* (bell), a tumbadora, a second trumpet, and a piano to the son conjunto (the son ensemble). The contemporary conjunto instrumentation, similar to that of salsa, thus took its initial form. Rodríguez also emphasized the *guajeo* (the tres and piano interlocking rhythmic patterns) and incorporated the tumbao, an ostinato pattern resulting from interlocking patterns played by the bass and conga. Additionally, he structured the horn arrangements and musical breaks around the *clave* pattern and integrated the rhythm section of bongos, congas, bass, campana, tres, and piano in such a way as to create a melodic-rhythmic unity also revolving around the clave. Rodríguez expanded the accompanying function of the tres to that of a solo instrument and re-emphasized the role of the *estribillo* (refrain). More important, he introduced a solo section referred to as *montuno*, in which the tres, piano, and trumpet players demonstrated their improvisatory skills. Yet another of Rodríguez's major innovative contributions was his incorporation of the mambo, which had been introduced by Israel "Cachao" López and his brother Orestes López, members of the *charanga* ensemble of Antonio Arcaño, into the dance halls of Cuba by the late 1930s. Using son conjunto instrumentation and the mambo, the compositions of Arsenio Rodríguez greatly influenced the Latin popular music of New York, which eventually produced many great salsa musicians such as Machito, Tito Puente, and Tito Rodríguez, all of whom incorporated mambo into their big bands, and to this day salsa musicians continue to interpret Rodríguez's compositions.

Dynamically, the range and energy of Rodríguez's conjuntos grew extensively, remolding, yet preserving, the traditional son form. In recent years there has been a retroactive, international fascination with a number of traditional son groups from Cuba, notably the Buena Vista Social Club and groups led by Compay Segundo, Abraham Ferrer, and Rubén González.

Since the 1930s specific musicians and bandleaders have played a central role in the development of Afro-Cuban dance music in the United States through various cycles of style and innovation. One of the earliest examples is that of Don Azpiazú, who relocated to New York with his band from Cuba and released his recording of composer Moisés Simons's "El manisero" (The Peanut Vendor). Shortly afterward "El manisero" was also recorded by Louis Armstrong, among many others, eventually becoming one of the most-played standards in American music. Also active in the United States was Cuban composer and bandleader Ernesto Lecuona, who composed standard songs such as "Siboney" and "Maria la O," in addition to chamber and piano pieces such as the now universally performed "Malagueña" from his *Andalucía Suite*.

MAMBO, LATIN JAZZ, AND SALSA

By the 1940s musicians, especially those of Cuban and Puerto Rican heritage, were largely developing their music in Spanish Harlem. In the 1950s, during the height of Latin music's popularity (especially for the mambo and cha-cha-cha), they catered to audiences in the highly popular Palladium dance hall in New York City. Many of these artists also achieved international acclaim, made highly successful recordings, and eventually received numerous prestigious awards ranging from Grammys (although mostly not until the 1980s) to governmental honors.

Machito (1908–1984), whose actual name was Frank Grillo, was—along with Mario Bauzá, who performed alongside him—perhaps the principal thrust of the New York Latin music movement. Machito emigrated from his native Cuba to New York in 1937, and by 1940 he had organized his own orchestra, Machito and His Afro-Cubans. Machito fronted the orchestra and was lead vocalist, while the arrangements of Bauzá, a saxophonist-trumpeter originally from Cuba, and pianist René Hernández were crucial to the development of this big band–styled ensemble. One of the principal innovations of the Machito orchestra was its blending of Afro-Cuban dance forms such as rumba, guaracha, and mambo with the musical qualities of the big band jazz and bebop movements so active in New York City at this time. Heavily exposed to the music of Duke Ellington, Count Basie, Chick Webb, Cab Calloway, Charlie Parker, and Dizzy Gillespie (Bauzá had played with both Webb and Calloway) in the Harlem district where they lived, Machito and Bauzá spearheaded the convergence of US and Latin musical styles, specifically those that eventually evolved into both contemporary salsa and Latin jazz. Exemplary of the "marriage" of jazz and Cuban music was the Machito orchestra's "Tanga" (composed in 1943, recorded in 1948), with its mambo-based structure, Ellingtonian palette of orchestral colors, and Basie-like blues-inspired riffs, considered by many aficionados to be the recording that best defines the emergence of Latin jazz.

A number of other respected musicians in the progressive Latin and jazz waves of the late 1940s had experimented with fusions of the Afro-Cuban and Afro-North American styles, but it was the association of trumpeter Dizzy Gillespie and Cuban conguero, vocalist, and dancer Chano Pozo (recommended to Gillespie by Mario Bauzá) that played the most prominent role in what would be referred to as "Cubop," the mixture of Afro-Cuban music and the progressive bebop style of Gillespie, Charlie Parker, Thelonious Monk, and others. Roberts (1972, 119) notes that "in Cubop, Latins and [North] Americans were trying to work together without losing any crucial elements of either style." This was in certain aspects challenging, because although there were Afro-based similarities between the rumba and the jazz "bop" styles, the Afro-Latin and Afro-North American musical traditions were at the same time quite different. Nevertheless, Pozo's impact on music in North America endured, symbolized through the fusion music known as Latin jazz. Prominent conguero bandleader Mongo Santamaría stressed that Pozo's essential contribution was the exposure he gave to the conga drum, which spearheaded its rise in popularity. Among the more important Pozo-Gillespie musical collaborations were the compositions "Algo-Bueno," "Afro-Cuban Suite," and the profound "Manteca," a basic conga riff inspired by Pozo that received wide acclaim as the successful blend of the two Afro-American styles. Among the many artists who continued the school of Latin jazz have been Mongo Santamaría, Chico O'Farrill, Cal Tjader, Willie Bobo, Tito Puente, Jerry González and the Fort Apache Band, Paquito D'Rivera, Arturo Sandoval, and Poncho Sánchez, among many others. A jazz big band that produced highly creative and experimental interpretations of Afro-Cuban music was that of Stan Kenton, which during the 1940s and 1950s recorded classics such as the *Cuban Fire* suite, "Machito," "Viva Prado," and "23° N—82° W." An excellent documentary on Latin jazz artists, *Calle 54*, was directed by Spanish filmmaker Fernando Trueba and released in 2001.

The exact origin of the mambo is the subject of much conjecture. As noted above, the music and dance of the mambo originated in Cuba, especially in the innovations of Cachao and Orestes López and Arsenio Rodríguez. The height of the mambo's popularity spanned the first half of the 1950s, and Pérez Prado was perhaps the most widely acclaimed mambo bandleader. Originally from Cuba, he went to Mexico in the late 1940s and established a highly successful orchestra, even backing up the Cuban *sonero* (singer of son) Benny Moré on a number of recordings. In 1955 Pérez Prado released a recording—"Cherry Pink and Apple Blossom White"—which he had done in Hollywood, California, for a film. It became the highest-selling record worldwide that year. As Roberts (1972) points out, Pérez Prado's mambo was not as popular among the Latin population in New York as were the mambo styles of Machito, José Curbelo, Tito Puente, or Tito Rodríguez. Internationally, however, Pérez Prado's success was unprecedented, and his musicianship should not be underestimated. The cha-cha-cha, which also became highly popular in the United States, had originally been popularized in Cuba by Orquesta Aragón in 1953. A product of the Cuban charanga ensemble, the cha-cha-cha was an adaptation of the second section of the original danzón, and the crisp texture of flute, violins, and timbales contributed to its mass appeal. In New York, the Dominican-born flutist and bandleader Johnny Pacheco emerged during the 1950s leading a charanga.

As the son still largely defined the musical concept of this developing Latin music movement, vocalists were among the major stylists of Afro-Cuban dance music in the United States, especially in the growing Latin community of New York. Three of the most influential (besides Machito) have been Miguelito Valdés, Tito Rodríguez, and Celia Cruz.

Miguelito Valdés, a sonero, became a major influence among audiences in the United States by the early 1940s. Originally from Cuba but based in New York for a number of years, Valdés sang with the orchestras of Machito and Xavier Cugat, and by 1947 he had formed his own band. As with Cugat, he also enjoyed substantial success in Hollywood movies, which during the period of his popularity included many films incorporating popular Latin styles such as rumba and mambo.

Singer-bandleader Tito Rodríguez (1923–1973), one of the first of many Puerto Ricans to achieve major status in Latin music in New York, represents one of the most important periods of the famous Palladium dance hall era and the international popularization of Latin dance music. After performing and/or recording with Xavier Cugat, Noro Morales, José Curbelo, Chano Pozo, Arsenio Rodríguez, and Machito, Rodríguez developed his own big band and by 1949 had achieved major success. The 1950s became the apex of Latin dance music at the Palladium, and Rodríguez, Machito, and Tito Puente became the dominant symbols of the movement. Some of Rodríguez's most popular recordings included "Vuela la paloma," "Cuando, cuando," "Cara de payaso," "Mama guela," and "Inolvidable," the last selling over a million copies.

Celia Cruz emigrated from her native Cuba to Mexico in 1959, where she remained until 1961 with the Cuban conjunto Sonora Matancera, an ensemble that had popularized Cuban dance music throughout the Americas. Ultimately Cruz would establish herself as the most popular vocalist in the era of the development of salsa, in the 1960s through the early 1990s, a tenure of unparalleled success among singers of the style. She continued to record not only with Sonora Matancera but also with bandleaders Tito Puente, Johnny Pacheco, Ray Barretto, and Willie Colón, among many others. She also concertized and recorded with her own orchestras, directed by her longtime husband Pedro Knight. Cruz was awarded a National Medal of Arts by President Bill Clinton in 1994. Her death in 2003 was covered extensively by the Latin American and world news agencies and was a deeply sentimental moment for millions of aficionados.

In the estimation of many experts, the artist who became the major stylist and innovator following the early career of Machito was bandleader Tito Puente (1923–2000). Of Puerto Rican heritage and a virtuoso musician on timbales and vibraphone, Puente began his dynamic career in his native New York, performing by the early 1940s with various artists, including his principal mentor, Machito. After serving in the Navy during World War II, Puente returned to New York, studied music composition and arranging at the Julliard School of Music, and played with the Piccadilly Boys, a group that never recorded. It was during this period that Puente first brought the percussion section of his orchestra to the front of the bandstand, an innovation that became a permanent standard for Latin dance bands into the 1990s. In 1948 Puente formed his own band and in 1949 recorded one of his early hits, "Abanico," featuring Cuban sonero Vicentico Valdés. During the 1950s Puente's band became internationally associated with the mambo and cha-cha-cha eras with arrangement of tunes such as "Ran kan kán" and "Pa' los rumberos." His *Dance Mania* album on RCA became a classic. With the advent of the 1960s and the beginning of the salsa era,

Puente continued as one of the principal stylists of Latin music, earning the name El Rey del Timbal (The King of the Timbales). Original tunes such as "Que sera mi china?" and "Oye como va," the latter made into an international radio hit by Carlos Santana's 1971 recording, became standard arrangements in the Latin music repertoire. Puente also led an important Latin jazz ensemble that featured many of the top Latin jazz artists of the 1980s and 1990s. Puente received the National Medal of Arts in 1997 from President Bill Clinton and six Grammy Awards, the last posthumously for an album he recorded with Eddie Palmieri months before his death on June 1, 2000, which was mourned worldwide.

Another bandleader of Puerto Rican background who became one of the major contemporary artists of Latin music based in New York City is Eddie Palmieri (b. 1936). Although he was highly active in the 1960s, when he led the innovative charanga-styled group Conjunto La Perfecta, it was during the 1970s that Palmieri made a great impact on the salsa and Latin jazz scenes, emerging as an innovative pianist-composer-arranger who dynamically experimented with the blending of progressive Latin Caribbean forms and contemporary jazz shadings. Palmieri's piano style, for example, often reflected the style of the then highly influential McCoy Tyner, who was associated primarily with the progressive jazz styles of the period. Classic albums recorded by Palmieri and featuring numerous first-rate Latin and jazz musicians have included *The Sun of Latin Music* (1974), *Unfinished Masterpiece* (1975), and *Arete* (1995). As of 2004 he had been awarded six Grammys.

A popular trend that evolved from the salsa movement in New York during the 1960s was *bugalú*. A blend of Latin rhythms and African American rhythm and blues, or soul, the style represented the close cultural and musical association of Latin and black music in the United States and what Juan Flores (1988) has referred to as a unique cultural "complementarity." There was also an ideological tie that developed between African Americans and Puerto Ricans in spaces such as the Bronx and other sectors of New York City, where the two cultures lived side by side and began to consolidate their political causes and goals during what was perhaps the most active national mobilization era of the civil rights movement. Leading bandleaders of bugalú included Joe Cuba, whose 1966 recording of "Bang Bang" sold over a million copies, Joe Bataan (of Afro-Filipino heritage and raised in New York), Ray Barretto, who recorded the 1963 hit "El Watusi," and Hector Rivera, who recorded one of the most popular bugalú hits in 1967, "At the Party." George Lipsitz (1994, 83–84) notes that Latin bugalú and salsa musicians played an important part in the disco craze of the 1970s, and late in the decade they began to play a crucial part as well in the rise of hip-hop in New York.

The many Puerto Ricans in New York and along the East Coast who have so closely identified with both Cuban and US jazz have played an important role in the crystallization of the hybrid salsa movement internationally, but especially in the Latin quarters of the United States. Lyrics sung in Spanish over a strong dance base have been fostered by a significantly growing US population whose Caribbean, Chicano/Mexican, and Central and South American composition continually enhances the Latino nature of the music. Additionally, as articulated by Max Salazar in so many of his writings, Latin music served as a catalyst for racial integration, with the Palladium era in New York being a metaphor for the interaction of not only diverse Latinos but also dancers and musicians of Italian, Jewish, African American, Anglo-American, and so many other heritages (see Salazar 2002). With an ever-growing multicultural awareness and the constant development of hybrid forms of expression within the United States, salsa has for many provided a mode of cultural expression that bridges and cures many intercultural conflicts and barriers. Its growth continues internationally.

An important artist who emerged from the salsa movement during the 1970s was Rubén Blades. Originally from Panama and trained in law, Blades ventured to New York where he worked for Fania Records and eventually established himself as a lead vocalist and prolific composer. His album *Siembra*, with arranger-trombonist Willie Colón, was released in 1980 and sold a record volume of units. Two of its tracks, "Pedro Navaja" and "Plastico," became known throughout Latin America, the United States, Europe, and Japan. Blade's song texts that addressed social and political issues of Latin American and the Latino sector in the United States gained him special recognition.

The 1980s witnessed a rather different mode of expression and new breed of salsa adapted to a more international pop sound, that of *salsa romantica*. Exponents included Luis Enrique (Nicaragua and United States), José Alberto (Dominican Republic), Eddie Santiago (Puerto Rico) and Marc Anthony (New York). Some singers of the older school—Lalo Rodríguez for example, who recorded with Eddie Palmieri in the early 1970s at the age of seventeen—successfully adapted to the new trend. Another phenomenon was the international success of Grammy-nominated Orquesta de la Luz, a salsa group from Japan that was influenced by the

New York style and whose recordings were originally produced in New York by Sergio George.

Afro-Cuban musical styles have become increasingly popular throughout the United States, with salsa and Latin jazz bands proliferating in cities such as Miami, Chicago, Phoenix, Philadelphia, Tucson, Houston, Dallas, and Albuquerque. In California, major exponents of the style have emerged since the 1940s, with the aforementioned Stan Kenton in addition to Cal Tjader, who was raised and learned to play music in the San Francisco area, eventually performing with the original jazz groups of Dave Brubeck. Inspired by the music of Machito and Tito Puente, he proceeded to form his own Afro-Cuban ensemble, and in 1957 Mongo Santamaría and Willie Bobo left Tito Puente's orchestra to join Tjader's ensemble. Tjader recorded prolifically on the Fantasy and Verve labels, including his classic *Soul Sauce* LP of 1964, which sold over 100,000 copies and helped popularize the word *salsa*. In 1966 he recorded an LP with Eddie Palmieri, *El sonido nuevo*. Among the many musicians to work with him were Armando Peraza, Al McKibbon, Jerome Richardson, Vince Guaraldi, Clare Fischer (composer of the cha-cha-cha standard "Morning"), Mark Levine, and Poncho Sánchez.

PUERTO RICAN MUSICAL TRADITIONS

In addition to playing a major role in the development of salsa and other styles in the United States, musicians of Puerto Rican heritage have also been important to the popularization of Puerto Rican musical genres. In New York, in particular, Puerto Ricans perform *plena*, bomba, and the *jíbaro* forms of *seis*, aguinaldo, and danza. Plena and bomba music and dance originally developed in the coastal towns of Puerto Rico and derive largely from African tradition. Active interpreters of plena and bomba have included Victor Montañez, Manuel "Canario" Jiménez, and the highly successful Rafael Cortijo and Ismael Rivera (the last three artists were based in Puerto Rico, but New York was a constant reference point). A highly influential bomba and plena group in New York during the 1990s was Los Pleneros de la 21, led by musician, teacher, and bandleader Juan Gutiérrez. The innovative group modernized the percussive instrumentation of the plena and bomba ensemble by adding electric bass, piano, cuatro, and additional percussion. Los Pleneros were widely imitated throughout the United States and Puerto Rico.

The jíbaro styles, especially popular during the Christmas season, have also played an essential role in the transplantation of Puerto Rican traditional music culture into the United States. In great part Hispanic-derived folk forms, they especially make use of the Puerto Rican cuatro, with ten strings grouped in five courses, in addition to the standard Spanish guitar and the guiro (gourd scraper). Influential in the formation of the contemporary *conjunto jíbaro* was the Puerto Rican *cuatrista* (cuatro player) Ladislao "Maestro Ladí" Martínez Otero, especially during the 1930s. He increased the popularity of the jíbaro style by incorporating a diversity of musical genres into the cuatro repertoire and enhancing the instrumentation to include two cuatros, bongos, bass, and congas. Several conjuntos jíbaros exist in the United States, especially in the larger cities of the Northeast and Midwest. Virtuosos on the cuatro include Yomo Toro (New York) and Edwin Colón Zayas (Puerto Rico). A major contemporary vocalist of the style is Andrés Jiménez.

MUSIC OF DOMINICANOS

The Dominican Republic has also had a major impact on the musical culture in the United States. The merengue, which originated there, is along with the Colombian cumbia one of the most popular dance rhythms throughout Latin American and the Latin quarters of the United States. The merengue that became internationally popular emerged from the *merengue cibaeño* (regional merengue from Cibao). Based on a fast tempo, the typical merengue ensemble included a button accordion, a metal rasp called a *güira*, a two-headed drum called a tambora, and often a saxophone or marimba bass-type instrument. Austerlitz (1997, 126) notes that the accordion-driven merengue, known as *perico ripiao*, became associated with Dominican national identity and also became an important symbol of and link to the Dominican culture and homeland in the United States—that is, New York City and other Northeastern urban industrial areas, where immigration from the Dominican Republic escalated dramatically following the political and social upheaval after the death of dictator Rafael Trujillo in 1961. Dominicans especially settled in the Washington Heights district in New York City, which they began to refer to as Quisqueya, the indigenous name for Hispaniola.

The first merengue bandleader to settle in the United States was accordionist Primitivo Santos. Santos, along with Joseíto Mateo, who worked extensively in the United States, made merengue available to Dominicans and other aficionados and helped increase its popularity. By the 1970s merengue had become one of the most popular dance styles in New York and other cities. New York–based merengue bands included the group Milly, Jocelyn y los Vecinos, which developed a local and international audience (Austerlitz 1997, 125–26). Artists from the Dominican Republic who have attained immense popularity in the United States and internationally include Wilfredo Vargas, Johnny Ventura, and Elvis Crespo, among many others. During the 1990s another Dominican style, bachata, became highly popular throughout Latin America and the Latin quarters of the United States, and it was internationalized largely through the recordings and performances of Juan Luis Guerra, who was awarded a Grammy in 1991 and whose group interpreted both the bachata and the merengue in addition to ballads and other types of arrangements. In 1997 Paul Austerlitz wrote an informative book titled *Merengue: Dominican Music and Dominican Identity*. Also of great significance is the 1995 book *Bachata: A Social History of a Dominican Popular Music*, written by Deborah Pacini Hernandez.

Contemporary International Styles

As the scope of this essay has focused on the musics of Mexican American (Chicano) and Latin Caribbean cultures in the United States, the obvious note should be made that there certainly exist in the United States many other Latin American and Spanish or Portuguese genres and their associated makers and audiences. Examples include Afro-Cuban folkloric rumba, the music of *santería*, and other Afro-Cuban and Afro-Brazilian religious traditions, the Argentine tango, Brazilian samba and bossa nova, flamenco, Central American forms, and contemporary/classical music from Latin America. In addition to Mexicans/Chicanos, Cubans, Puerto Ricans, and Dominicans, there are many Latinos in the United States of heritages originating in Colombia, Argentina, Brazil, Nicaragua, El Salvador, and all the other countries of Latin America.

With that in mind, however, I will stress here that this essay has primarily focused on the popular musical expression of the US border areas—that is, music related to the Mexican-Chicano Southwest and the Caribbean (Puerto Rican, Cuban, Dominican) Northeast. In a sense, music of these areas, on a geographical and historical basis, represents the concept of the US border, and given the fact that their geographic locations became the basis of two major bloody conflicts—the Mexican-American War (1846–48) and the Spanish-American War (1898)—it is not surprising that the cultures of these spaces and their related times would have had so much impact on and penetration into the musical life of the United States.

We should also remind ourselves that the interaction has been both negative and positive, with much "grey" in between; thus, the music reflects both sides and even more in between, especially so in a contemporary society where cultural and social hybridity—or to return to the spirit of this essay, the "mestizaje of it all"—can inspire creative blends and identities of both daily life and lifelong values.

There have been, in addition to the border blends, other international musical styles on both sides of the border that have been heavily appropriated by constantly changing values and their corresponding aesthetics. International styles have emerged in the United States from an external and an internal market of trade and have thus been either heavily imported or heavily exported by means of airwaves, recordings, cyberspace, and the video explosion that has spanned the 1980s to the present. Prime examples from the United States who represent a north-south directional line are artists such as Gloria Estefan, Tito Puente, Celia Cruz, Carlos Santana, and Cristina Aguilera, not to mention Madonna, Britney Spears, and *NSYNC. And there are the actual cross-border paradoxes, such as Los Tigres del Norte, who are from Sinaloa, Mexico, but live in San Jose, California. And then there are also the "grey" areas represented by artists such as Plácido Domingo, Wynton Marsalis, and Ravi Shankar, who concertize throughout the world, including Latin America.

Two of the examples above, Gloria Estefan and Los Tigres del Norte, might offer some insight into the state of contemporary international styles that have enjoyed the highest ranks of popularity simultaneously in the United States and Latin America, without even citing other sectors of the world market. Vocalist Gloria Estefan has made a major impact on both mainstream and Latino markets. Born in Cuba in 1957, Gloria Fajardo immigrated to Miami as a young child in 1960 with her family, leaving the island after the 1959 Cuban Revolution. Eventually she and her husband, Emilio Estefan, organized a Miami-based group called Miami Sound Machine, which achieved international recognition with its 1985 hit "Conga." The recording remained on the Top 10 charts in the United States for sixteen weeks. Gloria Estefan had numerous other international hits, in both English and Spanish, and for some time became the most popular artist in Latin America. Her album *Mi tierra*, released in 1993, was awarded a Grammy and established unprecedented record sales. Other singers that developed a "crossover" style that was in some ways similar to Estefan's, but during the late 1990s, were Ricky Martin and Marc Anthony. Martin created a sensational response in the international market with his recoding of "Livin' La Vida Loca" in 1999 and was featured on the cover of *Time* magazine.

The other example, Los Tigres del Norte, represents not only the phenomenal growth of the Mexican music industry in the United States but also the constantly growing penetration of Mexican culture, often referred to in California as the "Mexicanization" of the state. Los Tigres del Norte interpret the norteño style of Northern Mexico, highly related to the South Texas conjunto style previously critiqued. However, Los Tigres del Norte have achieved a massive cross-national audience composed of four distinct categories of aficionados: Mexicans living throughout Mexico; Mexican and other Latin American immigrants to the United States and other countries; native residents of other, especially Spanish-speaking, countries in Latin America in addition to Spain; and Chicano and other Latinos born and living in the United States. One of the most attractive features of the group, especially among immigrants to the United States, are the many immigration-themed corridos, rancheras, polkas, and cumbias included in their repertoire, as well as texts based on the drug world (e.g., *Corridos prohibidos*, 1988), corrupt Mexican politics ("El circo" and *Jefe de jefes*, 1997), and romance. In his book *Narcocorrido*, Elijah Wald offers the following perspective:

> Los Tigres are the kings of norteño, the Mexican country music that is one of the most popular styles in the United States and Central America. Though the Anglo media act as if the current Latin music boom were driven by Afro-Caribbean styles like salsa and merengue, Mexicans and Mexican Americans are by far the largest group of Spanish speakers in the United States, and Mexican bands account for roughly two-thirds of domestic Latin record sales. In this world, Los Tigres are like Willie Nelson and the Rolling Stones combined, the enduring superstars of down-to-earth, working-class pop. Their records sell in the millions, their concerts pack halls throughout the North American continent, and their songs have become part of the Mexican cultural heritage. They have never crossed over to Anglo fans for several reasons: First, their style is based on accordion-driven polkas and waltzes—not generally considered a sexy sound. Second, their music is old-fashioned and rurally rooted, a style disrespected by most trendsetting intellectuals and hipsters. Third, their most popular hits are narcocorridos, ballads of the drug traffic. (2001, 1–2)

It might be pointed out here that the narcocorrido, which has received much recent attention (Simonett 2001a, 2001b), is not so much a glorification of drug culture as a critique dressed in metaphor, satire, tragic drama, and historical tales of reality.

There are, of course, other dimensions to contemporary international styles germane to the concept of a US–Latin American border musical culture. Styles ranging from ballad and mariachi to rock and other styles—including those of Julio Iglesias (Spain), Vicente Fernández (Mexico), Juan Gabriel (Mexico), Luís Miguel (Mexico), José Feliciano (Puerto Rico and New York), José Luis Rodríguez (Venezuela), Pepe Aguilar (Mexico), Shakira (Colombia), Los Fabulosos Cadillacs (Argentina), Maná (Mexico), Juanes (Colombia), Alejandro Fernández (Mexico), and Alejandro Saenz (Spain), among hundreds of other international artists—illustrate the volume and diversity of contemporary popular styles marketed in a multibillion-dollar industry in Latin America, the United States, and other sectors of the globe.

The Music Industry and LARAS

As noted by Wald above, about two-thirds of the Latin American music recording product sold in the United States is that of Mexican regional styles, including norteño, ranchera, and banda, among others. Other statistics confirm the impressive sales of Latin American music; for example, recent statistics confirm the tremendous growth in the Latin music industry at about 25 percent during 1999, a rate of growth more rapid than that of non–Latin American recordings. Such statistics and interest in the US Latino sector and Latin America have certainly had effect on the executive heads of the music industry in the United States. It is no coincidence that the National Academy of Recording Arts and Sciences (NARAS) established the Latin Academy of Recording Arts and Sciences in 1997, with its first annual Latin Grammy Awards, an internationally televised show, in September 2000. Still thriving as of 2005, LARAS awards forty-three Latin Grammys annually, encompassing sixteen fields and forty-three categories. These fields are organized as follows:

General Field, 4 categories: Record, Album, Song, and Best New Artist of the Year.

Field 1—Pop, 3 categories: Best Female Vocal Album, Male Vocal Album, Pop Album by a Duo or Group with Vocal

Field 2—Urban, 1 category: Best Urban Music Album

Field 3—Rock, 4 categories: Best Rock Solo Vocal Album, Rock Album by a Duo or Group with Vocal, Alternative Music Album, Rock Song

Field 4—Tropical, 5 categories: Best Salsa Album, Merengue Album, Contemporary Tropical Album, Traditional Tropical Album, Tropical Song

Field 5—Singer-Songwriter, 1 category: Best Singer-Songwriter Album

Field 6—Regional, Mexican, 6 categories: Best Ranchero Album, Banda Album, Grupero Album, Tejano Album, Norteño Album, Regional Mexican Song

Field 7—Instrumental, 1 category: Best Instrumental Album

Field 8—Traditional, 3 categories: Best Folk Album, Tango Album, Flamenco Album

Field 9—Jazz, 1 category: Best Latin Jazz Album

Field 10—Christian, 2 categories: Best Christian Album (Spanish Language), Christian Album (Portuguese Language)

Field 11—Brazilian, 7 categories: Best Brazilian Contemporary Pop Album, Brazilian Rock Album, Samba/Pagode Album, Música Popular Brasileira Album, Romantic Music Album, Brazilian Roots/Regional Album, Brazilian Song (Portuguese Language)

Field 12—Children's, 1 category: Best Latin Children's Album

Field 13—Classical, 1 category: Best Classical Album

Field 14—Production, 2 categories: Best Engineered Album, Producer of the Year

Field 15—Music Video, 1 category: Best Music Video (1 song only)

The diversity and magnitude of categories in the LARAS Grammy process is self-evident. In addition to these awards, LARAS has honored a "Person of the Year" annually since its initial awards year of 2001, including vocalist Julio Iglesias, producer Emilio Estefan, vocalist Vicente Fernández, singer-songwriter and guitarist Caetano Veloso, and guitarist and bandleader Carlos Santana.

Latin America's proximity to the United States and Latin music's cultural impact, in conjunction with its global popularity and high record sales, prompted NARAS to form LARAS. In addition to the awarding of Grammys at an annual televised broadcast, which itself generates millions of dollars for the organization, LARAS's agenda includes the promotion of "creative freedom, music education, copyright protection, health insurance, and human services to promote the free flow of musical ideas across borders" (Greene 2003, 241). One of LARAS's principal goals in recent years has been to challenge the prevalent practice of music piracy in Latin America (primarily the selling of illicitly copied recordings). It has been estimated that as much as 50 percent of music recordings purchased in Latin America is pirated (Greene 2003, 243). From a critical perspective, however, the goals of LARAS on this issue must also be assessed from an equitable set of perspectives. How, for example, can one expect a Latin American citizen, whose average wages might be less than seventy-five dollars a week, to pay the same price for a CD (twelve to twenty dollars) paid by a US citizen, who makes a salary four or many more times greater? Yet the system has basically operated in this manner. Although considered "illegal" according to international law, is such piracy immoral? That is a very good and important question—one not so different from the issue of immigration.

The members of LARAS are primarily from Latin America, the United States, and Spain (although it is open to anyone anywhere who fulfills the required professional credits). The main offices of LARAS are located in Miami (although NARAS is based in Los Angeles). Thus far, all the televised awards shows have been produced in Los Angeles and Miami.

Conclusions

The concept and realities of Latino culture and "border" in the United States are constantly expanding and changing. With these political and social reconfigurations, the role of musical and artistic culture in general maintains a direct, relevant, and indelible effect on society in both the United States and Latin America. In a globalizing economy and world culture, the expanding, intercultural interface of music will hopefully play a major role in opening the borders of conflict, a theme so prevalent in working class Latino music. It is safe and wise to say that by the early twenty-first century, Latino music in the United States, from ranchera to Latin jazz to hip-hop, has reached heights never before imagined by a quickly changing music industry and American society.

Note

An earlier version of this essay appeared in *Ethnic and Border Music: A Regional Exploration*, edited by Norm Cohen. Westport, CT: Greenwood Press, 2007. Reprinted by permission.

Works Cited

Austerlitz, Paul. 1997. *Merengue: Dominican Music and Dominican Identity*. Philadelphia: Temple University Press.

Broyles-González, Yolanda. 2001. *Lydia Mendoza's Life in Music/La historia de Lydia Mendoza*. New York: Oxford University Press.

Bryant, Edwin. 1936. *What I Saw in California*. Santa Ana, CA: Fine Arts Press.

Campa, Arthur L. 1979. *Hispanic Culture in the Southwest*. Norman: University of Oklahoma Press.

Cobos, Ruben. 1956. "The New Mexican Game of 'Valse Chiquiao." *Western Folklore* 15, no. 2: 95–101.

Espinosa, Aurelio M. 1985. The Folklore of Spain in the American Southwest: Traditional Spanish Folk Literature in Northern New Mexico and Southern Colorado. J. Manuel Espinosa, ed. Norman: University of Oklahoma Press.

Flores, Juan. 1988. "Bumbún and the Beginnings of Plena." *Centro de Estudios Puertorriqueños Bulletin* 2, no. 3: 16–25.

García, Peter J. 1996. "The New Mexican Early Ballad Tradition: Reconsidering the New Mexican Folklorists' Contribution to Songs of Intercultural Conflict." *Latin American Music Review* 17, no. 2: 150–71.

Greene, Michael. 2003. "Building Bridges with Music: Spanning Latin Music's Diversity of Culture, Geography, Art, and Science." In *Musical Cultures of Latin America: Global Effects, Past and Present,* edited by Steven Loza, 241–44. Los Angeles: UCLA Department of Ethnomusicology and Systematic Musicology.

Grenet, Emilio. 1939. *Popular Cuban Music: Eighty Revised and Corrected Compositions, Together with an Essay on the Evolution of Music in Cuba*. Havana: Carasa.

Guerrero, Lalo, and Sherilyn Meece Mentes. 2002. *Lalo: My Life and Music*. Tucson: University of Arizona Press.

Guevara, Rubén. 1985. "The View from the Sixth Street Bridge: The History of Chicano Rock." In *The First Rock & Roll Confidential Report,* edited by Dave Marsh, 113–26. New York: Pantheon.

Jáquez, Candida. 2003. "El Mariachi: Musical Repertoire as Sociocultural Investment." In *Musical Migrations: Transnationalism and Cultural Hybridity in Latina/o America*, vol. 1. New York: Palgrave Macmillan.

Lamadrid, Enrique. 1994. *Tesoros del espíritu: A Portrait in Sound of Hispanic New Mexico*. With Jack Loeffler, recordist, and Miguel Gandert, photographer. Albuquerque: University of New Mexico Press.

———. 2003. *Hermanitos Comanchitos: Indo-Hispano Rituals of Captivity and Redemption.* Albuquerque: University of New Mexico Press.

Leger, James K. 2001. "Música Nuevomexicana." In *Garland Encyclopedia of World Music*, vol. 3, 754–69. New York: Palgrave Macmillan.

Lipsitz, George. 1994. *Dangerous Crossroads: Popular Music, Postmodernism, and the Poetics of Place.* London and New York: Verso.

Loeffler, Jack. 1999. *La Musica de los Viejitos: Hispanic Folk Music of the Rio Grande del Norte.* Albuquerque: University of New Mexico Press.

Loza, Steven. 1993. *Barrio Rhythm: Mexican American Music in Los Angeles.* Champaign: University of Illinois Press.

———. 1999. *Tito Puente and the Making of Latin Music.* Champaign: University of Illinois Press.

———. 2001a. "Hispanic California." *Garland Encyclopedia of World Music*, vol. 3, 734–53.

———. 2001b. "Latin Caribbean Music." *Garland Encyclopedia of World Music*, vol. 3, 790–801.

Lummis, Charles F. 1923. *Spanish Songs of Old California.* New York: New York: Schirmer.

Mendoza, Vicente, and Virginia R. R. de Mendoza. 1986. *Estudio y clasificación de la música tradicional hispánica de Nuevo México.* Mexico City: Universidad Nacional Autónoma de México.

Pacini Hernandez, Deborah. 1995. *Bachata: A Social History of a Dominican Popular Music.* Philadelphia: Temple University Press.

Paredes, Américo. 1958. *"With His Pistol in His Hand": A Border Ballad and Its Hero.* Austin: University of Texas Press.

———. 1995. *A Texas-Mexican Cancionero: Folksongs of the Lower Border.* Austin: University of Texas Press. First published in 1976.

Peña, Manuel. 1982. "The Emergence of Conjunto Music, 1935–1955." In *And Other Neighborly Names: Social Process and Cultural Image in Texas Folklore*, edited by Richard Bauman and Roger Abrahams, 280–99. Austin: University of Texas Press.

———. 1985a. *The Texas-Mexican Conjunto: History of a Working Class Music.* Austin: University of Texas Press.

———. 1985b. "From Ranchero to Jaitón: Ethnicity and Class in Texas-Mexican Music (Two Styles in the Form of a Pair)." *Ethnomusicology* 29, no. 1: 29–55.

———. 1989. "Notes Toward an Interpretive History of California-Mexican Music." In *From the Inside Out: Perspectives on Mexican and Mexican American Folk Art*, edited by Karana Hattersly-Drayton, Joyce M. Bishop, and Tomás Ibarra-Frausto, 64–75. San Francisco: The Mexican Museum.

———. 1999a. *The Mexican American Orquesta: Music, Culture, and the Dialectic of Conflict.* Austin: University of Texas Press.

———. 1999b. *Música Tejana: The Cultural Economy of Artistic Transformation.* College Station: Texas A&M University Press.

Pérez-Torres, Rafael. 2000. "Mestizaje in the Mix: Chicano Identity, Cultural Politics, and Postmodern Music." In *Music and the Racial Imagination*, edited by Ronald Radano and Philip V. Bohlman, 206–30. Chicago: University of Chicago Press.

Reyes, David, and Tom Waldman. 1998. *Land of a Thousand Dances: Chicano Rock 'n' Roll from Southern California.* Albuquerque: University of New Mexico Press.

Robb, John Donald. 1980. *Hispanic Folk Music of New Mexico and the Southwest: A Self-Portrait of a People.* Norman: University of Oklahoma Press.

Roberts, John Storm. 1972. *Black Music of Two Worlds: African, Caribbean, Latin, and African-American Traditions.* New York: Praeger.

———. 1979. *The Latin Tinge: The Impact of Latin American Music on the United States.* New York: Oxford University Press.

Rodriguez, Luis. 1980a. "Eastside Story, Part II." *L.A. Weekly,* August 15.

———. 1980b. "The History of the Eastside Sound." *L.A. Weekly,* August 1.

Rodriguez, Sylvia. 1996. The Matachines Dance: Ritual Symbolism and Interethnic Relations in the Upper Rio Grande Valley. Albuquerque: University of New Mexico Press.

Romero, Brenda M. 1993. "The Matachines Music and Dance in San Juan Pueblo and Alcalde, New Mexico: Contexts and Meanings." PhD dissertation, University of California, Los Angeles.

———. 1997. "Cultural Interaction in New Mexico as Illustrated in the Matachines Dance." In *Musics of Multicultural America: A Study of Twelve Musical Communities,* edited by Kip Lornell and Anne K. Rasmussen, 155–86. New York: Schirmer Books.

———. 2003. "The New Mexico, Texas, and Mexico Borderlands and the Concept of *Indio* in the Matachines Dance." In *Musical Cultures of Latin America: Global Effects, Past and Present,* edited by Steven Loza, 81–87. Los Angeles: UCLA Department of Ethnomusicology and Systemic Musicology.

Salazar, Max. 2002. *Mambo Kingdom: Latin Music in New York.* New York: Schirmer Trade Books

Sheehy, Daniel. 1997. "Mexican Mariachi Music: Made in the U.S.A." In *Musics of Multicultural America: A Study of Twelve Musical Communities,* edited by Kip Lornell and Anne K. Rasmussen, 131–54. New York: Schirmer.

———. 1999. "Popular Mexican Musical Traditions: The Mariachi of West Mexico and the Conjunto Jarocho of Veracruz." In *Music in Latin American Culture: Regional Traditions,* edited by John M. Schecter, 34–79. New York: Schirmer.

Simonett, Helena. 2001a. *Banda: Mexican Musical Life across Borders.* Middleton, CT: Wesleyan University Press.

———. 2001b. "Narcocorridos: An Emerging Micromusic of Nuevo L.A." *Ethnomusicology* 45, no. 2: 315–37.

Stevenson, Robert M. 1986. "Los Angeles." In *The New Grove Dictionary of American Music,* edited by H. Wiley Hitchcock and Stanley Sadie, 3: 107–14. New York: Macmillan.

Swan, Howard. 1952. *Music in the Southwest, 1825–1950.* San Marino, CA: Huntington Library.

Wald, Elijah. 2001. *Narcocorrido: A Journey into the Music of Drugs, Guns, and Guerrillas.* New York: Harper Collins Publishers Inc.

Works Consulted

Aparicio, Frances. 1998. *Listening to Salsa: Gender, Latin Popular Music and Puerto Rican Cultures*. Hanover, NH: Wesleyan University Press.

Barth, Fredrick. 1969. *Ethnic Groups and Boundaries*. Boston: Little, Brown.

Bateson, Gregory. 1972. "Culture Contact and Schismo Genesis." In *Steps to an Ecology of Mind*. San Francisco: Chandler.

Campa, Arthur L. 1933. *The Spanish Folksong in New Mexico*. Language Series Bulletin 4, no. 1. Albuquerque: University of New Mexico Press.

———. 1946. *Spanish Folk-Poetry in New Mexico*. Albuquerque: University of New Mexico Press.

Cornelius, Steven. 2001. "Afro-Cuban Music." *Garland Encyclopedia of World Music*, vol. 3, 783–89.

Crespo, Francisco. 2003. "The Globalization of Cuban Music through Mexican Film." In *Musical Cultures of Latin America: Global Effects, Past and Present*, edited by Steven Loza, 225–32. Los Angeles: UCLA Department of Ethnomusicology and Systematic Musicology.

Delgado, Kevin. 2003. "A Diaspora Reconnected: Cuba, Brazil, Scholarship, and Identity in the Music of Bata Ketu." In *Musical Cultures of Latin America: Global Effects, Past and Present*, edited by Steven Loza, 219–24. Los Angeles: UCLA Department of Ethnomusicology and Systematic Musicology.

Duany, Jorge. 1985. "Popular Music in Puerto Rico: Toward an Anthropology of Salsa." *Latin American Music Review* 5, no. 2: 186–216.

Fernández, Raúl. 2002. *Latin Jazz: The Perfect Combination/La Combinación Perfecta*. San Francisco: Chronicle Books.

———. 2003. "On the Road to Latin Jazz." In *Musical Cultures of Latin America: Global Effects, Past and Present*, edited by Steven Loza, 233–40. Los Angeles: UCLA Department of Ethnomusicology and Systematic Musicology.

Flores, Juan. 1988. "'Rappin', Writin', and Breakin'." *Centro de Estudios Puertorriqueños Bulletin* 2, no. 3: 34–41.

———. 2002. "Que Assimilated, Brother, Yo Soy Assimilao: The Structure of Puerto Rican Identity in the U.S." *Journal of Ethnic Studies* 13, no. 3: 1–16.

Haro, Carlos Manuel, and Steven Loza. 1994. "The Evolution of Banda Music and the Current Banda Movement in Los Angeles." In *Musical Cultures of Latin America: Global Effects, Past and Present*, edited by Steven Loza, 59–72. Los Angeles: UCLA Department of Ethnomusicology and Systematic Musicology.

Koegel, John. 2003. "Crossing Borders: Mexicana, Tejana, and Chicana Musicians in the United States." In *From Tejano to Tango*, edited by Walter Aaron Clark, 97–125. New York: Routledge.

Loza, Steven. 1984. "The Origins of the Son." *Aztlán: A Journal of Chicano Studies* 15, no. 1: 105–22.

———. 1992. "From Veracruz to Los Angeles: The Reinterpretation of the Son Jarocho." *Latin American Music Review/Revista de música latinoamericana* 13: 179–94.

———. 1994. "Identity, Nationalism, and Aesthetics Among Chicano/Mexicano Musicians in Los Angeles." In *Musical Aesthetics and Multiculturalism in Los Angeles*, edited by Steven J. Loza, 51–58. Selected Reports in Ethnomusicology, no. 10. Los Angeles: UCLA Department of Ethnomusicology and Systematic Musicology.

———. 2000. "Latin Jazz." In *Jazz: The First Century*, edited by John Edward Hasse. New York: Harper-Collins.

———. 2002. "Poncho Sanchez, Latin Jazz, and the Cuban Son: A Stylistic and Social Analysis." In *Situating Salsa: Global Markets and Local Meanings*, edited by Lise Waxer, 201–18. New York: Routledge.

———. 2003. "Introduction: Latin America, Mestizaje, and the Myth of Development." In *Musical Cultures of Latin America: Global Effects, Past and Present*, edited by Steven Loza, 5–18. Los Angeles: UCLA Department of Ethnomusicology and Systematic Musicology.

Loza, Steven, Milo Alvarez, Josefina Santiago, and Charles Moore. 1994. "Los Angeles Gansta Rap and the Aesthetics of Violence." In *Musical Aesthetics and Multiculturalism in Los Angeles*, edited by Steven Loza, 149–62. Los Angeles: UCLA Department of Ethnomusicology and Systematic Musicology.

Lozano, Danilo. 1990. "La Charanga Tradition in Cuba: History, Style, and Ideology." Master's thesis, University of California, Los Angeles.

Manuel, Peter. 1991. "Latin Music in the United States: Salsa and the Mass Media." *Journal of Communication* 41, no. 1: 104–16.

Manuel, Peter, Kenneth Bilby, and Michael Largey. 1990. *Caribbean Currents: Caribbean Music from Rumba to Reggae*. Philadelphia: Temple University Press.

Pacheco, Javier Barrales. 1986. "Salsa in San Francisco, 1974–1985: The Latin Music Experience." Master's thesis, University of California, Los Angeles.

———. 2003. "A Chicano in a Cuban Band: Okan Ise and Songo in Los Angeles." In *From Tejano to Tango*, edited by Walter Aaron Clark, 126–50. New York: Routledge.

Roberts, John Storm. 1999. *Latin Jazz: The First of the Fusions, 1880s to Today*. New York: Schirmer Books.

Sheehy, Daniel, and Steven Loza. 2001. "Overview (South American, Central American, Mexican, and Caribbean Musics." *Garland Encyclopedia of World Music* 3, 718–33.

Yanow, Scott. 2000. *Afro-Cuban Jazz*. San Francisco: Miller Freeman Books.

CHAPTER 2

The Origins of the Cuban *Son*

The term *son* has several meanings. In Latin America, it generally refers to a musical form that is played and danced. In Mexico, it has a history of association with that country's regional musical forms, including *son jarocho*, *son jalisciense*, *son huasteco* and others.

In Cuba, on the other hand, *son* does not refer to a specific or formal musical structure. Rather, it is a word that describes a particular sound and instrumentation, characterized by a certain feeling. It originally emerged from the black population in the rural districts of Cuba as a vehicle for entertainment at informal gatherings. In the early twentieth century, it migrated to the urban sector, eventually molding the entire landscape of Cuban popular music.

Raúl Martinez expresses the mixture that has become the son character:

> The *son* is probably the result of the mixture of certain African folk quick songs with which the negroes accomplished to make their rude works, mixed with the festive tunes which were brought to our Island by the first Spanish people. Both elements fused and being organized by the tunes of the guitar and the bongo, gave birth to the *son* as it is known to us today and to the typical orchestras that play it. (n.d., 8)

The Spanish and African influences, however, were not diametrically equal. "The *son* form was firmly based on African concepts, though with guitar-playing in a strong Spanish vein" (Roberts 1972, 97). Most original *sones* incorporated the African tradition of call-and-response vocals accompanied by complex rhythmic patterns played on the drums:

> In the cities *son* gained popularity among whites as dance and background music for social events and provided a major source of income for black performers. The complex African-derived rhythms, however, did not easily conform to the musical expectations of the whites, and out of economic necessity the performers simplified the rhythmic structure and

52

de-emphasized the *estribillo* (refrain), which consisted of call-and-response patterns. (Friedman 1976, 2)

The exact history of the son has been a subject of both uncertainty and fable. According to a document referred to as "La crónica de Hernando de la Parra," published in 1845 by José Garcia in *Protocolo de antiguedades, literatura, agricultura*, there existed in Havana a strong musical culture:

> Los Bailes y diversiones en la Habana son graciosos y extravagantes, conservan todavía en los primeros la rudeza y poca cultura de los indigenas, y en las segundas la escasez y ningunos recursos de una población que comienza a levantarse.[1] (2)

The chronicle included descriptions of four musicians of Havana, one of whom was Micaela Ginés. Eventually, Cuban musicologists reproduced the information in order to prove the existence of musical development in Cuba during the sixteenth century. Serafín Ramírez discussed it in his *La habana artística: Apuntes históricos* (1891), and in 1893, Laureano Fuentes Matóns actually composed the mythical "Ma Teodora" in *Las artes en Santiago de Cuba: Apuntes históricos* (1893), in which he claimed to have extracted from his father, D. José de la Cruz Fuentes (1764), information concerning Micaela Ginés and her sister, Teodora. Fuentes Matóns's evident desire was to place the historical importance of Santiago de Cuba on a level higher than that of Havana in relation to musical culture.

The whole affair has been quite a misfortune, for subsequent historians have relied upon the numerous secondary sources to confirm the imaginative documentation of de la Parra's chronicle. In writing *La música en Cuba*, Alejo Carpentier (1946) relied on such historical tradition and probably never referred to the original document. Two notable authors had detected certain contradictions in reference to the chronicle: Manuel Pérez Beato (*Los primeros días del teatro cubano*, 1927), and José Juan Arrom (*Historia de la literatura dramática cubana*, 1944).[2] The authenticity of the chronicle is finally negated in the article "Teodora Ginés: ¿Mito o realidad histórica?" by Alberto Muguercia Muguercia (1971). His four conclusions, based on intense primary research regarding the legitimacy of the "Ma Teodora" manuscript, abolish any credibility that may have theretofore been attributed to the following: the authenticity of "La crónica de Hernando de la Parra"; the possible existence of three of the four instruments described in the chronicle, for they had not been invented prior to 1598; the sixteenth-century origin of the documented son, "Ma Teodora," which was actually created by Fuentes Matóns in 1893; and the association established between the "Canción de ma Teodora" and Micaela Ginés's sister, Teodora, who was most likely part of Fuentes Matóns's fiction.

The earliest development of the son originated in the eastern portion of Cuba, extensively so in the areas of Guantánamo, Baracoa, and the peripheries of Santiago de Cuba. According to Helio Orovio (1981, 481), in 1892 the highly popular Nené Manfugás, one of the first musicians to popularize the *tres*, brought with him from Baracoa to Santiago de Cuba the first authentic tres to leave the countryside.

Carlos Borbolla (1975) cites the importance of the small rural folk groups called *bungas* in developing the son in the areas of Santiago de Cuba, Palma Soriano, Bayamo, Manzanillo, and possibly Guantánamo. Many of these bunga musicians were transients who moved from one sugar plantation to another with their instruments in search of *trabajo de zafra* (sugar harvest work). It was these small duo or trio groups from the province of Oriente who brought the identifiable son rhythm, marked by strong, syncopated anticipation, to Havana. Most of the bungas, however, remained as humble groups of little recognition in the rural sectors, unknown to the popular dance movements in the urban centers. Recognizing the significance of the "Ma Teodora" document, Borbolla elaborates on the possible origins of the son:

No conozco crónica alguna anterior al 1900 mencionando la modalidad son. Tampoco es descrito, durante los dos primeros decenios de este siglo, el son que iba a ser clásico: el que se conoció y remodeló del 1925 al 1940.

Sospecho que este son pudo haberse ido generando, o conformando, a fines del siglo pasado en conexión con el actual y en la provincia de Oriente, sin poder indicar, ni superficialmente, qué circunstansias ayudaron a originar su extraño toque anticipado, y curiosamente, soló en esta región.

Con cierta anterioridad a este 1900 dicho especial toque debió ser una fórmula privada, por así decir, que había ido sufriendo sus obligados acomodamientos antes de perfilarse tácitamente aceptada su escritura totalmente o posiblemente desconocida dentro del mundo de las bungas ya que la "escolástica musical teórica" no entraba en los conocimientos de los integrantes de ellas. Repitamos, fue la Habana la que supo trasladar el estilo al papel pautado a la orquesta de salón aunque todo un proceso preparalorio había pasado antes por el color y calor de los tríos al sexeto y de éste al septeto, ya un importante conjunto en el que entraba el contrabajo como instrumento adecuado para hacer resaltar, en las notas graves, el relieve importante de la anticipación. Este contrabajó formó un nuevo concepto sonoro en el género. Como sustituto del contrabajo con su necesaria técnica se pudo acudir en los más humildes conjuntos, a una caja sonora provista de flejes de acero vibrátil que emitían graves sonidos al pulsar los flejes. Se denominaba "marímbula" y poseía, en efecto, indudables cualidades para sustituir ciertos toques del contrabajo: los pizzicatos. Los primitivos dúos y tríos desconocían esta marímbula, parece que surge en nuestro siglo como una consecuencia habanerista. Su técnica era muy fácil. (1975, 153–54)

During both the rural and urban development of its musical form, the son acquired a distinctive style in both its musical and dance characteristics. These exhibited a large variety of influences that had not existed in the other forms and alluded heavily to either African or European traditions. Son, like rumba, was a developed form. Odilio Urfé (1973) remarks that the Cuban son contributed also in the integration of various instrumental groups, such as the *orquestas típicas*, which had existed from 1800 to 1930, to the *charanga* groups of Leopoldo Cervantes and Antonio María Romeu (1876–1955).[3] Collective interpretation by instrumental ensembles, then, began to mold a most distinctive Cuban sound. Urfé proceeds to comment on the social force of the son in dogmatic fashion:

Por su extracción, desarrollo, caractísitca sonora y coreográfica y uso social, el son cubano devinó historicamente como el medio de expresión más ideal y representativo para las capas humildes de la estructura socio-económico-politica de la Cuba de la post-primera Guerra Mundial y que en la producción del mencionado *Sexteto Habanero*, Miguel Matamoros (1893–1971), Bienvenido J. Gutiérrez (1904–1966) e Ignacio Peñeiro, concretó logros supremos; y teniendo como a su mas vibrante diapasón lírico al indiscutible, inolvidable e inmortal Benny Moré (1920–1963). (1973, 199)

An important element that typified the transition of son from the rural to urban sectors was the incorporation of guajira as a popular form. *Guajira* in Spanish can refer to a woman from the rural sector (for a man, *guajiro*), and it refers to the music of the Cuban countryside, the structure, text, and musical elements of which derive largely from Spanish musical tradition. Rhythmically, however, there is a definite African influence. Through the guajira, *trovadores* sing nostalgically of their country life, accompanying themselves on the tres. In the cities, melody and texts of the guajira were adapted to the son instrumentation, adding the *guajeo*, which was "interlocking melodic and rhythmic ostinato patterns based on the *clave* patterns" (Friedman 1977, 2).

The early son ensemble consisted of a tres, a *marímbula*, a *botija*, bongos, maracas, and claves. The tres is a six- or nine-stringed acoustic instrument resembling a guitar. The marímbula is constructed of a large resonating box with attached metal tongues; when plucked, they produce a bass-like sound. The botija is a large clay jug that is blown into to produce a note. The claves are two hard wooden sticks struck together; they provide a repetitive rhythmic basis to the son ensemble, producing either of the two clave patterns (fig. 1). The role of the claves is parallel to a specific trait of basic West African instrumental practice. The bongos provide the principle means for rhythmic melody and variation.

Figure 1. The two rhythmic patterns played by the claves.

The development of son has been characterized by three recognizable stages, each reflected by three separate musical groups, or conjuntos: the Sexteto Habanero, the Septeto Nacional, and the conjuntos of Arsenio Rodríguez. Although the son conjuntos had existed and were performing in the cities prior to 1918, it was the Sexteto Habanero that created the sound that was to be identified as typically son. The musical form was standardized by three voices, a bass replaced both the marímbula and botija, and guitar and trumpet were added to the conjunto. The use of bongos, claves, maracas, and tres remained, while the *laúd* (lute) was deleted.

The Septeto Nacional was actually performing at the same time as the Sexteto Habanero. The marked difference between the two groups developed in the late 1920s when the Septeto Nacional expanded the style of the son, which had been established by the Sexteto Habanero. This change was depicted by a greater Europeanization in the sound of both the Septeto Nacional and the other son conjuntos of the period, an influence owing to the fact that son was gaining international popularity through record distribution, a high tourist trade in Cuba, and performance of the son conjuntos in Europe, the United States, and elsewhere. The new style included vocal harmonies of greater complexity, expansion of the melodic range, and the addition of more ornamentation through the utilization of the trumpet. The tres became more dominant than before, although it would reach its pinnacle of importance during the era of Arsenio Rodríguez. Also of significance was the incorporation of a fixed, steady rhythm in the patterns played by the bongos, creating less freedom for improvisation and spontaneous interaction with the other elements of the conjunto.

Puerto Rico played an essential role in spreading the form and influence of the son when Puerto Rican musicians adopted the *septeto* style as performed by the Septeto Nacional and other son groups in Cuba. Both the Cubans and Puerto Ricans who migrated to the United States sustained and intensified the popularity of the son, especially in New York.

It was in the late 1930s that Arsenio Rodríguez expanded the son sound to return to the African-derived elements from rural areas, which had been simplified or omitted in the music of both the Sexteto Habanero and the Septeto Nacional. Simultaneously, however, Rodríguez did continue the trends of Europeanization that the two groups had initiated. Achieving a synthesis of African and European influences, Arsenio maintained the integrity and artistic quality of both elements. Instrumentally, he added to the son conjunto a *campana*, a conga drum, a second trumpet, and a piano. The contemporary conjunto was thus taking its initial form. In relation to stylistic innovation, Rodriguez emphasized the guajeo and incorporated the *tumbao*, which was "an ostinato pattern resulting from interlocking rhythms played by the bass and conga" (Friedman 1977, 3). Additionally, he structured the horn arrangements and musical breaks around the clave pattern and integrated the rhythm section of bongos, congas, bass, campana, tres, and piano in such a manner as to create a melodic-rhythmic unity revolving around the claves. Rodriguez expanded the accompanying function of the tres to that of a solo instrument and reemphasized the role of the *estribillo* (refrain). Importantly, he introduced a solo section, referred to as *montuno*, in which the tres, piano, and trumpet players demonstrated their improvisatory skills. Dynamically, the range and energy of Rodríguez's conjuntos had grown extensively, remolding yet preserving the traditional son form.

One of Rodriguez's major innovative contributions was his creation of the mambo, which was introduced into dance halls in 1937. Using son-conjunto instrumentation, the mambo, the conjuntos, and the compositions of Arsenio Rodríguez left a strong impression in the Latin popular music of New York, which produced Machito, Tito Puente, and Tito Rodríguez, all of whom incorporated mambo arrangements for their big bands. In the 1960s, many of his compositions were reinterpreted by salsa musicians.

Of special significance in reference to Rodríguez's *son montunos* was his use of them as vehicles of personal expression. Although many of his texts retained the traditional romantic themes of the earlier sones, he incorporated his own sentiments and philosophical perspective toward his community, racial pride, and Cuba.

The Musical Structure of the Son

The traditional son form is composed of two major sections. The first part, or verse, is a solo melody sung by the lead singer, usually comprised of a maximum of eight measures. The second part, called the montuno or the estribillo, demonstrates a more vivacious rhythmic character and exhibits a more sharply defined melody than the first part. The montuno or estribillo normally does not encompass more than four measures per phrase. The meter of the son is most frequently 2/4.

Figure 2. Example of an anticipated bass, as notated by Carlos Borbolla (1975, 152).

One of the son's most outstanding rhythmical characteristics is its use of a highly anticipated bass of unique character (fig. 2). Carlos Borbolla defines and notates this characteristic in such fashion:

> El son cubano, visto a través de su peculiarísima trama se le encuentra característicamente basado en la figura composicional denominada "anticipación" la que, en el caso de este género, es más rítmica que melódica.
>
> Se presenta como un sonido con valor de corchea o semicorchea y cuyo valor se suma, prolongándose, hasta un mismo sonido, de idéntico valor, al compás siguiente. (1975, 152)

Borbolla makes note of the fact that this compositional formula, representative of son, is unique among popular music and dance. Although other musical forms may demonstrate elements of anticipation, it is not as calculated or of such definite character as in son. Borbolla defines this characteristic in terms of musical structure. As illustrated in figure 2, the dominant accent of the son rhythmic pattern falls on the upbeat of the second count.

In his analysis of the son and its syncopated quality, Borbolla presents three variations in its use of anticipation. He emphasizes the point that these notations refer solely to the period of 1920 to 1940, in which son developed as a complete generic form, losing some pure original elements but assuming a more extensive musical complexity. Figure 3 illustrates anticipation occurring only in the uppermost voice. Conversely, figure 4 demonstrates anticipation only in the lower line, while the contrapuntal upper voice assumes more rhythmic freedom. Figure 5 is an example of anticipation in all voices but with closely corresponding rhythmic patterns.

Figure 3. Anticipation in the upper voice.

Figure 4. Anticipation in the lower voice.

Figure 5. Anticipation in all voices.

The unusual aspect of figure 5 lies in its use of a definite syncopation with the initial upbeat while eluding the same pattern in the following measures, which exhibit strong metric sonority.

Borbolla mentions the danza form as an integral component in the development and spread of son, making particular reference to "Las alturas de Simpson," a piece composed in 1879 by Miguel Faílde (1852–1921). Although of conventional danza style, Faílde's piece incorporated a novel use of two sections, each beginning with the same introduction. Four years later, in 1883, Raimundo Valenzuela (1848–1950) wrote "El combate," which displayed certain traits in the second and final part (at that time the danzón did not conform to the classic three-part form) that would characterize the eventual son. Valenzuela himself would eventually add the third part to the danzón structure, frequently using the extra section to display his trombone technique, which was considered to be quite proficient.

The son has retained its strong tradition and vigor since its emergence in Cuba in the early part of this century. Importantly, it has been a vehicle for a constantly evolving landscape of Cuban musical forms, including the bolero, the conga, the rumba, and, ultimately, the mambo, as exemplified through the efforts of Arsenio Rodríguez. The innovative quality of the son since its conception in Cuba has been its unique use of anticipation. It is for this reason that it has not dissipated as a tradition, for it has constantly conformed to the syncopation common to the wide array of Afro-Cuban rhythms. Moreover, it has proved to be a Cuban expression of musical, poetic, and social innovation.

The Son and Literature

A most intriguing phenomenon of the son in Cuba has been its relation to literature, especially that of Nicolás Guillén, a Cuban-born mulatto who exemplifies through his work the essence of what Ian I. Smart terms a "Spanish American Negritude" (1977, 73, 83). Considering that the basic framework of the son had grown from a neo-African tradition, strong in rhythm and sung in call-and-response style with an African nasal vocal quality, Guillén found a vehicle that seemed to parallel his mode of hybrid expression and "indicated that his poems were written in an attempt to bring to Spanish verse the verbal rhythms of the *son*" (83). He had been influenced strongly by the Sexteto Habanero and the Trío Matamoros, and "in 1930, at the height of the Afro ferment, his collection of eight short poems called *Motivos de son* were an instant success" (ibid.). As had occurred with the son in music, a poet had now wed African and Spanish elements to create another Cuban idiom, one of artistic and literary innovation.

Guillén's intent is to imitate the son song through his son poems. In the musical form, the introductory *largo* (verse) succinctly states the theme and is followed by the montuno, which is structured according to the antiphonal call-and-response form. During the montuno, the exchange between the lead singer and chorus further develops and resolves the original largo theme. Its use of repetition in the chorus characterizes the son quality of Guillén's poetry. Thematically, Guillén's poems also resemble the son song, for the text reflects black life and philosophy in addition to modifying certain Spanish linguistic norms. Guillén's first son poem, "Negro bembón," reads as follows:

> ¿Por qué te pone tan bravo
> cuando te dicen negro bembón
> si tiene la boca santa,
> negro bembón?

Bembón así como ere
tiene de to;
Caridad te mantiene,
te lo da to.

Te queja todavía,
negro bembón;
sin pega y con harina,
negro bembón,
majagua de dril blanco,
negro bembón; (1967, 39)

Although Guillén's son technique has not yet fully been analyzed, a vital aspect of his son is the neo-African poetic rhythm. Guillén has used verbal inventions to maximize this rhythmic effect, but designs them with both thematic discretion and reference to African vocabulary, especially that of the Yoruba language. A prime example would be his poem "Sensemayá," which evokes a title similar in sound to Yemaya, the Yoruba name of the mother of Shango.

Guillén's son poems mark the beginning of his significant poetic achievement. Ideologically, his poetry has portrayed "his total commitment to justice" (Smart 1977, 85) and in the words of another analyst, "takes its place at the very heart of the struggle for freedom" (Fanon 1963, 233). Importantly, however, he has been able to interface his intellectual perception with a Cuban popular form, the son having become his vehicle for success. In a eulogy for Benny Moré, the popular Cuban musician of son, Guillén included the following thoughts:

> Los dioses mueren jovenes . . . había una correspondencía profunda entre aquel hombre de tan directa sensibilidad popular y las angustias, las esperanzas, las luchas y victorias de su gente. . . . Su arte les comunica la misma permanencia de la fuente en que bebieran. Así es como nace ahora de su muerte para no morir mas el hombre a quien toda Cuba ha llorado "con lágrimas que mojan," según el decir de nuestro gran poeta, pero cuya voz suena como nunca, sin pasar ni apagarse en el aire nuestro de cada día. (Guillén 1963)

The Son and Social Change

The son and its implications of social expression—here is an inevitable topic for discussion. From the rural trovadores to the popular son conjuntos of Arsenio Rodríguez to "*la nueva trova*" of contemporary Cuba, the son has characterized and expressed country life, racial barriers, and the political penetration of revolution in Cuba.

René López cites the importance of the son through Cuba's social history. In the 1930s, for example, Antonio Machín became popular with songs such as "Pobre mi Cuba" in addition to "Suavecito," a guajira thought to be quite bold at the time. López discusses Machín's music and its political connection. "He talked about bad conditions in Cuba in music. The guajira gives conditions. This is close to the 'lamento' and there is a connection to African protest historically . . . black lament. 'Amor de mi patria' is another of the revolutionary songs; it is about Martí . . . I want to show readers that there is a history—that the revolution did not just come; that there was a struggle" (López n.d., 2).

Referring to Benny Moré, López states that the popular Cuban musician "really reflected the 'sentimiento del pueblo' (sentiments of the people) because he was a non-conformist. He used to sing in the streets for pennies. . . . I think Benny Moré was foremost than anything a Cuban . . . a strong Cuban; and I think that his reason for returning to Cuba (in 1953) was to make a band that reflected more his sentiments and feelings of Cuba. . . . He was a rebel . . . a very strong rebel and in a way that pleased the public" (López n.d., 6, 7–8).

Music in Cuba, then, has played a nationalistic role in its transmission of significant social comment through a popular idiom. Although Benny Moré's attitude of "non-conformity" may not have been directly political, the message was quite apparent in the sones of Arsenio Rodríguez, as previously discussed. López remarks upon the historical significance. "Today in Cuba, music certainly reflects an attitude of people with an awakened consciousness, (more so) than it did before; although things were dealt with before. I can bring you records all the way back from 1927 that talk about conditions. They always were there. There had to be some outlets for them and they are there. Arsenio's little tunes in the 1930s and '40s really reflect intense protest" (López n.d., 9).

In Cuba today exists "la nueva trova," an outgrowth of the traditional *trova*, which originated in the boroughs of Santiago de Cuba during the nineteenth century. The nueva trova movement is inspired by the Cuban revolution and has spread throughout various countries of Latin America. With the cessation of diplomatic ties with the United States, the market for Cuban music changed considerably and North American influence diminished. The motivation of the young trovadores, therefore, is to revitalize Cuban national music while incorporating the element of social protest. Contemporary artists such as Silvio Rodríguez and Carlos Puebla use this folk idiom to convey themes of social relevance within the context of Cuba's society and political philosophy.

The eight-member Grupo Moncada exemplifies the nueva trova movement through its wide repertoire, which includes songs based on slave chants interpreted on wooden boxes similar to those used by the slaves in Cuba as drums. The group also incorporates rhythms and musical structures typical to modern Cuba and Latin America in general. Playing a total of forty-one instruments, the group makes use of local folkloric varieties, such as the Andean charanga guitar and the *quena* flute, when interpreting music of other nationalities. The musicians of Moncada represent a variety of professionals, including teachers of French and English, an economist, and students of music and engineering. With a travel schedule throughout Cuba and many other countries (including the United States), the group regards their music as a link with different world cultures and as an effort of "rediscovering Cuba's music tradition and interpreting it in the content of Cuba's present political position and past political experiences" (*Cuba Update* n.d., 2).

In compiling research of recently published Cuban musicologists, the ideational element is quite explicit in their perspectives, especially when discussing the importance of retaining a "national folklore" through Cuban music. The Marxist approach illustrates itself clearly in the following passage from Odilio Urfé's "Busquejo histórico":

> Por nuestra parte, y, como resultado de un cuidadoso analisis musicologico de enfoque marxista, hemos podido detectar, identificar y aislar una amplia variedad de elementos propios del complejo sonero cubano que, unidos a otros procedentes de los sectores marginados de la poblacion negra y chicanos de la Norteamerica anglo-sajona, del Africa negra y arabica, del Caribe, Brasil e India, han posibilitado la "fabricación" en cadena de los híbridos POPS que en gran intensidad se vienen esparciendo como una epidemia hacia amplias y lejanas áreas del mundo.
>
> Por estas razones y por ló que respecta a Cuba debemos evaluar con sumo cuidado cuándo en verdad la música cubana, de autentica fisonomía, gana terreno en la palestra internacional, o, tambien cuándo incluye positivamente en el desarrollo de una determinada expresion foranea, ya que estos hechos no pueden confundirse con otro que se deriva de COMO LOS ELEMENTOS DE LA MUSICA CUBANA SON UTILIZADOS como materia prima para la elaboración de líneas de mercancías de consumo masivo, pero con etiqueta imperialista y neocolonialista. (1973, 200)

Urfé's statement refers to commercial exploitation of a national folklore. He is expressing Marxist doctrine in relation to music and Cuba's intent to retain its art devoid of the "imperialist market." Urfé's perspective is vital, for it symbolizes a thought process that has reflected Cuba's national policy, and, therefore, its music. It is part of a cultural reality.

The missing link, however, seems to lie in the existence of a cultural "vacuum" between two exceptionally strong musical cultures—those of Cuba and the United States. A resultant factor of political barriers is a lack of communication between dedicated artists preoccupied not so much with political ideologies, but rather with their artistic capabilities of expression and expansion. No amount of political indoctrination or rhetoric will ever impede the creative potential of the arts, for they symbolize all forms of ideology, including those of the political institutions which frequently seem to create an artificial barrier between political diplomacy and cultural diplomacy.

Notes

An earlier version of this essay appeared in *Aztlán: International Journal of Chicano Studies Research* 15, no. 1 (1984). Copyright 1984 by The Regents of the University of California. Reprinted by permission of the UCLA Chicano Studies Research Center Press.

1. Quoted in Muguercia Muguercia (1971, 56).
2. See Muguercia Muguercia (1971, 57–58). Both Pérez Beato and Arrom are discussed in relation to the works cited and their respective observations.
3. See Urfé (1973, 199).

Works Cited

Arrom, Jóse Juan. 1944. *Historia de la literatura dramática cubana.* New Haven: Yale University Press.
Borbolla, Carlos. 1975. "El son, exclusividad de Cuba." *Anuario interamericana de investigación musical* 11: 152–55.
Carpentier, Alejo. 1946. *La música en Cuba.* Mexico City: Fondo de Cultura Económica.

Cuba Update. n.d. "The Nueva Trova Song Movement of Cuba." Press release no. D-877. New York: Center for Cuban Studies.

Fanon, Frantz. 1963. The Wretched of the Earth. Translated by Constance Farrington. London: Penguin.

Friedman, Robert. 1976. "Puerto Rican and Cuban Musical Expression in New York." Liner notes for Caliente=Hot, 80244-2. Recorded Anthology of American Music, Inc. New York: New World Records.

Fuentes Matóns, Laureano. 1893. Las artes en Santiago de Cuba: Apuntes históricos. Santiago: Juan E. Ravelo.

Garcia, José. 1845. "La crónica de Hernando de la Parra." In Protocolo de antiguecdades, literatura, agricultura, vol. 1. Havana: M. Soler.

Guillén, Nicolás. 1963. "Benny." Unpublished manuscript. Archived at the Center for Cuban Studies, New York.

———. 1967. Sóngoro cosongo, motivos de son, West Indies, Ltd., España. Buenos Aires: Losada.

López, René. n.d. Unpublished interview. Archives of the Center for Cuban Studies, New York.

Martínez, Raúl. n.d. "La estudiantina." Program notes for "Festival de Música Popular Cubana," Matanza, 8–15.

Muguercia Muguercia, Alberto. 1971. "Teodora Ginés: ¿Mito o realidad histórica?" Revista de la Biblioteca Nacional José Martí 13, no. 3: 53–85.

Orovio, Helio. 1981. Diccionario de la música cubana: Biográfico y técnico. Havana: Ediorial Letras Cubanas.

Pérez Beato, Manuel. 1927. "Los primeros días del teatro cubano." El curioso americano, año 60, no. 1: 26–29.

Ramírez, Sarafín. 1891. La habana artística: Apuntes históricos. Havana: E. M. de la Capitanía General.

Roberts, John Storm. 1972. Black Music of Two Worlds: African, Caribbean, Latin, and African-American Traditions. New York: Praeger Press.

Smart, Ian I. 1977. "Some Thoughts on the African Contribution to Spanish-American Literature." Ufahamu: A Journal of African Studies 7, no. 3: 73–91.

Urfé, Odilio. 1973. "Bosquejo histórico sobre el origen y desarrollo del complejo musical y coreográfico del son cubano." Revista de la Biblioteca Nacional José Martí, 64 (January–April): 197–202.

Works Consulted

Bianchi Ross, Ciro. 1975. "Benny Moré: El barbaro del ritmo." Cuba internacional, February, 48–19.

Biblioteca National José Martí. 1973. "Bongo, maracas y marimbula: Ciclo de son." Revista de la Biblioteca National José Martí 65, no. 1: 197–202.

Cohen, Martin. 1978. *Understanding Cuban Rhythms.* Vol. 1. Palisades Park, NJ: Latin Percussion Inc.

Grenet, Emilio. 1939. *Popular Cuban Music: Eighty Revised and Corrected Compositions, Together with an Essay on the Evolution of Music in Cuba.* Havana: Ministry of Education.

Hart, Armando. 1977. "La música cubana." *Bohemia* (Havana), no. 6, February 11.

Knight, Franklin W. 1970. *Slave Society in Cuba during the Nineteenth Century.* Madison: University of Wisconsin Press.

León, Argeliers. 1974. "Notas para un panorama de la música popular cubana." *Boletín de música* (Havana), no. 24: 4–14.

Martin, Edgardo. 1977. *Panorama histórico de la música en Cuba.* Havana: Cuadernos CEU, Universidad de la Habana.

Martinez Furé, Rogelio, ed. n.d. *Conjunto Folklórico Nacional de Cuba.* Havana: Consejo Nacional de Cultura.

Martínez Rodríguez, Raúl. 1977. "La rumba en la provincia de Matanzas." *Boletín de musica* (Havana), no. 65: 15–27.

Nketia, J. H. Kwabena. 1972. "Sources of Historical Data on the Musical Cultures of Africa." In *African Music.* Paris: La Revue Musicale. Paper presented at a meeting organized by UNESCO, Yaoundé, Cameroon, February 23–27.

Ortiz, Fernando. 1974. *La música afrocubana.* Madrid: Ediciones Júcar.

Roberts, John Storm. 1979. *The Latin Tinge: The Impact of Latin American Music on the United States.* New York: Oxford University Press.

Ruiz, Ramón Eduardo. 1978. *Cuba: The Making of a Revolution.* Amherst: University of Massachusetts Press.

Sauer, Carl Ortwin. 1966. *The Early Spanish Main.* Berkeley: University of California Press.

Stevenson, Robert M. 1975. *A Guide to Caribbean Musical History.* Lima: Ediciones Culturas.

Suchlicki, Jaime. 1974. *Cuba: From Columbus to Castro.* New York: Scribner.

Szwed, John F., and Roger D. Abrahams. 1978. *Afro-American Folk Culture: An Annotated Bibliography of Materials from North, Central, and South America and the West Indies.* Philadelphia: Institute for the Study of Human Issues.

Timossi, Jorge, and E. López Oliva. 1963. "Donde nace lo cubano." *Cuba* 2, no. 18: 62–75.

CHAPTER 3

From Veracruz to Los Angeles
The Reinterpretation of the *Son Jarocho*

This article consists of two sections. In the first, I will briefly describe the stylistic development of the *son jarocho* in Veracruz, Mexico, emphasizing how elements from various musical traditions were reinterpreted and fused in its formation. In the second, I will attempt to demonstrate how such processes of stylistic reinterpretation continue in the present day by examining the disparities between two versions of a specific son jarocho as performed in Veracruz and East Los Angeles. Through a comparison of these two versions, and in particular the study of the role of the son jarocho played in the early 1970s Chicano movement in the Los Angeles area, I explore some of the general determinants of musical tradition and innovation.

Origins

The son jarocho is a song and dance form originating in Veracruz, Mexico. The genre is a stylistic amalgam of influences derived from the Spanish colonizers of Mexico, from Africans taken to New Spain as slaves, and from the indigenous population of the southeastern region of Mexico. Initial development of the form occurred during the seventeenth and eighteenth centuries. In earlier Spanish parlance, the term *son* literally meant "a sound which is agreeable to the ear" (Sheehy 1979). In a formal sense, son texts closely resemble poetic forms popular during the early colonial period in Mexico, such as the *copla*, *coplilla*, and *letrilla*. These short verses frequently made reference to bawdy or picaresque subject matter. As early as the sixteenth century, genres such as the copla were criticized by the Catholic clergy in Mexico for being in "bad taste." The first documentation of the son as a distinct musical and poetic form dates back to 1776, when it was officially banned during the Spanish Inquisition, most likely on the grounds that it was blasphemous or immoral. This was a period, after all, in which the views and practices of the leaders of the Catholic Church in all Spanish colonies were strictly enforced.

Toward the end of the eighteenth century, Mexican Indians, blacks, and mestizos came to adopt a number of the musical genres introduced by the Spanish, but they modified them to suit the stylistic preferences of their respective social groups. *Sonecitos regionales* (regional little sones) developed in this way throughout the country and became very popular. Particularly well-known examples of the son regional include "La bamba," "El besuquito," and "La india valerosa." The sonecito still exists today in the form of the son jarocho, as well as the *arabe*, another song and dance genre.

Sonecitos continued to be sung even with the eventual decline in popularity of the Spanish *tonadilla*; the dances earlier associated with it continued evolving among the mestizo population. Representatives of the Inquisition officially condemned the performance of regional sones during the eighteenth century, for the dances were viewed as sexually suggestive and the son texts often considered obscene or anticlerical. It is possible that the repression of sexually suggestive or politically oppositional texts led to the widespread use of metaphors and double entendres in the son.

In the aftermath of the Mexican War of Independence (1810–21), a quest ensued for Mexican identity, especially within the country's mestizo population. In most cases, mestizos considered themselves neither Indian nor Spanish, and thus they sought a means of expressing their newly acquired nationalist sentiment in a distinctly "Mexican" way. It is among the mestizos, even today, that one finds the most intensive cultivation of popular forms such as the jarabe, the romance, and the son. Regional allusions and patriotic identification with one's hometown, state, and country have long been a prominent element of son texts.

In Mexico today, the term *jarocho* is an adjective used to refer to the Atlantic seaboard of Veracruz or to someone or something from that area. The Veracruz area probably became associated with this term as a result of the perceived characteristics of its inhabitants. The word *jarocho*, still used in parts of Spain, means "brusk," "out of order," or "somewhat insolent."

Interest in the son jarocho tradition persists strongly in the Veracruz area. Due to overall changes in musical production and dissemination in Veracruz, however, the jarocho style has changed in recent decades. Marketing and commercialization have affected the son jarocho not only in musical terms but also with respect to the relationship existing between performer and audience. Instead of playing for lodging, food, and other nonmonetary incentives, the jarocho musician now typically demands a cash payment for performances; he or she is also a more versatile musician, adept at musical styles not necessarily associated with the jarocho region. Social changes thus clearly correspond to changes in the musical culture of Veracruz. The appeal of the son jarocho remains strong among the Mexican population of the United States as well. A recent rise in the number of touring *folklórico* groups (dance troupes) has exposed increasing numbers of Chicanos to jarocho-style dance music.

Instrumental and Structural Form

Typically, the instrumentation of the son jarocho ensemble includes from one to four of the following instruments: *arpa veracruzana* (Veracruz harp), *jarana* (a small folk guitar, played with a large plectrum), a *requinto jarocho* (also a small folk guitar); and sometimes the violin. When only one of these is performed solo, it is usually the jarana because this instrument by itself can provide both the necessary rhythmic and harmonic accompaniment. The most typical son jarocho ensemble consists of the arpa, jarana, and requinto jarocho, with the violin occasionally replacing the requinto. The most popular of the instruments among Veracruzanos are the jarana and the arpa, both of which help define the harmonic form of the genre. Different groupings of the conjunto jarocho tend to characterize regional substyles within the Veracruz area.

The musical example that I have chosen for comparative analysis is a standard son jarocho, "El Canelo." The two recorded versions discussed here represent unique interpretations of the piece taken from two distinctly different centers of Hispanic culture. The Veracruz version, performed by José Aguirre Vera (jarana, *pregonero*), Jose Aguirre "Cha Cha" (harp, *coro*), and Cirilio Promotor (requinto, coro), was originally a part of the repertory analyzed by Daniel Sheehy (1979) in his dissertation on the son jarocho. Sheehy recorded this performance in Tlacotalpan, Veracruz, during a live performance. The second version of the same son was recorded in a studio by the Chicano group Los Lobos del Este de Los Angeles (now known as Los Lobos) on their first LP, an independently produced project (New Vista Records, 1977) in Los Angeles, California.

"Canelo" can be roughly translated as "cinnamon." In the context of this song, "El Canelo" is used as the nickname of someone with brown skin. The text consists of a set of *versos* (verses) and *coros* (choruses) that contain both nonsensical and humorous subject matter.

Versos

¿Dónde vas, Canelo, caramba	Where are you going, Canelo
Tan de madrugada?	So early in the morning?
A buscar lechuga, Canelo	To look for lettuce,
Pa' la ensalada. [JAV and JAC]	For the salad.

Y el amigo mono, Canelo	And the monkey friend, Canelo
Se cayó de un palo	He fell from a branch
[Y en] el aire dijo, Canelo	And in the air he said, Canelo
"Válgeme San Pablo."	"Oh St. Paul, find me worthy."

Canelo murió, caramba	Canelo died, oh no
Lo van a enterrar	They're going to bury him
Cuatro zopilotes, Canelo	Four buzzards, Canelo
Y una águila real.	And a royal eagle.

Estribillos

Ya retripa, tripa, retripa	Tripe, tripe, tripe
Tripa de vena'o	Deer tripe
Mi mamá no quiere, Canelo	My mother doesn't want, Canelo
Que coma pesca'o	Me to eat fish
Y si acaso fuera, Canelo	And if I were to, Canelo
Que sea bacalao.	That it would be codfish.

Ya retripa, tripa, retripa	Tripe, tripe, tripe
Tripa de mapache	Raccoon tripe
Mi mamá no quiere, Canelo	My mother doesn't want, Canelo
Que yo me emborrache	Me to get drunk
Y si acaso muera, Canelo	And in case I die, Canelo
Que sea con tepache.	May it be from drinking *tepache*.

Ya retripa, tripa, retripa	Tripe, tripe, tripe
Tripa de cochino	Pig tripe
Mi mamá no quiere, Canelo	My mother doesn't want, Canelo
Que yo tome vino	Me to drink wine
Y si acaso muera, Canelo	And in case I die, Canelo
Que sea del refino.	That it would be in a dignified way.

Sheehy ascribes the *compás* (ostinato pattern) shown in figure 1 to "El Canelo" as performed among informants during his fieldwork in Veracruz. This rhythmic notation defines the basic nuclear pattern of the *compás* without providing specific *maniqueos* (strumming patterns). Sheehy notes

Figure 1. The compás *(ostinato)* pattern of "El Canelo," as transcribed by Daniel Sheehy (1979, 160).

that "the most distinguishing aspects of the [son jarocho] compás are its meter, length of the nuclear pattern, and harmonic pattern" (1979, 160), which can be represented as shown in figure 2.

Figure 2. *Meter and harmonic pattern of the "El Canelo" compás, as transcribed by Daniel Sheehy (1979, 160).*

The nuclear rhythmic pattern performed in Los Lobos' version of "El Canelo" basically adheres to the above compás notation. The jarana, requinto jarocho, and guitar in the Los Lobos version all perform double stroke maniqueos on each quarter-note beat of the 3/4 meter, which results in a continuous eighth-note strumming effect. Los Lobos musicians do not employ the harp in their rendition of this son jarocho, nor do they incorporate the harp into any of their other arrangements; instead, *guitarrón*, the mariachi bass instrument, substitutes for the harp. The eighth-note patterns performed by Los Lobos establish the compás schematic shown in figure 3. Arrows denote the direction of the maniqueo strokes employed by Los Lobos, one of approximately seventy-five typical jarocho strumming patterns cited and notated by Sheehy (1979, 106–10).

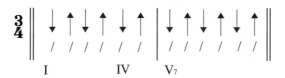

Figure 3. Compás pattern of "El Canelo," as performed by Los Lobos.

An extensive variation of textual structure is frequently associated with the performance of the son jarocho. As mentioned, the dominant textual models are derived from Iberian literary forms (Sheehy 1979, 153). The stanzas of "El Canelo" are in coplas (couplets), which consist of sets of four-line octosyllabic phrases in which the second and fourth lines rhyme or assonate. In the following example, these lines are marked "B" and "D":

A. ¿Dónde vas, Canelo, caramba
B. Tan de madrugada?
C. A buscar lechuga, Canelo
D. Pa' la ensalada.

Most son jarocho melodies are syllabic rather than melismatic. The primary concern for the performer is that the second and fourth lines assonate, and not that the stress patterns of the text exactly conform to those of everyday speech. In actual practice, the number of syllables in each line may be less than eight; in such cases, an extended syllable or pause in the text delivery maintains the desired correspondence with the length of the musical phrase.

The lyrical form of the son jarocho does not necessarily imitate verbatim the classic Spanish copla form either. The term *copla* is used by both musicians and non-musicians from the Veracruz area to refer to any of a number of traditional verse forms (except the *decima*). The copla model in the son jarocho tradition is used loosely as the basis, but not the ultimate determinant, of improvised expression.

The verse structure of "El Canelo" in actual performance adheres to the following structure; ABAB/CDCD EFEF/GHGH/IJIJ. Each four-line copla is typically divided and repeated in the following manner:

A. ¿Dónde vas, Canelo, caramba
B. Tan de madrugada?
A. ¿Dónde vas, Canelo, caramba
B. Tan de madrugada?
C. A buscar lechuga, Canelo
D. Pa' la ensalada
C. A buscar lechuga, Canelo
D. Pa' la ensalada.

E. Ya retripa, tripa, retripa
F. Tripa de vena'o
E. Ya retripa, tripa, retripa
F. Tripa de vena'o
G. Mi mamá no quiere, Canelo
H. Que coma pesca'o
G. Mi mamá no quiere, Canelo
H. Que coma pesca'o
I. Y si acaso fuera, Canelo

J. Que sea bacalao
I. Y si acaso fuera, Canelo
J. Que sea bacalao.

As most sones jarochos have strophic melodies, Sheehy provides transcriptions outlining the basic melodies of the fifty-six sones that he collected in Veracruz. The strophic melody of the "El Canelo" version documented by Sheehy is notated in figure 4. In contrast to the Veracruz version transcribed by Sheehy, the strophic melody of Los Lobos' "El Canelo" represents a different adaptation of the son in terms of rhythm and melodic contour, as notated in figure 5.

North American culture in general and commercial music seem to have influenced Los Lobos' interpretation of the son jarocho. Both the performers' use of Spanish and their overall vocal inflection reflect an involvement with English and with African-American musical genres such as R&B and rock. Widely variant levels of proficiency in Spanish among the group's members have necessitated a process of adaptation to and imitation of recorded music from Mexico in order to create a homogeneous performance style based at least partially on the son jarocho. Even singer César Rosas, who is fluent in Spanish, changed his vocal style in the process of incorporating music with Spanish lyrics into the Los Lobos repertory.

The decision on the part of Los Lobos musicians not to include the harp in their version of the son jarocho represents a noteworthy break with the Veracruzano performance tradition. Some precedent exists for this decision, however; many mariachi groups, when performing the son jarocho, do not have access to the harp and also tend to interpret jarocho genres without it. Both Los Lobos and other groups have adapted the son jarocho, performing it with what they consider to be "the essentials" of the form's instrumentation: jarana and requinto. The guitarrón, as in the case of the mariachi in the early twentieth century, has replaced the harp in these cases, possibly because of the stronger bass foundation it provides. The transcription in figure 6 is that of the instrumental, requinto-led introduction to Los Lobos' version of "El Canelo," a section that also serves as the nuclear rhythmic and melodic model of their arrangement.

Reinterpretation: An Amalgam of Invention and Tradition

In my dissertation (1985) examining the musical life of the Chicano people of Los Angeles, I concluded that Los Lobos' conscious adoption of and stylistic adaptation to Mexican musical genres represented an

Figure 4. Strophic melody of "El Canelo," as documented by Daniel Sheehy.

Figure 5. Strophic melody of "El Canelo," as performed by Los Lobos.

Figure 6. Introduction to "El Canelo," as performed by Los Lobos.

affirmation of their ethnic origin and identity. The form of nationalism that evolved among mestizos in Mexico during the nineteenth century is not substantially different from the political spirit and awareness among twentieth-century Chicanos, who are mestizos of a particular sort themselves. Los Lobos and their music epitomize and are a part of the 1970s Chicano movement, as illustrated by their promotion of numerous forms of Hispanic-influenced music, including the son jarocho and their well-known rockabilly-norteño style.

Musical expression of this sort has played a crucial role in the construction of Chicano identity in Los Angeles, involving the complex appropriation of numerous stylistic components. The musical style created by Los Lobos and other Chicano performers from East Los Angeles in the early 1970s can be theorized as a series of interpenetrated layers of ideologically charged sonic elements which were consciously fused to form a particular musical style. The study of style presupposes an awareness of the semiotic content, or significance, of various musical components and the ongoing processes of group definition in society by means of which all members position themselves in relationship to various "traditions."

In an important sense, "tradition" was the ideal that Los Lobos sought to express through their reinterpretation of Mexican music. A large part of the group's desire to appropriate folkloric jarocho genres into their repertory was based on an urge not only to preserve such music but also to promote it as a viable art form in an urban and, in many respects, a culturally hostile environment. For a number of years, Los Lobos performed Mexican-derived music almost exclusively, playing at weddings, parties, dances, and numerous college and other institutional affairs. Their musical preferences, as mentioned, were heavily influenced by the dynamics of the Chicano movement of the early 1970s, in which the valorization of Hispanic culture became a paramount goal. Activists felt that the maintenance of Chicano identity required the active support of and involvement in a multiplicity of Mexican traditions and the formal, equitable recognition of those traditions.

In an interview I conducted with Los Lobos band members, Louie Pérez offered one explanation for the group's initial attraction to the son jarocho, which manifested itself around 1972, after all four members had graduated from high school.

> It was a collective kind of experience that we had. We all started to go toward listening to something that was a lot different. So what happened was that we all went back to our houses, to our mothers' records, looking

into all that stuff. . . . The artistic kind of thing that really turned us on was the music . . . music of our own culture. That's why we pursued it for so many years. (Loza 1985, 310–18)

In the same interview, César Rosas stated that his first musical experiences involved listening to the recordings his parents owned. The artists included Mexican ranchera singers such as Lola Beltrán, Amalia Mendoza, Miguel Aceves Mejía, and a number of well-known mariachi performers. Because his mother was from the state of Jalisco, where the mariachi originated, such music assumed a dominant presence in the family household.

We were involved in Mexican music. . . . I'm just saying that we're just a bunch of Mexicans that grew up in East L.A. It was 1973, and we started playing Mexican music because we felt that it was a good thing to do. We were the first East L.A. band—a group of East L.A. kids who enhanced this Mexican music because we felt that it was something that was really important to do at the time . . . important for our peers, important for our culture, important for the community, and to awaken a lot of people and say, Look-it, man, Mexican music is a beautiful thing, and you shouldn't be ashamed of it. (Loza 1985, 317)

Rosas's comments reflect his conceptions of his own identity and help explain the group's decision to develop a more consciously Mexican-influenced musical style and to openly promote it as an oppositional aesthetic model. David Hidalgo, another Los Lobos member, describes further dimensions of this process of aesthetic reappropriation and the importance of audience response to the eventual determination of the group's unique style.

The thing was . . . after we broke the ice and people decided that they could accept what we were doing, everybody was longing for what we were doing. Everybody had that need in them that hadn't been fulfilled or something. But we were playing this music that people said, "Oh yeah, that's what I grew up with," and so it started to click. Like the first gig we played in Florence at the American Legion, it was a *tamalad* and we only knew about five songs, and we kept playing them over and over again. That was the first time that we played somewhere where there was old folks, there was kids dancing, there was teenagers, everybody was partying together. Before that it was mostly for whatever crowd you were playing for. But we got all these folks up and everybody was dancing. It was like, "What is this?" I never had that feeling before. (Loza 1985, 318)

This new feeling made the experience important for the group. Conrad Lozano noted, "We were just doing it [at first] for the fun of it because we wanted to do it; but when we saw the effect . . . we had on the people, we started getting a little bit more into it and we started developing it" (Loza 1985, 318). The response of the community thus reinforced Los Lobos' venture and solidified the group's decision to continue with its experiment. A process synthesized from various aesthetic systems had been fashioned in response to specific cultural and ideological needs.

The stylistic eclecticism of Los Lobos, whose repertory includes everything from Latin American genres to Mexican-influenced pop and rock and roll, and who prominently feature Mexican and other folkloric instruments such as guitarrón, vihuela, jarana, and charango, is not a standard formula for commercial success in the music industry. David Hidalgo offers the following perspective on this issue.

> We were playing the [Mexican] folk music and we believed that it would take us somewhere else. It was always like an art to us. We always felt that it wasn't for the cantina, it wasn't for the bar room. This is beautiful music, this is our culture. We wanted to take it out and we wanted some people to hear it and check it out and enjoy it. (Loza 1985, 320)

The idea of reclamation plays an essential role in Los Lobos' reliance upon Mexican-influenced musical repertoire. In a study that I conducted in 1982 (which became the pilot study for my dissertation research) with four young Chicano musicians in Los Angeles, including one member of Los Lobos, I was given some useful advice by folklorist Alicia Gonzalez, then teaching in the Department of Anthropology at the University of Southern California. Gonzalez suggested that arguably the most significant aspect of the cases examined through my study was the unique social and cultural environment of Los Angeles and the extent to which it may have contributed to the formation of the syncretic musical styles associated with Los Lobos and other groups. Chicano musicians in Los Angeles of the 1970s developed a particular musical style; its creation involved in large part a process of "reverting" to and revalorizing musical forms marginalized by the US commercial music industry. The prominence of Mexican or "neo-Mexican" musical genres in the repertory of Chicano musicians in Los Angeles after 1970 represents a marked stylistic shift and suggests a preference not easily discernible ten years earlier.

The factors inducing artists to reaffirm or reinforce previously repressed aesthetic predispositions are both complex and multidimensional. Within any marginalized social group, and particularly within those living in urban, multicultural environments, a number of conflicting stylistic influences typically play a role in the development of collective cultural expression. In East Los Angeles, especially during the apex of the Chicano movement, resistant artistic production took the form of murals, poetry, theater, and music. The son jarocho as incorporated into this movement was transformed from a regional stylistic marker (associated primarily with Veracruz) into one with an entirely different set of associations and meanings. I would suggest that the modified son jarocho form and its performance in Los Angeles became a dominant cognitive metaphor for Los Lobos, referencing the Mexican nation and nationalist sentiment, a nostalgic yearning for rurality, a particular sense of Chicano "tradition," and a united Chicano resistance in Los Angeles to the cultural hegemony of the United States all at once.

Los Lobos, and many others with similar experiences, do in fact comprehend some of the jarocho lyrics they sing in a manner not so different from that of Veracruzanos. The veiled references and subtleties of the son jarocho texts, however, are probably not understood in the same way by musicians in Los Angeles as they are by those from the Mexican gulf coast. Two of the four Los Lobos musicians, for instance, do not speak Spanish fluently. In addition, the text of "El Canelo" is highly colloquial and anything but transparent for Spanish speakers unfamiliar with jarocho slang.

In terms of the overall aesthetic system linking musicians to their music, however, a number of similarities do exist between the performers of "El Canelo" in Veracruz and those in East Los Angeles. In both of these "worlds" the performance of music manifests a particular life style and worldview. One of the principal sentiments associated with musical performance in both Veracruz and East Los Angeles is one of regional cultural pride. Examples throughout the world demonstrate that one of the most powerful effects produced from the performance of regional or national music is a sense of solidarity derived from knowledge that it has (ostensibly) originated in the performer's own society (for example, Texas Mexican conjunto music, Louisiana Cajun styles, Chicago blues, Italian opera, and so on). Son jarocho, wherever it is accepted and performed, is a music with many nuances of meaning that are shared in such communities by musicians and spectators alike.

As noted in the analysis of Los Lobos' version of "El Canelo," both the linguistic and musical inflections of the group have been affected and cognitively contoured by exposure to North American commercial music. Singing in Spanish was an entirely new experience for many band members. Some learned Spanish in the act of memorizing the jarocho lyrics; others transformed the Veracruz-style Spanish used by regional jarocho musicians into a version of the language with which they felt more comfortable. These transformations affected not only the performance of the son jarocho but also the manner in which it was heard and evaluated by Chicanos throughout Los Angeles and eventually consumers around the world. International dissemination of the Los Lobos jarocho style was assured with the release and promotion of *La pistol y el corazón* in 1989, which garnered a Grammy Award and included two sones jaroches, including "El Canelo."

Also noted in previous analysis were the changes made by Los Lobos musicians in traditional son jarocho instrumentation, especially the replacement of the harp by the guitarrón. Although the decision to exclude the harp was intentional, it was not part of the group's original plan. The major factor in the decision not to include the harp in the ensemble was the departure of Frank Gonzalez from the group, the only member who could play the instrument well.

Following the release of *La pistola y el corazón* in 1989, Los Lobos embarked on a national thirteen-city tour, exposing audiences from Los Angeles to New York to their version of the son jarocho and other regional styles of Mexican music. The group performed not at educational institutions or folk art exhibitions, but rather in large theaters as part of a major commercial venture. Apparently the group was considered worthy of promotional backing because of the recent release of the soundtrack to the film *La Bamba*, recorded by Los Lobos. "La bamba," the film's title track, held the number one position on US pop music charts for three weeks in 1987, and it eventually sold over three million copies, achieving the status of a triple platinum single. The song reached the number one position on pop charts in at least twenty-six other countries as well.

Los Lobos' blue jeans and blue-collar shirts hardly resemble the white, sun-repelling cotton loin of the mid-century jarocho musician in Veracruz, nor does the urban and intensely multicultural milieu of the Los Angeles area have much in common with Tlacotalpan, Veracruz. George Lipsitz (1990) has noted the postmodernist, deconstructive modus operandi of Chicano musicians such as Los Lobos and suggests that their modes of musical expression represent a decentered and contradictory form of cultural expression, yet one that represents well their present-day life experience. One wonders whether the musical preferences of Veracruz musicians today demonstrate the same sorts of stylistic mixing and contradiction that can be found in the music of Los Lobos, owing to the economic and cultural influences of the United States there.

A Conceptual Configuration

My studies of the musical culture of Chicanos in Los Angeles have emphasized the development and maintenance of syncretic musical forms. Melville
J. Herskovits originally defined syncretism as "the tendency to identify those
elements in the new culture with similar elements in the old one, enabling
the persons experiencing the contact to move from one to the other, and
back again, with psychological ease" (1945, 57–58). Herskovits continues,
stating that syncretism can be understood as a form of reinterpretation.
Robert Baron (1977) states that Herskovits defines reinterpretation as
"a process by which old meanings are ascribed to new elements or new
values give old forms a different cultural significance" (212). As examples
of syncretism, Herskovits cites the identification of saints of the Catholic
Church with African deities among Afro-Caribbean and Latin American
groups. In particular, he describes Afro-Cuban *santería* as a religion fusing
the elements of Yoruba beliefs with those of Catholicism.

In assessing such cultural metamorphoses, the notion of collective will
can be useful. When confronted with the imposition of dominant cultural
practices, the marginalized segments of a macroculture may develop any
number of syncretic cultural practices that function to integrate mutually
contradictory ideological spheres. One way in which such integration can
and frequently does manifest its presence is through music, visual art, and
other expressive modalities. In the case of Los Lobos' reinterpretation of the
son jarocho and other musical genres, one might suggest that dissatisfaction
with Anglo-American cultural and social institutions in the lives of California Chicanos led to the eventual formulation of a collectively resistant
aesthetic system. This system can be considered syncretic to the extent that
it demonstrates both the cultural and stylistic effects of mainstream musical
styles on Chicano taste and also the presence of stylistic formulations that
derive from styles not associated with the North American mainstream.
The Chicano movement of the early 1970s, therefore, both "fed into" and
was "fed by" cultural enterprises such as those epitomized by Los Lobos. The
stronger sense of identity, social power, and cultural legitimacy achieved
in the wake of the Chicano movement among Mexican Americans was
accomplished in large part through a collective process of musical appropriation and reinterpretation.

It is in the processual interaction of what are commonly referred to as
"tradition" and "innovation" that one can perceive the constantly evolving dimension of expressive culture. As a tool for the conceptualization of

these relationships, I have sketched the rotational graphic below (fig. 7). It provides, for me, a representation of the whole process of development of a new, or emergent, aesthetic. The effect of this processual complex might be referred to by the term *aesthetic cognition*.

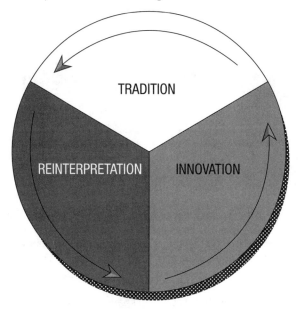

Figure 7. Aesthetic cognition: A hypothetical configuration.

Conclusion

The history and musical characteristics of the son jarocho in all of its present-day incarnations are richly textured and varied and merit further research and documentation. Studies by Sheehy (1975, 1979) and others have been indispensable in the construction of the first two portions of my analysis, which concern the early history and musical characteristics of the genre. But it is difficult, and perhaps futile, to attempt to isolate the origins of a form that is now understood to be in a state of constant reinterpretation. Through the juxtaposition of two versions of "El Canelo" I have attempted to focus on the reinterpretive and constructed aspects of musical "tradition" in both Veracruz and Los Angeles. I have relied on data and observations based on ten years of fieldwork and documentary research to support various hypotheses about the nature of reinterpretation and innovation. These concepts will hopefully become the subject of further inquiry, as Chicano music in Los Angeles and elsewhere undergoes further stylistic change.

Notes

An earlier version of this essay appeared in *Latin American Music Review/Revista de Música Latinoamericana* 13, no. 2 (1992). Copyright 1992 by University of Texas Press. All rights reserved.

    1. Group members also appeared in the film.

Works Cited

Baron, Robert. 1977. "Syncretism and Ideology: Latin New York Salsa Musicians." *Western Folklore* 1, no. 3: 209–25.

Herskovits, Melville J. 1945. "Problem, Method and Theory in Afroamerican Studies." *Afroamerica* 1: 5–24. Reprinted in *The New World Negro*. Bloomington: Indiana University Press, 2004.

Lipsitz, George. 1990. "Cruising Around the Historical Bloc: Postmodernism and Popular Music in East Los Angeles." In *Time Passages: Collective Memory and American Popular Culture*, edited by Stanley Aronowitz with Sandra M. Gilbert and George Lipsitz, 133–62. Minneapolis: University of Minnesota Press.

Loza, Steven. 1985. "The Musical Life of the Mexican/Chicano People in Los Angeles, 1945–1985: A Study in Maintenance, Change, and Adaptation." PhD diss., University of California, Los Angeles.

Sheehy, Daniel E. 1975. "Speech Deviations as One of the Determinants of Style in the Son Jarocho of Veracruz, Mexico." Master's thesis, University of California, Los Angeles.

———. 1979. 'The Son Jarocho: The History, Style, and Repertory of a Changing Musical Tradition." PhD diss., University of California, Los Angeles.

Works Consulted

Herskovits, Melville J. 1938. *Acculturation: The Study of Culture Contact*. New York: Augustin.

Loza, Steven. 1982. "Acculturative Patterns in Music Within the Chicano Community of Los Angeles." Paper presented at the Southern California Chapter Conference, Society for Ethnomusicology, March.

———. 1993. *Barrio Rhythm: Mexican American Music in Los Angeles*. Champaign: University of Illinois Press.

Stevenson, Robert. 1952. *Music in Mexico*. New York: Thomas Y. Crowell.

Valle, Victor. 1988. "The Changing Sounds of Mariachi Music." *Los Angeles Times*, March.

CHAPTER 4

Marginality, Ideology, and the Transformative Expression of a Chicano Musician
Lalo Guerrero

> They couldn't conceive of a Mexican sitting up there and singing
> Bing Crosby songs. So naturally the Anglos would get the jobs.
> And so I saw I wasn't going to make any money. I reverted
> to singing Mexican music.
> —Lalo Guerrero

Perhaps more than anyone performing today, Lalo Guerrero epitomizes the bicultural expression and experience of the Chicano musician. A first-generation Mexican American and recipient of the NEA's 1991 National Heritage Award, Guerrero is, at age seventy-seven, considered a living legend among Chicanos of the Southwest and in Mexico.

Guerrero's observations, derived from numerous formal and informal interviews I have conducted since 1984, inform the ethnographic profile presented in the first half of this work.[1] In order to situate this material within a theoretical context, I then apply a variety of analytical frameworks that collectively represent the issues of marginality, ideology and transformative expression. Additionally, I draw on the ideas of George Lipsitz (1990), who has developed analytical constructs directly applied to the study of Chicano musical culture in East Los Angeles.

Ethnographic Profile

CHILDHOOD

Lalo Guerrero was born in Tucson, Arizona, in 1916, five years after his parents had emigrated from Mexico. Lalo's father worked for Pacific Railroad as a boilermaker. As his parents spoke no English, Lalo and his siblings learned the language when they started school. They communicated with other schoolchildren in English and spoke Spanish in the home.

Lalo was influenced early in his life by his mother's music. She learned to play the guitar and sing when she was a young girl (although Lalo does not know where). Lalo said that she sang quite beautifully and that if she were a young woman today, she would probably be a professional singer. He quickly pointed out, however, that in the early 1920s there was little opportunity for a woman, particularly a Mexican woman, to become a professional entertainer. Lalo was musically enculturated in the home by listening to his mother, who started to teach him the guitar when he was fourteen or fifteen years old. In addition to singing, Lalo's mother also danced to such forms as the Spanish *jota aragoneza* and the *paso doble*.

From his mother Lalo learned the music of the old country, Mexico. This included rancheras, traditional folksong, and romantic song. In school he was exposed to American (US) culture and began to assimilate the music that was popular during the 1930s. Influences upon him at that time included Al Jolson, Russ Colombo, Rudy Vallee, and eventually Bing Crosby. Lalo maintained his Mexican music repertoire along with a variety of tunes popular in the United States. His exposure to popular music had been mostly through radio and motion pictures. Having never studied music formally, Lalo learned songs by ear. He has since composed hundreds of his own songs.

Childhood conflict in relation to being Mexican remains a vivid memory for Lalo, who has often described the environment at his school in a Mexican barrio in Tucson. The children were not allowed to speak Spanish in the classroom, although they spoke nothing but Spanish on the playground. Lalo once recalled that they were scolded for speaking Spanish in front of a teacher, "apparently so that we would master the English language." He also recalls having very few Mexican American teachers, and it was not until junior high school that he finally attended school with Anglo-Americans. "I felt a little out of place. It was given a negative connotation. . . . I had an inferiority complex because supposedly everything that was Mexican or Mexican-oriented was second rate and pretty soon you got the feeling that you were second rate."

This feeling of displacement inhibited Lalo from performing in Spanish; he wanted to sing and play contemporary American music of the era. In an interview he stated, "I don't want to sound boastful, but I could sing and play in English the popular American songs of the day as well as any

Anglo person." Lalo actually wanted to succeed in the American music field more than in the Mexican field because he was living in the United States and "wanted to be in the mainstream." He again pointed out, however, that in the 1930s (his high school years and thereafter) there were few opportunities for Mexicans or those of Mexican descent to become popular singers. There was widespread discrimination, and even though he could perform as well as the Anglos, he could never get work because of his Mexican physical features:

> They couldn't conceive of a Mexican, especially one who looks as Indian as I do, sitting up there and singing Bing Crosby songs. So naturally the Anglos would get the jobs. I'm talking about the nightclubs and the theaters and that kind of thing. And so I saw I wasn't going to make any money. I reverted to singing Mexican music.

It was actually out of necessity that he continued to sing and perform in Spanish. There were ample opportunities in Tucson at the time because of the large Mexican American population. In addition to the discrimination, Lalo also recalled that these were Depression years and that bad economic conditions forced him to perform in the Mexican sector. He needed the money.

THE INDUSTRY

Guerrero performed in Mexican nightclubs and bars and for dances, playing with trios, duos, and four- and five-piece groups. He became interested in going to Mexico to have his songs recorded and published, especially because he was composing in different Mexican musical styles. Eventually he went to Mexico City and had two songs recorded which later became very big hits and which to this day are standards in the Mexican repertoire. These were "Canción mexicana," recorded by Lucha Reyes, and "Nunca jamás," recorded by Trío Los Panchos and Javier Solís.

Although success seemed imminent for Guerrero in Mexico, he experienced disappointment when he attempted to perform there. He stayed in Mexico for approximately one year, hoping to achieve musical success and credibility. He was labeled a "pocho," a person born in the United States of Mexican descent and who has assimilated American traits, and the stigma of being from the United States prevailed among Mexican entrepreneurs and other musicians. Lalo also attributed this experience to some resentment on the part of the Mexicans:

> The Mexican people from Mexico have the feeling that we Mexicans who came to the United States were turncoats or traitors; and then, of course, being better off economically over here, there was a certain amount of jealousy I suppose, which is natural, and I think that was the reason. To this day, we still have some of that.

Lalo also discussed the Los Angeles record companies that became quite profitable in the Mexican community. Mexican music recorded in Mexico was generally unavailable in the United States. The local companies therefore recorded mostly Mexican and Chicano artists working in Los Angeles, including Adelina García, Las Hermanas Padilla, Anselmo Alvarado, Rubén Reyes, and Lalo himself. In addition to their local success, these record companies, with no competition from Mexico, produced records that became popular throughout the Southwest—California, Arizona, New Mexico, Texas, and Colorado.

Concerning the assortment of styles with which he became interested, Lalo has continually voiced his feeling that versatility was always a priority in his performance and compositional philosophy. In the 1940s, for example, he composed songs that incorporated the Cuban forms popular at the time, such as the rumba and mambo, and others in the popular swing style of the big band era. Lalo adapted Spanish words to the swing numbers and, along with the Latin forms, recorded them on Imperial Records.

The recordings attained considerable popularity, particularly with the zoot-suiters in Los Angeles. When Luis Valdez wrote the highly successful play *Zoot Suit*, he asked Lalo for permission to adapt some of his music, which had been discovered on old 78 rpm records of the 1940s. Four of Lalo's songs were included in the play and motion picture versions of *Zoot Suit*. He received royalties for music that he had composed thirty-five years before.

Although he had never actually become a zoot-suiter, he performed as a vocalist at the Mambo Club, frequented by many young Mexican Americans dressed in zoot suits. Lalo himself never wore the zoot suit and explained his association with the zoot suit culture:

> I never wore it because I was always introverted. Although I was a performer, I was a little shy. I had very many friends among the zoot-suiters and I learned to talk their language. Many of them would come over to dance where I played. They were strictly into swing. They hadn't gone in for the Latin music. This was before the mambo.

Lalo also noted that "*los pachucos*," or the zoot-suiters, were attracted to the swing sound in a way that seemed to reflect the phenomenon of their caló language, a dialect of Spanish and often referred to as a slang form. It was at this time that Lalo also started to compose in the Latin style, which was becoming more and more popular, even among the young zoot-suiters. Instead of adapting his lyrics to swing, Lalo began to compose songs in the form of the popular Cuban guaracha, which incorporated Spanish verse in a more fluid and natural manner. In some cases, he incorporated both styles, such as in "Vamos a bailar," which begins with a swing tempo, followed by a mambo, and then a return to swing. Lalo also used themes related to the cultural realities among Chicanos of the period, such as the use of caló in the lyrics. He even applied the theme of smoking marijuana in the song "Marijuana Boogie." Lalo clarified as follows:

> That plant [marijuana] has been around for ages; it was very popular in the days of Pancho Villa. Among the pachucos, zoot-suiters, it was used very widely. They always had it. They always used to offer me some. Boogie-woogie was very much in at the time. I said, "Well why not write something for these guys that identified with 'Marijuana Boogie.'" They loved to do the swing because this was during the war and that was what was in. You remember how they used to do the jitterbug!

IDENTITY

I asked Lalo about artists, especially Mexican Americans, who make professional compromises, such as name changes. He laughed and remarked that he looks too Mexican, so that even if he did change his name, "it wouldn't do any good." Vikki Carr changed her name (her surname was Cardona), a move that helped her enter the mainstream more easily. Lalo believed that Vikki Carr did not disclose she was Mexican American until it became popular to do so. Lalo also mentioned Andy Russell, whom he had known in the 1940s, when Russell was internationally popular and had recorded the hit "Besame mucho." Lalo remarked that Andy was not particularly Mexican in physical appearance, that he could be identified as Italian or of most any other background. In Lalo's view, Russell had to change his name (from Andrés Rábago) in order to "break in" to the entertainment business. Lalo stated he too would probably have changed his name had he looked less Mexican and "a little bit more *guero*" (colloquial for light complexioned). He wanted the success of an Andy Russell, whose appearance and name change were definite advantages. (Lalo pointed out, however, that Andy Russell had great talent and was a product of East Los Angeles.)

In regard to entering the mainstream in Los Angeles, Lalo said he had no trouble finding work in Los Angeles as long as he was performing in the field of Mexican entertainment. The success Guerrero enjoyed in Los Angeles launched his career in 1948. He was quite popular on records for twelve years and composed numerous songs that became hits on the radio. He also owned his own nightclub. He appeared on a variety of television shows during that era, such as *Latin Time*, hosted by Lupita Beltrán, *Fandango*, hosted by Joe Rodríguez and sponsored by Reingold Beer, and *Latin Cruise*, hosted by Bobby Ramos, a very popular Mexican American bandleader and singer.

Although content with the exposure he received in Los Angeles, Lalo would still have enjoyed additional success in Mexico City. He felt that if a person were successful there, he would be successful internationally. He did take occasional tours and professional dates in Mexico City, but for short periods only. His family was in Los Angeles, and he could not afford to maintain a home in each country. He repeated that he could think of very few Mexican American artists, save Russell and Carr, who have been successful in Mexico, completing his thought by saying, "And there's been many, many good ones."

Why Lalo Guerrero is today more well known among the young Mexican Americans than someone like Andy Russell, who was also from East Los Angeles, is another point of interest. Guerrero has explained that because he performs for young people at various locations, such as college campuses, the youth are exposed to his music and songs and consider him somewhat of a pioneer in the field of Chicano expression. He has written and recorded many songs that identify with the Chicano movement, such as corridos or ballads about César Chávez, Ruben Salazar, and other figures who symbolize the political struggle of Chicanos. He has also adapted many American heroes to the Mexican experience ("Elvis Pérez" in place of Elvis Presley and "Pancho Claus" instead of Santa Claus). Lalo Guerrero has intended throughout his career to identify with his community, to which he feels he belongs. He operated his nightclub (Lalo's) in East Los Angeles for fourteen years, where he enjoyed many happy times and made many special friends. When questioned about the issue of "Chicanismo" and the Chicano movement of the 1970s, Guerrero has always expressed a proactive position and political perspective. For him, the term *Chicano* has never implied a negative connotation, as it has for some. He recalled that when he was a boy during the 1920s and 1930s, his mother would always say with pride as she was singing or playing, "Soy pura Chicana," or "Soy pura Chicanita."

Satire and "Chicanismo"

> I've always had a flair for writing comedy, and through the years, in
> Spanish, I had quite a few hits of novelty songs like "La minifalda de
> Reynalda," "La flaca," "Maruca," and "El guero aventado," many comical
> songs in Spanish. But I've [also] written a lot of satirical things in English,
> but always with a Mexican flavor. Or I'll take a Mexican controversial
> subject and put it into a satirical song like . . . "No Way José," which is
> about the illegal alien problem, the undocumented worker problem. It
> seems that there's a very fine line between comedy and tragedy.

Although a social problem may represent an unfortunate situation, Lalo
Guerrero attempts to extract the humorous aspects that project from
"inside" the issue or personality. Both positive and negative attributes of a
controversy therefore become humorous and thus quite human. Lalo stated
that he writes these musical satires "as they come," and he says, laughing,
"I'm an opportunist . . . I jump on the subject. Sometimes I take criticism."
Lalo recalled that his satirical songs gained popularity when he wrote "The
Ballad of Pancho Lopez" in 1955. Although it was financially successful for
him, he received considerable criticism from the Chicano community for
presenting a Chicano stereotype in the lyrics. For this reason he no longer
performs the song.

Queried as to whether the stereotype of the Chicano people has
affected him negatively, Lalo explained that after receiving the "Pancho
Lopez" feedback, he realized that the community was correct in critically
responding to the song.

> It was kind of a putdown, but at the time I was hungry. I was starting and
> I needed the bread and maybe I shouldn't have done it, but I don't think
> it was really that bad. At that time the community was very sensitive
> about that. But I never did it again and I promise I won't do it anymore.
> The ones I do now . . . they're not derogatory in any way or stereotyping
> the Chicano. They're just about the Chicano situation.

I asked Lalo if he has ever found the criticism from the Chicano community
overly harsh or whether he has considered it a product of a nationalist
reaction. One example I gave was the presentation of the song "Granada"
as the theme song for Mexico during the opening ceremonies of the 1984
Olympic Games in Los Angeles. Lalo commented that although the song is
Spanish-based in terms of musical style and has a Spanish title (Granada is
a city in Spain, to which the song was dedicated), it was written by a Mexican, Agustín Lara. Lalo said the choice of the song did not really offend
him. At the same time, he pointed out that on Spanish-language television

programs, such as *Siempre en Domingo*, musicians are seen performing "poor imitations of rock 'n' roll." He added:

> Now if they were doing good rock 'n' roll, I'd say all right. Why don't they do our music, Mexican music? I can see a José José, a Juan Gabriel . . . marvelous . . . but you have all these groups who are playing bad rock 'n' roll and that is what is dominating the whole scene down there.

Lalo proceeded to emphasize that in Mexico, especially Mexico City, more and more commercial American music from the United States is heard on the radio, on television, and in the nightclubs. Referring to the Chicanos in the United States, Lalo commented that he believes they are "more Mexican here than they are down in Mexico." His perspective is that Mexicans in the United States, to a varying extent, appear to maintain traditions more so than in certain urban areas of Mexico, possibly because being away from their native country makes them want to honor the culture and land of their parents. Lalo also added that the issue of rock music is international in scope, and that badly executed forms of rock are performed throughout the world.

Lalo is now semiretired and has lived in Palm Springs for the past seventeen years. There he entertains on a lighter schedule, performing about two nights a week at Las Casuelas Nuevas. He still writes songs and parodies and attempts to have some of his own material recorded by other artists. For the past twenty years he has worked on a series of children's records called "Las Ardillitas" (The Little Squirrels). The records have been very popular in Mexico, where he has recorded them with the Mexican division of Capitol Records, and have become a tradition during the Christmas season. He stated that he has many fans between the ages of five and twelve years, and that he has found the project very gratifying. It is the only recording work with which he is presently active, although Linda Ronstadt has been performing and has tentative plans to record Guerrero's "Canción mexicana." (Ronstadt's father, Gilbert, was a close musical associate of Guerrero's during his days in Tucson.)

Lalo notices the recent trends in music in the Eastside of Los Angeles and compares the idea of a "new wave" among Chicano musicians to what he was involved in almost fifty years ago. He is very proud of his son Mark, whom he considers a very talented songwriter in the rock field, and of the other young Eastside musicians of today. On the concept of the "Eastside Renaissance," a term coined by the Chicano musician and writer Rubén Guevara with reference to the 1980s flowering of Chicano artistic expression in East Los Angeles, Lalo reflected by saying, "I'm very much for it. The process continues."

Cultural Analysis

The ethnographic data compiled from my documented work and communication with Lalo Guerrero provide a strong basis for the integration of the various theoretical models I have selected for analysis. Especially useful are Guerrero's reflections on his ideological perspective in regard to his social experience of marginality. Through his life experiences, Guerrero has generated a constantly transforming musical style that incorporates traditional musical forms from both Latin America and the United States. Ideologically, the most salient features of his musical expression represent the sentiment and motives of conflict, human value, ethnicity, politics and humor.

ENCULTURATION

Johannes Wilbert's model for the study of enculturation provides a framework for comprehension that is visualized through a three-dimensional concept of process, time and space. According to Wilbert, enculturation is "a process in which informal and nonformal modes of teaching alternate in frequency and in intensity throughout the learner's life" (1976a, 20). Wilbert poses an empirical question: "During (1) infancy, (2) childhood and (3) adulthood, how are skill-training, socialization, and moral education effected in a particular environment, society, and culture?" (23).[2] When this question is asked about the musical life of Lalo Guerrero, the responses gathered from the ethnographic interview depict the evolution of his musical life.

As seen in the ethnographic profile of Guerrero, the musician-composer was enculturated early in life in a rich musical ambience, one dominated by his mother's fondness for and ability in musical expression, specifically Mexican musical expression. She was Guerrero's principal resource for early skill training in voice, guitar, and language. She reinforced ethnic identity in a positive way, although the out-of-household socialization process evoked negative factors in her son's enculturation within his environment, society, and culture. Guerrero experienced and learned, both formally and nonformally, in a matrix of environments: his household, his barrio, Anglo society, school, and eventually his musical activities. He interacted with intersecting and often conflicting personalities within his family, among his teachers, and eventually in his musical audiences.

Culturally, Guerrero's experiences illustrate an early understanding and cognition of his ethnicity and its aesthetics, ranging from musical expression to religion. Fidelity to Mexican culture became a motive for cultural maintenance and thus learning. The dual quality of this enculturation was maintained by Guerrero's bicultural experience. One example of this process was the conflict imposed upon him with respect to his two languages: Spanish was not permitted in elementary school. Another example is his desire to sing US popular music, which was eventually discouraged because of his physical features, considered a detriment to such a goal. This conflict led Guerrero to develop his own ethnic art form ("ethnic" in terms of mainstream art forms in the United States) as a US citizen.

REINTERPRETATION AND IDEOLOGY

The theoretical application of reinterpretation of culture, syncretism, and ideology also serves as a vehicle for the analysis of the musical culture discussed here. Within the context of this study, the process of reinterpretation appears to be characterized by the development and maintenance of particular musical styles practiced by Chicano musicians in Los Angeles. The spawning ground for such development has been augmented by the adaptability of a transcultural Mexican musical framework of style, form, and philosophy.

The now classic theories of Melville J. Herskovits in relation to syncretism and reinterpretation are applicable in this study as well. Herskovits originally defined syncretism as "the tendency to identify those elements in the new culture with similar elements in the old one, enabling the person experiencing the contact to move from one to the other and back again, with psychological ease" (1945, 57–58). Applying this perception to Mexican-Chicano musical hybridizations reinforces its validity, although Herskovits's definition does not account for the expansion and mutation that occur within the new culture. Recognizing this, Herskovits later made clear that reinterpretation characterized all aspects of culture change. Moreover, he considered syncretism a form of reinterpretation and defined the latter as a process by which new elements ascribe old meanings, or by which old forms are given through new values a different cultural significance (see Baron 1977, 212). As examples of syncretism, Herskovits (1945) cited the identification of saints of the Catholic Church with African deities within the process of acculturation, a prime element in the formation of *santería*, the Afro-Cuban religion.

The cross-comparative and interacting musical expression of Lalo Guerrero provides an example of such a process. In his composition "Canción mexicana," Guerrero utilizes a traditional Mexican genre often used to portray romantic and/or nationalistic sentiments or spirit. The text of the song alludes to the beauty of symbols or sentiments particular to Mexico while the equivalent cultural meaning in the United States is questioned:

Pa' hacer pesos de a montones
no hay como el americana.
Pa' conquistar corazones
no hay mejor que el mexicano.

(To make a lot of money
There's no one like the American.
But to conquer hearts
There's no one better than the Mexican.)

Additionally, Guerrero interpolates into "Canción mexicana" nationalistic genres, melodic themes, and lyrics, such as "Cielito lindo," a *son jalisciense*, and "La adelita."

Also exemplary of syncretic, reinterpretive application of form, style and philosophy are Guerrero's "Chucos suaves" and "No Way José." "Chucos suaves," the energetic guaracha composed during the mambo-infused era of the 1940s and eventually used in Luis Valdez's play and film scores of the production *Zoot Suit*, incorporates a textual theme and linguistic style that imply a specific reinterpretation of the pachuco's forebears. Caló was a dialect that borrowed from and adapted both Mexican and Chicano clichés in linguistic structure, tonal contour, and vocabulary. Similar yet different forms or reinterpretations of the dialect existed from Mexico City to the border region of El Paso to Los Angeles. Thematically, the text of "Chucos suaves" provided a self-identity for the pachuco through light, but coded, metaphoric and highly symbolic expression. The song not only permitted the pachuco cult to examine its role as a subculture with various meanings but also enabled the pachuco to remove his mask and reveal himself to at least a larger public within his own subculture (Mexican-Chicano society), which often was unable to understand the pachuco and his zoot suit ritual. More than merely a physical symbol of race and fabric was perceived. There was also song and dance.

Cada sábado en la noche	Every Saturday night
Yo me voy a borlotear	I go dancing
Con mi linda pachucona	With my beautiful pachucona [girl]
Las caderas a menear.	To shake some hips.

Ella le hace muy de aquella	She's really something
Cuando empieza a guarachar	When she starts to dance the guaracha
Y al compás de los timbale	And to the rhythm of the timbales
Yo me siento petatear.	I really feel like dancing.
Estribillo	*Chorus*
Chucos suaves, bailan rumba	Fine dudes, dance the rumba
Bailan la rumba y la zumba	Dance the rumba and the zumba
Bailan guaracha sabrosón	Dance the tasty guaracha
Y el botecito y el danzón.	And the botecito and the danzón.
Carnal, pongase abusa'o	Wake up brother
Y los tiempos han cambia'o	The times have changed
Usted está muy aguita'o	You, sir, are very tired
Y hasta buti atravesa'o.	And even with the buti, out of step.
Antes se bailaba el swing	They used to dance the swing
Boogie-woogie, jitterbug	Boogie-woogie, or jitterbug
Pero esto ya torció	But all that has changed
Y esto es lo que sucedió.	And this is what has taken over.
Estribillo se repite	*Repeat chorus*

The syncretic quality of "Chucos suaves" is that of a transculturated AfroCuban guaracha popular at the time throughout Latin America, especially among Mexicans in Mexico and the United States. Here Guerrero evoked a nationalistic tendency by lauding the greater popularity of Latin dance forms such as the rumba, zumba, *botito*, guaracha, and danzón (mostly Cuban transculturations). In place of specific Mexican nationalism, Guerrero now conveyed his metaphor and satire through a syncretic Latino adaptation and hybridization, for the Chicano had himself emerged in such a fashion.

The satire "No Way José" is dressed in a unique cloak of syncretism. Singing in English with a Mexican accent, Guerrero employs a humorous text to express the futility of an undocumented Mexican immigrant's search for "a promised land." An innovative feature is the use of a vaudeville or early Broadway form and style. Versed with the metaphoric text and vocalized with the identifiable stereotyped accent, the song represents in thematic form a contemporary Chicano corrido reflecting the large corpus of early twentieth-century border corridos analyzed by Américo Paredes (1976) through a conceptualized framework of intercultural conflict.

My name's José González
I come from Monterrey
I came up to the border
One bright and sunny day
I told the immigration man
I go to USA.
He looked at me and laughed
This is what he say.

Chorus

No way, José
No way you go to USA
No way, José
If you no got no papers,
You don't go to USA.

But I am very stubborn
And I jumped the fence next day
I took the Greyhound bus
And went to East LA
I wound up washing dishes
For fifty cents a day
I told the man "I want a raise"
This is what he say.

No way, José
No way you get a raise today
No way, José
If you don't got green card
You don't get a raise today.

The hybridization of Mexican and US cultural features within an urban infrastructure might therefore be applied to a theoretical analysis of the concepts of syncretism, reinterpretation, and ideology in relation to Mexican-Chicano musical tradition in Los Angeles. Robert Baron posits folklore as perhaps concentrated and condensed forms of "ideological symbols," which are clarified by Clifford Geertz who, as Baron notes, "sees man as realized through symbolic thought, constructing symbolic models which create the capabilities by which he is defined" (Baron 1977, 210). Recognizing that social order is problematic, the resultant process causes the human to make itself "a political animal through the construction of ideologies which are schematic images of a social order which is chronically mal-integrated" (210). Baron speaks of the "power" of these symbols, referring to their capacity to grasp, formulate, and communicate social realities that elude the tempered language of science (see Geertz 1973, 210).

SYMBOLIC AND SOCIAL DRAMA

Important to this study is the work of José Limón, specifically his article "Texas-Mexican Popular Music and Dancing: Some Notes on History and Symbolic Process" (1983). Limón applies ethnography, social history and cultural analysis to the study of a different Mexican-Chicano subculture, both in terms of regionality and musical expression and/or style.

Limón's purpose is to explore an "ethnically defined expressive cultural system" (1983, 229) through the application of Victor Turner's (1969, 1974) concept of "comparative symbology" and to integrate such analysis in a historical reflection of Texas-Mexican social subordination. Limón stresses the importance of identifying culturally significant activity and symbolic behavior through the concept of cultural expression. The analysis of symbolic performances can yield an appreciation of social dynamics only if it grasps the essence of such behavior (Peacock 1968, 256). Limón concludes that "induced and accelerating sociocultural disruption, change and marginalization mark the fate of Mexicanos in this country" (1983, 231). Although Texas Mexicans challenged their position of marginalization politically, economically, and culturally, their resistance was never complete. In actuality, the social position of this ethnic group continued to "shift from a relatively more stable sociocultural state of affairs (both in Mexico and in pre-Anglo village life in the Southwest) to a state of dislocation, subordination and increased acculturation" (231–32).

Limón proceeds to relate this shift in sociocultural stability to the symbolic action of expressive performances, specifically music and dancing. He notes that during the 1930s and 1940s there occurred "a definite shift in the social context of performance from familial-ritual scenes to public, profit-oriented situations devoted exclusively and centrally to the performance and enjoyment of music and dancing" (1983, 232). After providing brief ethnographies of the dance and music social context, genres, and themes—or, as he terms them, "the various components of this mass expressive behavior" (235)—Limón offers a tentative anthropological interpretation of and hypothesis for the growth and intensification of such behavior since 1945. Here he applies Turner's comparative symbology phase of "social drama" by which "significant and culturally revealing symbolic action emerges and develops structurally when a historically and momentarily stable 'perduring system or set or field of social interaction' is thrown into crisis through the appearance of a specific, essentially political, disagreement between (usually) two sets of actors" (235).[3] Recognizing that Mexicans in Texas historically constitute a society undergoing continuous sociocultural change through processes such as acculturation, Limón states that such a "breach of previously stable social relationships" has resulted in cultural marginality (237). Limón takes Texas Mexican popular music and dancing to be "a cultural contradiction containing both elements of nationalistic/class resistance and acquiescence to the dominant social order," and considers its possible role as "redressive action in the service of both contenders in the social drama in the TexasMexican community and the dominant, largely Anglo, society" (238).

Although Limón's analysis appears to serve as a logical model for the ethnography presented here, questions emerge about its political, regional, and musical applications on a parallel or comparative basis to musical tradition among Mexican Chicano artists in Los Angeles. Whereas Limón has isolated a relatively organic framework, the conjunto-*orquesta* relationship, here I have focused on an individual's musical style on the basis of genre, political implication, and individual artistry. In addition to the musical life of Lalo Guerrero, isolated cases applicable to Limón's concepts include the 1960s to 1970s Eastside band circuits in Los Angeles, the 1940s adaptation and hybridization of vogue styles among the zoot-suiters, the new wave musicians from East Los Angeles, the mariachi culture in Los Angeles, and the many Mexican social club dances in Los Angeles (see Loza 1985, 1993). Differing in contexts while related in aspects, a model based on Limón's analysis would generate a variety of dimensions for analysis.

INTERCULTURAL CONFLICT

Américo Paredes has applied the concept of intercultural conflict to the Texas-Mexican border experience as expressed through music, specifically traditional folk types—for example, corridos, *danzas mexicanas*, romances, and huapangos. (Paredes 1976 describes sixty-six folk songs of the lower Texas-Mexico border.) In relation to the "*orquesta*-conjunto nexus," Manuel Peña (1985, 30) has posited two hypotheses on the relationship between the two musical styles. His first is a proposal that a dialectic worked itself out through the two styles, orquesta and conjunto, within a framework of emerging class difference and conflict among Texas Mexicans. This signified an intrinsic class operating within Texas Mexican society. Peña's second hypothesis, linked to the first, builds on a more "synchronic" base and "posits orquesta and conjunto as symbolic projections of a Texas-Mexican social structure that was solid enough to survive both the disruptive effects of interethnic contact with American society and the fragmentation introduced by class differences" (30).

Peña (1981) expressed the specifics of this conflictual duality, noting that changes in the social structure transformed into changes in musical (and dance) structures. "The move toward assimilation by some segments of Chicano society was countered by a corresponding move by the proletariat to strengthen its cultural position. And the music-and-dance innovations symbolically articulated this move" (294). Peña also notes that both US and Mexican musical styles have maintained powerful influences on the conjunto and, more so, on the orquesta, which, according to Peña,

> expresses the cultural duality . . . of Chicano society, it functions as a kind of symbolic style-switching . . . allowing Chicanos access to both Mexican and American socio-musical systems. The outspoken *orquesta* leader Little Joe has perceptively interpreted this dual access as demonstrating the "flexibility" of Chicanos. (295)

Peña thus cites these symbolic structures as processes representing an esoteric-exoteric factor (Jansen 1965) operating on the principles of cultural confrontation and accommodation (Barth 1969; Bateson 1972), "or what Paredes (1976) has described more specifically as the intercultural conflict between Chicanos and Anglos. It is against this backdrop that conjunto and *orquesta* have played out their dialectic" (Peña 1981, 295).

Whether such a specific dialectic exists in Mexican/Chicano musical expression in Los Angeles is debatable. Certainly Lalo Guerrero represents Peña's conceptualizations of duality and Little Joe's perception of a "flexibility" among Chicanos. Guerrero's "No Way José" expresses intercultural conflict as does "Canción mexicana," the latter predating the former by forty-five years. One major difference, however, can still be attributed to the lack of any particular regional musical style comparable to the stylistic development examined by Peña in South Texas, which is based on the emergence of two distinct yet related ensemble genres and their repertoires.

Mexican Chicano musicians in Los Angeles have assimilated, changed, and perhaps introduced a variety of musical styles that originated in both Mexico and the United States. The existence of such a clarified dialectic posed by Peña in relation to the conjunto-orquesta relationship, however, is more difficult to detect in Los Angeles, although such a possibility might exist through cross-comparative variables of musical practice in relation to meaning and history. The ethnographic profile and cultural analysis of Lalo Guerrero's musical expression and philosophy in this study, however, show that intercultural conflict is clearly a consistent issue and an analytical factor. Various social and artistic metaphors have pervaded Guerrero's life, from his early childhood ethnic conflicts to his eventual cultural satire in song.

THE UNITY OF DISUNITY

In addition to various dimensions of conflict, the issues modeled through enculturation, reinterpretation, and symbolic process represent active metaphors of marginality, ideology, and transformative expression. The "decentered and polyglot nature of popular culture" (Lipsitz 1990, 149) in Los Angeles has provided artists such as Lalo Guerrero with an interactive dialectic of accommodation and contradiction, access and rejection, and co-optation and resistance. George Lipsitz has perceived this ambience and experience as "juxtaposed multiple realities": "Caught between the realities of life in their community and the hegemony of Anglo-capitalist culture, Chicano artists fashioned a bifocal music accessible from both inside and outside their community" (149). Lipsitz thus cites this "postmodern" culture as a "multivocal and contradictory culture that delights in difference and disunity" that "seems to be at the core of contemporary cultural conscious-ness" (135). In assessing the metamorphosis of the Chicano musician in Los Angeles, Lipsitz would consider Lalo Guerrero as one of a "historical bloc" of "organic intellectuals" using the techniques and sensibilities of postmodernism. Within Mexican American Los Angeles this strategy was characterized by the pursuit of self-preservation that ideally would foster and propel the unique and distinctive cultural traditions of Chicanos into the mainstream of mass popular culture (136). In many cases this became the pattern; in other cases it did not.

Lalo Guerrero certainly fits the Lipsitz perception of the organic intel-lectual (which I assume has been derived from Antonio Gramsci), a notion that I would extend to describe the synthesized philosopher, not bound to the literary, analytical tradition of academia.[4] The role of the artist is, after all, to express, to compose, and to enact. Whether symbol or belief, the artistic process and individual experience represent an ideology that perhaps transcends even the most classical definitions of culture. Charles Seeger's (1961) time-tested warning about the limitations of verbal rhetoric still confronts my conscience as I apply these verbal, literary models for analysis.

Nevertheless, I believe the analysis presented here is valid. Through the integration of some versatile theoretical notions, I have not only probed the meaning of Lalo Guerrero's musical expression but also attempted to decipher part of its motive. This represents much more than a thesis of cause and effect; rather, the analysis examines a multidimensional human matrix that can be conceptualized as such and, in the spirit of postmodernism, as both "unified and disunified." History provides us with ample evidence of the highly creative consequences that emerge from the most marginal quarters of society. Lalo Guerrero has not only symbolized and tested such a hypothesis; he has verified it.

Notes

An earlier version of this essay appeared in *NARAS Journal* 4, no. 1 (1993). Printed by permission of the GRAMMY Foundation.

1. Section I of the article is based on a video taped interview, one of nine conducted in October, 1984, for my PhD dissertation (Loza 1985), which surveyed the musical life of the Mexican/Chicano people in Los Angeles from 1945 to 1985. The research was made possible through a grant from the Institute of American Cultures at UCLA, administered through the ULA Chicano Studies Research Center. Profiles based on these interviews are also included in my book *Barrio Rhythm: Mexican American Music in Los Angeles* (1993).

2. Wilbert (1976a, b) illustrates the model as a three-dimensional cube encompassing the elements of the three empirical questions.

3. Here Limón quotes from and refers to Turner (1974, 38).

4. See, for example, Gramsci (1971).

Works Cited

Baron, Robert. 1977. "Syncretism and Ideology: Latin New York Salsa Musicians." *Western Folklore* 1, no. 3: 209–25.

Barth, Fredrik. 1969. *Ethnic Croups and Boundaries.* Boston: Little, Brown.

Bateson, Gregory. 1972. "Culture Contact and Schismogenesis." In *Steps to an Ecology of Mind: Collected Essays in Anthropology, Psychiatry, Evolution, and Epistemology,* 71–82. San Francisco: Chandler Publications.

Geertz, Clifford. 1973. *The Interpretation of Cultures.* New York: Basic Books.

Gramsci, Antonio. 1971. *Selections from the Prison Notebooks*. Translated by Quintin Hoare and Geoffrey Nowell Smith. New York: International Publishers.

Herskovitzs, Melville J. 1945. "Problem, Method and Theory in Afroamerican Studies." In *The New World Negro: Selected Papers in Afroamerican Studies*, 55–58. Bloomington: University of Indiana Press.

Jansen, William. 1965. "The Esoteric-Exoteric Factor in Folklore." In *The Study of Folklore*, edited by Alan Dundes, 43–51. Englewood Cliffs, New Jersey: Prentice-Hall.

Limón, José. 1983. "Texas-Mexican Popular Music and Dancing: Some Notes on History and Symbolic Process." *Latin American Music Review* 4, no. 2: 229–46.

Lipsitz, George. 1990. "Cruising Around the Historical Bloc: Postmodernism and Popular Music in East Los Angeles." In *Time Passages: Collective Memory and American Popular Culture*, edited by Stanley Aronowitz with Sandra M. Gilbert and George Lipsitz, 133–62. Minneapolis: University of Minnesota Press.

Loza, Steven. 1985. "The Musical Life of the Mexican/Chicano People in Los Angeles, 1945–1985: A Study in Maintenance, Change and Adaptation." PhD. diss., University of California, Los Angeles.

———. 1993. *Barrio Rhythm: Mexican American Music in Los Angeles*. Champaign: University of Illinois Press.

Marks, Morton. 1974. "Uncovering Ritual Structures in Afro-American Music." In *Religious Movements in Contemporary America*, edited by Irving Zaretsky and Mark Leon, 60–134. Princeton: Princeton University Press.

Parades, Americo. 1976. *A Texas-Mexican Cancionero: Folksongs of the Lower Border*. Champaign: University of Illinois Press.

Peacock, James L. 1968. *Rites of Modernization: Symbolic and Social Aspects of Indonesian Proletarian Dances*. Chicago: University of Chicago Press.

Peña, Manuel. 1981. "The Emergence of Conjunto Music, 1935–1955." In *"And Other Neighborly Names": Social Process and Cultural Image in Texas Folklore*, edited by Richard Bauman and Roger D. Abrahams, 280–99. Austin: University of Texas Press.

———. 1985. "From Ranchero to Jaiton: Ethnicity and Class in Texas-Mexican Music (Two Styles in the Form of a Pair)." *Ethnomusicology* 29, no. 1: 29–55.

Seeger, Charles. 1961. "Semantic, Logical, and Political Considerations Bearing upon Research in Ethnomusicology." *Ethnomusicology* 5, no. 2: 77–80.

Turner, Victor. 1969. *The Ritual Process: Structure and Anti-Structure*. Chicago: Aldine Publishers.

———. 1974. *Dramas, Fields, and Metaphors*. Ithaca: Cornell University Press.

Wilbert, Johannes. 1976a. "Introduction." In *Enculturation in Latin America: An Anthology*, edited by Johannes Wilbert, 1–27. Los Angeles: UCLA Latin American Center Publications.

———. 1976b. "To Become a Maker of Canoes: An Essay in Warao Enculturation." In *Enculturation in Latin America: An Anthology*, edited by Johannes Wilbert, 308-358. Los Angeles: UCLA Latin American Center Publications.

Works Consulted

Herskovits, Melville J. 1938. *Acculturation: The Study of Culture Contact.* New York: Augustin.

Limón, José. 1983. "The Rise, Fall and 'Revival' of the Mexican-American Corrido: A Review Essay." *Studies in Latin American Popular Culture* 2: 202–7

Loza, Steven. 1992. "From Veracruz to Los Angeles: The Reinterpretation of the *Son Jarocho.*" *Latin American Music Review/Revista de música latinoamericana* 13, no. 2: 179–93.

Paredes, Américo. 1968. "Folk Medicine and the Intercultural Jest." In *Spanish-Speaking People in the United States,* edited by June Helm, 104–19. Seattle: University of Washington Press.

Peña, Manuel. 1980. "Ritual Structure in a Chicano Dance." *Latin American Music Review* 1, no. 1: 47–73.

Velez-Ibáñez, Carlos G. 1983. *Rituals of Marginality: Politics, Process, and Culture Change in Central Urban Mexico, 1969–1974.* Berkeley: University of California Press.

CHAPTER 5

Identity, Nationalism, and Aesthetics among Chicano/Mexicano Musicians in Los Angeles

Within this paper my aim is to examine a cross section of musical forms incorporated and stylized in a movement by contemporary musicians and their audiences representing the Chicano/Mexicano culture in the city of Los Angeles, California. The styles examined include rhythm and blues (R&B), rock, rap, mariachi, and banda. Theoretical issues discuss and address identity expressed through nationalistic motives, vogues, or trends in these styles, by which I mean ethnic affirmation through an interaction of the traditional and innovative.

Ultimately, such artistic "movements" must be considered from an aesthetic viewpoint, understanding that the development of new, emerging aesthetics in the four styles examined here represents various dynamics and a diversity—as Los Angeles is diverse—of changing expression and the cognition of such expression. The guiding principle that I will use to explore aesthetic frameworks is the concept of tradition as a cyclical, regenerative process involving the experiences of both reinterpretation and innovation (Loza 1992, 15–16).

The anthropologist Jacques Maquet has helped develop a field called aesthetic anthropology. Maquet (1979) issues a basic argument concerning the exclusive use of empirical data for the assessment of cross-cultural aesthetics. Maquet's principal admonition is that we not only consider the collective patterns and processes of any culture but also assess the specific character and thought of the individual artist when probing art as a cultural product. Maquet also suggests that the aesthetical domains of culture be evaluated from a "material culture" framework built on the foundation of the productive, societal, and ideational factors involved in the making of art. The issues of identity and nationalism, as I have used them in this critique, are correlated to the three levels of Maquet's triad.

In this essay and project I continue to develop a concept I employed in an article that I wrote assessing the reinterpretation of a regional Mexican style by a popular Los Angeles group of Chicano musicians, Los Lobos (Loza 1992). In that study I designed a circular model that could serve as an indicator of the aesthetic process among societies that have experienced a dual locus of culture—in this case, the Mexican American experience as expressed through what I referred to as the "sonic power" of musical expression. I offered the hypothesis that the cyclical movement of tradition, reinterpretation, and innovation employed by musical groups such as Los Lobos is a response to an intense artistic desire and motivation to reaffirm tradition through a variety of reinterpreted yet fresh innovative art forms. This cognition is not necessarily or primarily conceptualized verbally; it can be a predominately "sonic" metamorphosis and style development. Thus, the aesthetic becomes an active, *art-performed* form of analysis that is much superior to the verbal expression of any concept of formal aesthetic considerations. When I have talked and written about this exciting process, I have also referred to it as one of "cultural reclamation." Concepts of identity and nationalism are certainly components of this process, as they are of the four styles that I briefly analyze in this essay.

Rhythm and Blues and Rock

This question has arisen frequently: Why have Chicanas and Chicanos, especially in Los Angeles, adapted so thoroughly to black music? Responses to this question have included rationales ranging from the two cultures' affinities for dance improvisation and singing to the value of socialization—the notion that much Mexican music has functioned in much the same way as the musical rank in African American society. Other conjecture has focused on the sociopolitical relationship of Mexican and African Americans. Many musicians, however, have not detected this connection, insisting on the "primal" aesthetic of the music (see Loza 1992, 223–24).

The musical styles of R&B and rock have been, through the last fifty years, among the major musical ambits of Chicanos in the United States, especially so in Los Angeles. Jump blues evolved in the 1930s and 1940s from bands like those of Cab Calloway, Count Basie, and Louis Jordan. By the end of World War II, Los Angeles artists such as Roy Milton, Joe Liggins, and Johnny Otis had gained national popularity. Milton recorded a national hit, "R. M. Blues," on the Los Angeles–based Specialty Records. He was among the many swing artists who became major influences among Mexicans in Los Angeles. In 1952, black saxophonist Chuck Higgins attained a major national hit with his instrumental single "Pachuco Hop," originally aired by Los Angeles disc jockey Hunter Hancock. Mexicans in East Los Angeles began listening to Hancock daily, especially after he switched to radio station KGFJ, the first to broadcast exclusively the music of African Americans (Guevara 1985). Jump blues and doo-wop were becoming part of Chicano musical vocabulary. By 1958, the influence of these styles would metamorphose into numbers such as Chuck Rio's (Danny Flores) national number one hit "Tequila," a hybrid of Latin and the R&B-jump-rock matrix.

To outline the diversity of identity among Los Angeles Chicanos as personified through the styles of R&B and rock, I have chosen two examples: Li'l Ray Jiménez's recording "I (Who Have Nothing)," recorded during the early 1960s, and Teresa Covarrubias's "The Cry," recorded by her with the group The Brat in 1991.

Li'l Ray Jiménez, originally from Delano, California, had been a vocalist for the original Thee Midniters before gaining considerable recognition as a soloist in East LA. He was offered a recording contract with Motown Records and had also been scheduled to record with Sam Cooke. Neither opportunity ever materialized, and "I Who Have Nothing," recorded on Eddie Davis's Rampart label and which attained successful regional radio play in Southern California, was the closest Jiménez ever came to attaining the national recognition many believed he was worthy of. "The Cry," recorded by Teresa Covarrubias almost thirty years after Jiménez's local hit, provides another example of high-quality Eastside rock that never really left Los Angeles. The Brat competed with some of the most popular punk, new wave, and hard rock bands in Los Angeles during the 1980s, but national distribution eluded this group also, in spite of the fact that the CD it was included on, *Act of Faith*, was produced by the highly respected and influential Paul Rothchild, producer of another former LA band, The Doors, the first rock band to achieve five successive albums with each selling over one million units.

Blues is an element that has certainly become part of the fabric of American music. Throughout the diverse musical repertoires developed by Chicano artists, the blues element has served as a basic cultural referential point from Los Lobos' classic recording of their Ellingtonesque "Kiko and the Lavender Moon" to Poncho Sánchez's adaptation of James Brown tunes over Latin R&B rhythms. "The Cry" of The Brat references the blues as much as Li'l Ray's "I Who Have Nothing," and both songs denote the metaphor or emotional expressions of "a cry" in a special way. This notion is further examined in my book *Barrio Rhythm* and refers to the formation of a "Chicano" musical style in Los Angeles demonstrative of "certain commonalties" among the artists:

> Vocal and instrumental tone and inflection, improvisational motives, harmonic progressions, rhythmic references and preferences, training in technique, and vocal/instrumental voicing all exhibit some specific commonalties that frequently cross-identify the styles of various Chicano musicians; that is, they apply to the venue of tone and inflection, as in the case of singer Li'l Ray Jiménez and his nephew, Mike Jiménez. Both possess a wide range and have a lyrical "cry" quality in the higher register, especially at the ends of phrases in ballads. Improvisationally, a commonality often exists in terms of melodic solo passages imitative of Mexican or other Latin American styles. Harmonic progression in English ballads (or "oldies") is often similar to Mexican bolero standards from the 1940s to 1960s. (Loza 1993, 271–72)

Thus, in my estimation, there exists an interactive influx and outflux of time and space in the factors of identity, adaptation, and the aesthetics of African American musical practice as interpreted and defined by Chicano musicians. Such intersection can be culturally evaluated from both social and musical bases of analysis. These bases, in effect, can support each other formidably in developing related hypotheses of how and why Chicana and Chicano musicians have responded so intensely to the ambit of R&B and rock.

Rap

One of the most intriguing, and to me, exhilarating, phenomena to occur in urban America within the past fifteen years, and especially in Los Angeles, is that of the rap "movement." The "gangsta rap" associated with Los Angeles has shifted the political boundaries of the rap genre and hip-hop culture largely to that city. "Given the recent political events such as the Rodney King verdict and the 1992 rebellion, LA-based rappers have become important in terms of their critiques of both life in Los Angeles and American society as a whole" (Alvarez and Santiago 1994). Chicano rappers in Los Angeles have been an essential link in this movement.

One of the first Chicano rap artists to achieve both local and national recognition through his recording has been Kid Frost (Arturo Molina). His initial 1990 hit "La raza" is a classic example of the US Latin infusion of the rap format through a bilingual setting. Not only did the bilingual format of "La raza" affirm the Latin engagement with rap, but the recording enlisted a third-generation reinterpretation of a tune composed and originally recorded during the early 1960s by Los Angeles jazz musician and band leader Gerald Wilson.[1] It was then reinterpreted and recorded a second time by the group El Chicano in 1970, at which point it became one of the various rallying anthems of the Chicano movement in Los Angeles. Finally, Kid Frost's 1990 reinterpretation expanded the instrumental yet political metaphor with the addition of a text overtly dedicated to the expression of the Chicano struggle, epitomized through the humor and tragedy of gang warfare, but juxtaposed with the exclamation of Chicano pride.

Kid Frost's creative work, however, cannot be assessed solely through his "La raza." On a subsequent album he collaborated with other Latino rappers in a project called *Latin Alliance*. One selection from the album, "Latinos unidos," interlaces Latin-R&B musical texture (both sampled and recorded live) and rhythmic flavor; bilingual historical referents and interpretations of the Mexican southwest, Puerto Rico, and Nicaragua; and direct commentary on issues related to minority politics and inter-cultural conflict. Other compositions on the album include themes based on reflections on American identity, lowrider and boulevard culture, the political wars of Central America, and gangsta raps that image violence, discrimination, incarceration, immigration, the Border Patrol, and romance.

In assessing the issues of cultural identity and ethnic nationalism, the aesthetics of rap expression emerges as a highly charged vehicle among a constantly growing corps of young Chicano/Latino contemporary rap artists. Although the aesthetic of rap has webbed itself internationally as a preferred expression of youth culture in a variety of languages, its relation-ship to Latinos in the United States as part of African American music is not simply an artistic interaction, dialectic, or experiment. Rather, it is reflective of neighborhoods such as South Central Los Angeles, almost exclusively populated by Latinos and African Americans, where cultural turf may not meet in private households, but certainly does on the streets. Rap has been a point of synthesis and inevitable value to the young members of this geographical sector of a so-called city whose assumed power brokers in the media consistently not only ascribe marginal labels to the inhabitants of South Central and the Eastside but also literally fear entrance through the portals of these neighborhoods. The Harbor and Pomona Freeways are not the favored city ways of many a record executive or even record buyer.

Mariachi

Mariachi culture in Los Angeles is yet another example of what I will refer to as a "movement." One of the distinguishing characteristics of this musical style in Los Angeles has been the innovative establishment of various restaurant-based "show" mariachis, epitomized by the most prestigious ensembles such as Mariachi Los Camperos de Nati Cano, Mariachi Los Galleros de Pedro Rey, Mariachi Sol de México de José Hernández, and Mariachi de Uclatlán de Mark Fogelquist. Contrasting this highly lucrative ambiance of musical spectacle, however, are the hundreds of freelance, *al talón* mariachis, many of them lining the street curbs of the donut shop corner of Boyle Avenue and First Street, known as "La Boyle," where a kiosk is planned to be built in recognition of this Mexican tradition reinterpreted and re-enacted from places such as Mexico City's Plaza de Garibaldi.

Two practitioners of the restaurant-based mariachis provide an informative juxtaposition of both contrasts and parallels. In his development of Mariachi Los Camperos, director Nati Cano, who emigrated to Los Angeles during his twenties and is now some sixty years of age, has been largely credited as the first to reap extensive success from the dinner show format. Los Camperos is considered to be one of the finest mariachis in the world. Cano's musical philosophy has been one of "purism"—his goal has been to maintain the mariachi traditional style while innovating the context of its presentation to a constantly growing Mexican and non-Mexican public. As a recipient of the NEA's National Heritage Award, he has been given national recognition as an artist fostering one of the major traditional art forms in the country.

In many ways contrasting with Nati Cano is José Hernández, the director of Mariachi Sol de Mexico. Although an adherent of the traditional rancheras and other forms traditionally performed by the mariachi, Hernández, who is in his mid-thirties, has chosen to also highlight his mariachi format with the interpretation of songs representing another aesthetic layer of the bicultural Mexican American context—indeed, his context. Hernández's arrangements and adaptations of songs such as "New York, New York" and other English-texted popular tunes attest to this innovation—one that has attracted a special brand of attention especially among many of the "baby-boom" Chicana and Chicano aficionados who consciously identify with and appreciate the juxtapositions of such styles—in effect, an aesthetic molded bilingually, bimusically, and biculturally.

On the line of parallels, however, it is also significant to highlight the similarities in the musical and business strategies of Cano and Hernández. They are proactive cultural entrepreneurs. Both have established restaurants with mariachi shows, both have recorded and performed with Linda Ronstadt, both have instituted scholarship foundations for young musicians, both have participated as performers and clinicians in the major mariachi festivals throughout the Southwest, and both have lauded the "renaissance" of mariachi among the young Mexicano/Chicano musicians north of the US-Mexico border. These are conscious actions to provide economics and extend the radius of audience and the pool of artists concurrently.

The youth emphasis of the latter movement ultimately and explicitly addresses the issues of identity, nationalism, and the emerging aesthetic among young Chicano musicians and audiences in the United States. The proliferation of student mariachis at the high school, middle school, and even primary school levels is another contemporary phenomenon taking place in every major city of the Southwest and beyond. A tradition once scoffed at by many an identity-complexed Chicano youth thirty years ago has landed in a current niche of time and space that must be regarded as a movement of rapid reversal, cultural reclamation, and aesthetic liberation.

Banda

Finally, I arrive at a most recent phenomenon in Los Angeles—one that still bears a necessary period of evaluation, but one that has exploded on the scene in a most unexpected fashion. As I completed the final drafts of my book *Barrio Rhythm* five years ago, banda music in Los Angeles was just a beginning "craze." It is now a colossal wave. As a media and social force, it is reminiscent of another major movement among people of Mexican heritage in the last forty years—that of the Chicano movement. Certainly, the banda craze in Los Angeles bears a resemblance to the mambo and cha-cha-cha craze of the 1950s in New York City, there largely generated by the Cuban and Puerto Rican sector, although many non-Latino aficionados eventually also became associated with that movement.

The banda craze in Los Angeles is one of a more specific nationalist character—namely, a Mexican character. The banda ensemble format can be traced historically and stylistically to the traditional *banda sinaloense*, originally developed at the turn of the century in the state of Sinaloa, Mexico. It is rightfully one of the long recognized and colorful styles in the ample variety of regional music in Mexico. Consisting primarily of woodwind and

111

brass instruments, the distinctive instrumentation of the Sinaloa style has become the standard of the contemporary banda. It has, of course, undergone major innovation. A lead vocalist is now a standard element in the formerly traditional instrumental format, and electric bass usually replaces the traditional tuba. A modern drum set and Cuban-style timbales are now situated as the percussion section, formerly characterized by a battery, or *tamborazo*, of marching band cymbals, bass drum, and snare drum (although timbales and congas had already been in use in the Sinaloa style).

The dance aspect of banda, referred to as *la quebradita* is, according to observations, the real heart of this socio-artistic experience. Although the quebradita, the tango-like "break" choreography executed at many of the banda night clubs and dances throughout Los Angeles, is usually the focal point of discussion, I have noted that the essential dance steps conform somewhat to combinations of the genres performed by the banda, ranging from a polka beat to tropical rhythms to traditional Mexican sones. A dance style has emerged that is at times a hybrid of *cumbia*, norteño, Tex-Mex, and zapateado. At many dances the actual quebradita is never actually executed because of space limitations.

In assessing the factors of identity, nationalism, and the emergence of a collective aesthetic in the making of the current banda phenomenon, it has been useful to think in terms of both the movement's social force and its artistic representation and regeneration. One of the principal reasons for the international media exposure of this style is the ascension of banda-ranchera–formatted radio station KLAX, known as "La Q" and spearheaded by disc jockey Juan Carlos Hidalgo. In August 1992 KLAX moved into the number one spot according to Arbitron ratings for the city of Los Angeles, surpassing the syndicated KLSX morning talk show hosted by Howard Stern, which had previously held the number one rating. The radio industry immediately reacted in an almost bewildered manner (the terms "shock waves" in the industry were used by *Music Connection* magazine), not only unable to explain this demographic "alarm clock" but also unable to develop immediate and competitive marketing strategies to regain top ratings. The Spanish-speaking public of Los Angeles is simply not part of the mainstream radio industry. Almost two years since the rating changed over, KLAX still retains the top Arbitron ratings for Los Angeles.[2]

Aside from this debate over the commercial success of banda, the more important question arises as to why this style has captivated so many so quickly. Unlike in culture and character when compared to the older waves of European immigrants, and no longer a racial minority, the Latinos who make up an estimated 41 percent of Los Angeles's population are not so different from other cultural masses that frequently feel the need for renovation in art, fashion, and other stylistic and philosophical pursuits. Primarily a working-class people, both Mexican immigrants and US-born Chicanos have opportunized the moment to "jump on the banda wagon," a vogue in which they are not vulnerable to pressure to assimilate to a North American musical style, but where they can reclaim and renovate their own tradition while defying the commercial seduction and standards of MTV and its related industry. As I said in an interview with Rubén Martínez for a cover story in the *Los Angeles Times Magazine*:

> People are saying that we don't want to look like Prince or Madonna. We can wear our boots and hats. The Vaquero style is important as a symbol. When a Mexican puts on the suit, just like in the old days you put on a zoot suit, you can walk into that club and be proud that you're a Mexican. (Martínez 1994, 12)

Another issue reinforcing the social and aesthetic needs of the Mexican/Chicano aficionados of banda is the current heavy dose of anti-immigration rhetoric being used to blame immigrants for California's economic problems. Politicians have been largely responsible for much of this rhetoric, which resonates with those in search of easy answers to complex social and historical problems. As Martínez so aptly wrote, "While Governor Pete Wilson, Senators Barbara Boxer and Dianne Feinstein and many other pols in the state rant about the 'immigration problem,' the more pertinent issue might be this: When will they learn to dance the quebradita?" (1994, 10). Recently, KLAX disc jockey Juan Carlos Hidalgo announced his mock candidacy for governor of California, referring to his incumbent opponent as "Pupi Wilson."

Forging a Collective Analysis

In the brief presentation I have made here, covering four distinct musical styles utilized by Chicanos/Mexicanos in Los Angeles, I have attempted to highlight some basic issues of identity, nationalism, and aesthetics as both social and artistic motives and to offer the viewpoint that these two motives are interactive in the current movement.

The four styles, or "movements," represent a diversity of artistic form, "content," and expression. This variation should not surprise those of us involved in the study of Chicano/Mexicano culture in the United States, especially when centered on diverse societies in Los Angeles, itself a mammoth, interacting framework of both cultural integration and segregation. An important fact that we must realize as scholars of Chicana/o studies is that Chicano society itself has continually diversified according to growing differences in age, gender, sexuality, social and economic class, religion, politics, immigration status, identity, and language. The dynamics of these sometimes artificial divisions often go well beyond such categories and logic. The explanations for why, for example, one second-generation Chicana, living in Los Angeles, immerses herself in the banda cultural network while another second-generation Chicana refutes the style and embraces rap have yet to be explored. As I sat and watched ten thousand Mexicanos and Chicanos dancing to live bandas at the Memorial Sports Arena in Los Angeles in April 1994, I found myself reflecting on how culturally engaged I felt, yet at the same time, how actively disengaged. The context was not part of my present social or musical network in spite of my cultural relationship to it.

Indeed, much of the media has recently described the city of Los Angeles as a riot-torn, burned-out, mud-slid, smog-laden, earthquaked, drive-by-shot remnant of twentieth-century civilization. *Time* magazine recently featured on its cover the question, "Is the City of Angels Going to Hell?"[3] New Yorker David Rieff has written a book titled *Los Angeles: Capital of the Third World* (1991). My reaction to much of this is a suggestion. Let us not think of Los Angeles or any other world city as either "third world" or "first world." The changing pattern of cultures and multicultural ambits in contemporary society simply is occurring too rapidly, and at an increasing pace, to set such a limited description for the human race. The Mexicans in Los Angeles have begun a "reclamation" of much more than music. But music speaks loudly, and the Mexicans may hold some answers for not only the City of the Angels, but for the imminent reality of a multicultural world.

Notes

An earlier version of this essay appeared in *Musical Aesthetics and Multiculturalism in Los Angeles*, edited by Steven Loza. Selected Reports in Ethnomusicology, no. 10. Los Angeles: UCLA Ethnomusicology Publications, 1994. Copyright 1994 by the Regents of the University of California.

1. It is important to point out that Wilson had become directly involved with Chicano-Mexicano culture. He married a Mexican woman and became actively engaged with Mexican culture, especially that of bullfighting. His "Viva Tirado" was named in honor of Mexican bullfighter Juan Tirado.

2. I do not suggest that banda will compete politically with the intensity and dynamics of the Chicano movement, initiated during the 1960s. As a popular movement, however, banda has penetrated a level of media influence that is unprecedented. Additionally, although its political force and stature is still a matter of metamorphosis, banda is highly political.

3. See the cover of *Time* 141, no. 16 (1993).

Works Cited

Alvarez, Milo, and Josefina Santiago. 1994. "Los Angeles Rap Music: Historical Aspects and Mexican-American/Chicano Case Studies." Unpublished term paper, UCLA.

Guevara, Ruben. 1985. "The View from the Sixth Street Bridge: The History of Chicano Rock." In *The First Rock and Roll Confidential Report*, edited by David Marsh, 113–26. New York: Pantheon.

Loza, Steven. 1992. "From Veracruz to Los Angeles: The Reinterpretation of the *Son Jarocho*." *Latin American Music Review/Revista de música latinoamericana* 13, no. 2:179–94.

———. 1993. *Barrio Rhythm: Mexican American Music in Los Angeles*. Champaign: University of Illinois Press.

Maquet, Jacques. 1979. *Introduction to Aesthetic Anthropology*. Malibu, CA: Undena Publications.

Martínez, Rubén. 1994. "The Shock of the New." *Los Angeles Times Magazine*, January 30, 10.

Rieff, David. 1991. *Los Angeles: Capital of the Third World*. New York: Simon & Schuster.

Selected Discography

Kid Frost. 1990. *Hispanic Causing Panic*. Pump Records.

East Side Revue: 40 Hits by East Los Angeles' Most Popular Groups. 1966 [1969]. Rampart. Distributed by American Pie. Includes "I Who Have Nothing" by Li'l Ray Jiménez.

El Chicano. 1970. *Viva Tirado*. MCA.

Gerald Wilson Orchestra. 1970. *The Best of the Gerald Wilson Orchestra*. World Pacific Jazz Records.

Los Lobos. 1992. *Kiko*. Slash/Warner Bros.

———. 1993. *Just Another Band from East L.A.: A Collection*. Slash/Warner Bros.

Mariachi Los Camperos de Nati Cano. 1992. *Canciones de siempre*. Peer Southern Productions, Inc. (Polygram Latino).

Mariachi Sol de Mexico. 1991. *New York, New York*. Discos Penix.

The Brat. 1991. *Act of Faith*. Tune Bomb Music Company.

CHAPTER 6

Latin American Popular Music in Japan and the Issue of International Aesthetics

Since especially the 1930s, Latin American music has played a dynamic role in Japanese society. The aesthetic for Latin American and Spanish popular music and dance has pertained not only to imported performing artists and recordings from that sector but also to the emergence of a major group of Japanese performers who have adapted Latin American and Spanish styles. Examples vary from the Argentine tango to Spanish flamenco, from the Cuban mambo to Mexican mariachi and boleros, and from Guatemalan and Mexican marimba ensembles to the current Caribbean and New York City salsa styles.

In this preliminary analysis, I offer some tentative hypotheses based on the following questions: 1) Why has an aesthetic of Latin music developed so strongly in Japan, as in Europe and Africa and other non-Latin American populations? 2) Why has the same pattern not occurred among the non-Latin population of the United States, which in terms of media and cultural exposure has more access, contextually and geographically, when compared with Japan and the other areas cited? 3) How does the development of a Latin music aesthetic in Japan represent an apparent international aesthetic of Latin music? Does Latin music and dance (e.g., mambo, cha-cha-cha, modern salsa), like African American music and dance in the United States, among other musical traditions, have a particular set of aesthetic traits and traditions that possibly cross the boundaries of culture, society, and language in a particularly unique way worldwide?

For this essay, I dedicated a good portion of my time in Tokyo during the last ten months to conducting interviews with various Japanese artists of Latin American music in addition to attending a variety of related live performances and researching some of the documented recordings and literature. I have also made substantial notes on the importation of Latin American music artists via the recording industry and live performances.

The Interviews as Analysis

The richest source for this fieldwork has been a number of interviews that I conducted with the following artists (identified with their approximate ages): Antonio Koga (54); Sam Moreno (48); Yoshiro (56); Yoshihito "Chiquito" Fukumoto (35); Nora (35).

In my conversations with these five artists, which at various points were quite intense and personal, I inquired of their opinions on the following issues: 1) Why and how did they develop a Latin American music aesthetic? What prompted their interest? 2) Why has Latin American music been so vital in Japan (in addition to many other foreign styles) and even more so than in many sectors of the United States, where much of it has evolved (e.g., salsa, mariachi, etc.)? 3) Is the Spanish language a factor in the acquisition and development of Latin American music performance in Japan?

Two of the artists, Nora and "Chiquito" ("small guy"), in their previous roles as members of the highly successful salsa ensemble Orquesta de la Luz, concertized at Madison Square Garden in New York City. In 1990 the group's first LP, *Salsa caliente de Japan*, became a platinum album, maintaining the number one spot in *Billboard* magazine's Latin Tropical sales chart for eleven consecutive weeks. In 1995 Orquesta de la Luz was nominated for a Grammy Award in the Latin Tropical category. The unprecedented success of this group has been debated from many perspectives. Some have speculated on the group's "exotic" and "foreign" personification of salsa as a "plus factor" in its acceptance by the Latin music industry and public.

But there is more to the equation than this facet of identity and novelty. For any salsa ensemble to perform at Madison Square Garden in New York's major salsa festival with leading Latin music artists such as Tito Puente and Oscar De Leon, or at the Universal Amphitheater in Los Angeles with Celia Cruz, demands a musical interpretive skill and an aesthetic, cultural sensibility that measure to the highest of standards in the field—otherwise, Puente and De Leon would neither "sit in" nor tour with the band, nor would the highly demanding, dance-oriented Latin music aficionados support an inferior musical product. This is not to say that Orquesta de la Luz's musical interpretations should necessarily be compared "across the board" with Latin American artists, especially in the area of vocal interpretation.

Referring then to both Nora and Chiquito, I have been able to enhance my understanding of their musical philosophies as related to Latin music because of their articulate responses to my cultureloaded questions. For example, in response to the issue of singing in Spanish, Nora commented that she speaks much better English than Spanish (characterized by the fact that I interviewed her in English) and that her earlier musical preferences were based on soul and R&B, influenced especially by artists such as Donny Hathaway and Chaka Kahn. Her decision to begin singing salsa began during the 1980s, and in 1984 she co-founded, with percussionist Gen Ogimi, the group Orquesta de la Luz. Groups in Tokyo such as Orquesta del Sol had already existed since ten years prior to this and highly influenced Orquesta de la Luz. For Nora, one of the immediate advantages of the music was that she found Spanish much easier to pronounce than English, largely due to similar inflections and more vowelbased characterization, among other elements in common with the Japanese language. By 1989 Orquesta de la Luz was a major sensation with the Tokyo public, and in 1990 the group was offered a recording contract with BMG and toured North America and Puerto Rico. The group continued to tour for six consecutive years in the United States, Latin America, Europe, and Asia, releasing a number of albums and garnering various radio hits.

It was also of great interest to me to ask Nora for her views on one of the main issues I raise in this paper—that of Japanese musicians developing salsa in a much more critical mode than non-Latin Americans in the United States. Her immediate response was that there are "many reasons," including: 1) the pronunciation of Spanish (often more difficult for non-Latin Americans in the United States than for Japanese); and 2) the "image" of Latinos in the United States, where she speculates that culture and society is "not really mixed [but] separate" in terms of African Americans, Latinos, and others. She referred to these as "different blocs" that are "separate" and that basically "protect their own culture." She noted that the United States is not one race or one nationalism. Thus, Nora feels that the image of salsa, the music of Latinos, has been influenced by these sets of circumstances, prejudices, and conflicts.

Nora's comments reinforce some of the hypotheses I have been thinking on. Again, one of my principal points is the paradox illustrated by the number of high-quality salsa groups from Japan, Holland, and Germany, among other countries around the world, while a vacuum exists within the non-Latino sector of the United States, apart from many instrumentalists, especially brass and woodwind musicians performing with salsa groups there (but not vocals or percussion, by and large). The dance clubs are also similarly polarized, a situation far different and contrary to the integrated social context of the New York Palladium era of the 1940s and 1950s. With the contemporary polarization of the races and culture in the United States, I have hypothesized this dichotomy to be possibly linked to the following issues: linguistics, ideology of art, growing international aesthetics, and class or ethnic prejudices and psychological factors resulting from ethnic/class polarization. In his yet unpublished paper on Orquesta de la Luz and the globalization and Japanization of Afro-Caribbean music, "'Salsa no tiene frontera': Orquesta de la Luz or the Globalization and Japanization of Afro-Caribbean Music," Shuhei Hosokawa makes the following observation:

> For Latinos, an all-*gringo* salsa band, if any, would be less surprising but more threatening and scandalous than Orquesta de La Luz. This is because such a band may annihilate in a rather invading manner the assumption about ethnic hierarchy inside which Latinos and *gringos* have been living for centuries. It may intimidate and subvert the Latino identity which is formed not only by their own biological and familial heritage but also by their constant confrontation with and astute repression by the Anglo-American society. (29–30)

Especially essential to an international perspective in Hosokawa's analysis is his integration of what might be referred to as native theories, and specifically that of *kata*—the Japanese conceptualization and philosophy of learning, tradition, spirituality, morals, perceived attention to detail, and the surface aesthetic—in effect, a form of aesthetic theory. Additionally, Hosokawa incorporates into his analysis *nihonjin-ron*, a term referring to "popular discourses on Japan and its particularity" (30); thus, the issue of Japanese identity and its related cultural values as an international actor becomes essential fodder for analysis or a deeper understanding.

In representing various issues of identity, trumpeter "Chiquito" Fukumoto, also formerly of Orquesta de la Luz, made a number of observations based on his own personal perspectives and experiences. He believes that much of the Japanese affinity for Latin music is related to the Japanese traditions of dance, drumming, and melody—the latter which he associates with meaning and the soul. On a related basis, many musicians in Japan have pointed out to me the similarity they feel between the Japanese *enka* song style and the Latin American romantic bolero. Highly influenced by artists such as Eddie Palmieri, Tito Puente, Luis "Perico" Ortiz, and Jerry González, all of Puerto Rican heritage, Chiquito currently leads a Latin jazz group named Latin Yaro (*yarô* means "guys"), which has released three albums on a Japanese label.

Responding to the issue of the Japanese versus non-Latino US salsa activity, Chiquito noted that in Japan people enjoy taking ballroom Latin dance lesson and learning other related things (e.g., Afro-Cuban drumming, *santería* chants, music lessons) and that Latin music thrives without much ethnic conflict. He also noted that although a number of US horn players (e.g. Brian Lynch, Mike Mosley) have performed extensively with Latin bands in New York City, singers and percussionists of similar background are rare in such contexts. He stated, "That might be related to American history. . . . There are hard social issues between groups in the US. . . . Subconsciously, some people perhaps think that Latin music makes people reflect on these conflicts. That's why Latin music is so important to Latin people. . . . [It is] their identity as a culture . . . as a race." Chiquito also noted that he is impressed by the musicality of Japanese Latin musicians and by the fact that Latinos in the United States have accepted these musicians as part of the Latin musical context.

Interestingly, the prime motivation for the recent break-up of Orquesta de la Luz was the desire to break out of the strict salsa mold and its pressure to maintain popular repertoire and commercial success in the Latin market. Both Nora (who has recently released her own solo LP internationally) and Chiquito expressed the fact that as Japanese, they have multimusical philosophies, and they want to incorporate these influences into a more multistyled context, that of combining elements of Latin, R&B, jazz, and Japanese artistic concepts.

My discussions with Antonio Koga, Yoshiro, and Sam Moreno have also profoundly enhanced my understanding of the Japanese Latin American music aesthetic. Antonio Koga's stage name is derived from the name of an Argentine guitarist who inspired him and his teacher, a well-known Japanese composer, who encouraged Koga to pursue Latin American guitar styles and music. It was during his high school years and after going through an Elvis Presley phase that Koga heard the Mexican-based Trío Los Panchos and decided that he wanted to play the guitar-formatted romantic style. He began to combine Latin American, flamenco, and Japanese styles in his guitar performances. Like Nora, he expressed the fact that Spanish was much easier for him to sing than English (again, the interview, however, was conducted in English and with a Japanese translator). He noted the similarity between Spanish and Japanese accents. By the age of twenty, Koga had become quite popular throughout Japan, and he hosted a weekly television musical variety program for five years. He also proceeded to record a number of albums. Chu Chu Navarro of Los Panchos composed a song for Koga—"Se llama Fujiama"—which became a hit in Latin America and Japan. Other Latin American musicians and composers whom he befriended included Laurindo Almeida, Luiz Bonfá, Lucho Gatica, Andrés Segovia, and Armando Manzanero.

When I asked Koga why Latin music is so popular in Japan, he responded with a number of ideas, including "same human feelings, our common Mongolian ancestors" and the fact that "we like parties, festivals, and the happiness of music." He also referred to the words of the songs that express both sadness and happiness, much like Japanese *enka*. He also stressed the importance of rhythm as another similarity between the cultures.

One of the significant aspects of Antonio Koga is that of his current role as president of AMLAN—Asociación de la Música Latinoamericana de Nippon. A major thrust in the organization's purpose is that of developing young Japanese artists in Latin American musical idioms. Concerts, competitions, and recordings are produced by AMLAN's sixty-plus membership throughout each year. Koga has acted as the group's president through the past nine years. One of Koga's current projects is the planning of an international Latin American music festival in Okinawa, a place that he considers to be very influenced by, and similar to, Latin American culture and society. Recently, Koga directed an AMLAN musical tour to Cuba and Mexico.

Singer Yoshiro, whose career spans the last forty years of singing styles ranging from Mexican styles to Latin pop to salsa, also offered a great level of insight on the issue of Japan and Latin American music and culture. As a young singer he began singing professionally at the US military base near Tokyo, interpreting mostly American music such as that of the Platters, Paul Anka, etc. However, he eventually began to develop much interest in Latin American music and, like Antonio Koga, was highly influenced by Trío Los Panchos, in addition to Cuban bandleader Pérez Prado, who became highly popular in Japan during the 1950s and 1960s. In 1974 Koga was invited to Venezuela to sing, and he eventually became quite popular there, especially on television programs where he would sing standard Latin American songs dressed as a kabuki performer, mixing the two concepts. He also performed extensively in Colombia, Puerto Rico, Miami, and Mexico, where he lived for some time.

Yoshiro made a point of telling me that in Japan there is interest in many foreign musical traditions, including those of North America, France,

Italy, European classical music, reggae, and many others. He also pointed out that the organization for French music in Japan is much larger than AMLAN, comprising over five hundred members. He feels, however, that the interest in Latin American music is growing at a rapid pace, as with the music of China and other Asian countries. He feels this is due in large part to shifting interests of Japanese society to places other than the United States and Europe.

Like the other artists I have spoken with here, Yoshiro also commented on the compatibility of singing in Spanish as compared to English. However, he also senses not only a linguistic compatibility with Latin music but also various connections with regard to lifestyle, philosophy, lyrics, sentimentalism, and an emphasis on rhythm. He made a point to tell me that Japanese males, like Mexican males, also cry ardently and openly to songs expressing the passion of life. He also referred to the fact that there are 200,000 Japanese (*nikkei*) from Latin America who now reside in Japan, mostly from Brazil and Peru, but also from Mexico and other countries. Latin American musical styles as played by groups such as Los Diamantes—Japanese Peruvians who now reside in Okinawa—are receiving daily radio play throughout Japan. On a final note, it was interesting to me that Yoshiro also spoke of a spiritual connection that he felt with Latin American music, and this is largely why he has dedicated his life to it.

The final artist with whom I conducted an extensive interview was Sam Moreno, whose actual name is Osano Hagegawa. Moreno is a common last name in Latin America, and it is also a term denoting a darker complexion, which is why Sam chose the name, as he is of a dark complexion. As a young guitarist and singer in Nagoya, in central Japan, his musical preferences were quite different from those of his peers, and he was heavily inspired by Mexican singers such as Miguel Aceves Mejía, Pedro Infante, Lola Beltrán, and the mariachi tradition. Recordings were his principal source for learning. Sam believes that much of his affinity for Mexican music is related to the Japanese *enka* style, in which sentimentalism, lost love, and romance are expressed. As with other artists I have presented here, Sam also felt very comfortable singing in Spanish as compared to singing the English songs that were more popular in Japan, a situation that also made him realize that it would be more difficult to market Latin American music here. The market for North American music was highly established and commercially oriented. Sam pointed out that his Japanese aficionados, however, enjoy his interpretations of Mexican rancheras, boleros, huapangos, and sones because of their beautiful melodies and song form, even though they cannot understand the lyrics.

Sam Moreno has become the most notable interpreter of Mexican music in Japan, and this is due to both his musical talent and his entrepreneurial skills. He lived in Mexico for some years early in his career, and he has command of a large song repertoire and guitar techniques based on traditional Mexican genres and styles. He has authored a songbook in Japan of Mexican and other Latin American popular songs, with both the music harmonic accompaniment and texts provided in Spanish with Japanese translations. He has recorded an LP with a leading mariachi in Mexico City, and he has also recently opened a Mexican restaurant in the Ebisu section of Tokyo called "El Rincon de Sam," where he and other local artists of Latin American music perform. He presently plans to form a mariachi, Japan's first, in the near future. During the interview, I might add, Sam and I sang a couple of Mexican rancheras as we sipped our small shots of tequila, and we reflected on our feelings about the music and related to each other in a very Mexican way. It all made me quite happy, and it was quite special.

Related to the story of Sam Moreno is that of another artist whom I have been able to work with musically here in Japan. Her name is Junko Seki, and she has become a very well-known and respected mariachi singer in both the United States (where mariachi is presently thriving as never before) and Mexico. Only twenty-six years old, I believe she has a very brilliant career ahead of her. She performs in the United States with Mariachi Cobre, one of the top mariachi ensembles there. She has sung in festivals at numerous venues, including the Hollywood Bowl Mariachi Festival, the Guadalajara Mariachi Festival, and the Tucson Festival, where she sang in trio format with Linda Ronstadt and Vikki Carr.

Yet another example of such a phenomenon is that of vocalist Noriko, a Japanese interpreter of Latin tropical and Latin ballads now based in Miami. She has had major successes in Venezuela, where she recorded an album on the Sony label. Her ability to sing in Spanish is, in my opinion, one of extraordinary exception. Like Junko Seki, she is penetrating the Latin American public and market in its native setting, and doing so at a very high artistic level.

Reflecting on the Analysis

As a way of concluding, I will reiterate some of the questions and tentative hypotheses I have raised. For example, what has the interplay of Latin American musical aesthetics signified for Japan as an integral actor in the development of Latin American music as a major popular music of world distribution? My answer to this is that Japan is one of the countries leading the way in this movement, and I have attempted to present here some of the apparent effects of the Japanese context. On a crosscultural, comparative basis of analysis, what are the aesthetic factors that should be considered for a meaningful understanding and conceptualization of the dynamic role that Latin American culture has played in Japanese culture? Here, I would say that we must also expand our observations and panorama of expressive culture in such an assessment, for along with music, Latin America has also had a great impact in Japan in terms of literature, visual art, philosophy, and historical and religious studies. I also feel that by working through direct discourse with artists, as I have attempted to do in this study, that the issues I have raised come to better light. Additionally, it is in this way that we can better come to relate to such artists as our fellow theorists, analysts, and intellectuals.

Has this aesthetic only influenced Japanese society and art, or has it also had a retroactive impact in Latin America, the Latino United States, and other parts of the world? I would respond here by pointing to the experience of Orquesta de la Luz or Junko Seki, artists who are demonstrating that Latin American and other cultures have listened with very open ears. These artists have not only penetrated other cultures, but are also being penetrated culturally from without in a very interactive, intercultural, yet culturally collective way. Finally, how have issues of linguistics, nationalism, and identity played into this matrix of international exchange of performing arts? These are among the issues that I believe have characterized the experiences of the artists I have encountered in Japan.

I have presented some related data and analysis here, but I would also point to other related contexts presently evolving, for example, the Los Angeles–based group Hiroshima—Japanese Americans who incorporate R&B, jazz, Latin, and Japanese traditional instruments with good commercial success—and the Okinawan groups Los Diamantes and Nēnēs, the latter which, in addition to Okinawan and Japanese traditions, utilizes numerous world styles, including the Mexican ranchera form, and has drawn from musicians such as David Hidalgo of Los Lobos. It is my feeling that comparative analysis may indeed provide us with a clearer concept of an international aesthetic as related to not only a Latin American but also an emerging world artistic culture.

Where To from Here?

I am only making a beginning with the topic of this paper, and I am merely scratching the surface of a huge concept. I have collected enough data to fill a book, which I feel the topic merits, but I am not sure I am the one to do it. I believe there might be someone here in Japan—perhaps Professor Hosokawa, for instance—who can lend some insight. But I also believe that we do have a unique and collective opportunity with this topic of Latin music in Japan, as with so many other cross-cultural, aesthetic issues in this country, to perhaps create a highly interesting matrix of comparisons and hypotheses. Concerning the issue of an international aesthetic and the development of global aesthetics as an essential area of study so timely in our contemporary era of cultural interchange, I question the idea that we are still bound by actual boundaries in this world or draped by banners, flags, or colors. I see neither our musical, artistic present nor future as a horizon marked any longer by "centers" of aesthetic understanding or origin. The world has become a small place, and the artists of Latin music in Japan can substantiate such a claim.

Note

An earlier version of this essay appeared in *Popular Music: International Interpretations*, edited by Toru Mitsui, 391–97. Proceedings of the Ninth International Meeting of the International Association for the Study of Popular Music, Kanazawa, Japan, August 19. Kanazawa: Kanazawa University Graduate Program in Music, 1998.

CHAPTER 7

Identity, Nationalism, the Aesthetics of Latin Music, and the Case of Tito Puente

In the realm of Latin American music and Latin American culture in general, the issues of nationalism and identity have been common analytical and figurative concepts. From the "nationalistic" use of folk and indigenous materials in the music of composers Heitor Villa-Lobos and Carlos Chávez to the use of song as political metaphor and protest, identity has been a dominant issue in Latin American culture and, I might add, world culture through the centuries.

The present momentum in the formulation of "salsa" musical and dance expression has been largely associated with a variety of identities. These have included associations based on a number of cultural constructs, such as religion, ethnicity, politics, change, innovation, and the artistic virtuosity of the venerated master musician, dancer, or performer—the high priest of a religion of art.

The diversity of such underlying constructs extends beyond the major historical artistic basis of contemporary Latin music, that of the Afro-Cuban musical tradition. Although still firmly based on the foundation of Afro-Cuban forms, the expressive framework of Latin musicians has evolved stylistically and varied extensively in terms of context, theme, and nationalist or ethnic sentiment. The music has also become quite universal, with salsa groups such as Orquesta de la Luz from Japan becoming Grammy Award nominees. Nonetheless, even among Latino artists, who constitute the majority of the contemporary Latin music enclave, the many innovators and stylists have come not only from New York and the northeast United States, representative of their local Cuban, Puerto Rican, or Dominican population, but also from other sectors of the United States (especially California and Florida) and, perhaps more significant in terms of historical precedent, from various sectors of Latin America. Many Afro-Cuban forms evolved in other parts of Latin America—for example, Mexico, home of Cuban Pérez Prado's orchestra—in a sphere of social and national context separate from that of the New York Palladium and its New York ambience. Artists such as Oscar D'León from Venezuela, Rubén Blades from Panama, Lobo y Melón from Mexico, and a large number of conjunto groups from Puerto Rico—for example, Cortijo, Ismael Rivera, Sonora Ponceña, and El Gran Combo—have emerged as messengers of salsa and Latin music no less important than the New York artists. Additionally, the social messages of the style have addressed this ever-growing geographical terrain. Although significantly more directed toward a "pop" market, salsa may now have a broader appeal across the Latino world than ever before, especially given the inter-American popularity of "salsa" artists such as Marc Anthony, José Alberto, Lalo Rodríguez, Luis Enrique, Tito Nieves, Grupo Niche, Joe Arroyo, Gloria Estefan, and Juan Luis Guerra (whose style is actually based on the Dominican merengue and bachata dance forms), among many others, all representing various Latin American countries or US Latino sectors (the evolution of salsa as a pan-Latino development and symbol has been significantly examined by Frances Aparicio [1998]).

In the light of these observations concerning the evolving identities, markets, and aesthetics of Latin music, I feel compelled to raise in this study an issue that has become a focal point for some contemporary scholars: the "Cubanization" of Puerto Rican culture and musical expression, particularly in New York City. In his article "Puerto Rican Music and Cultural Identity: Creative Appropriation of Cuban Sources from Danza to Salsa," Peter Manuel confronts the "issue of cultural identity" that "has been particularly controversial and active among Puerto Ricans" (1994, 249). Manuel notes that "Puerto Rican nationalist intellectuals as well as popular opinion have long embraced salsa—for example, as opposed to rock—as a characteristically (albeit not exclusively) local music." Manuel's aim in the article is not to question the "validity of the virtually unanimous Puerto Rican conception of salsa and danza as local in character" but "to explore the process by which Puerto Ricans have appropriated and resignified Cuban musical forms as symbols of their own cultural identity." He does note, however, a "potential contradiction" concerning historical "fact" and the origins of the music: "A significant qualification and potential contradiction lies at the heart of the allegedly indigenous character of salsa and its island antecedents, for in stylistic terms, most of the predominant Puerto Rican musics, from the nineteenth-century *danza* to contemporary salsa, have been originally derived from abroad—particularly from Cuba" (249).

In my estimation, such analytical viewpoints are problematic. For one thing, many Puerto Ricans might question the point of concentrating on the idea that "most of the predominant Puerto Rican musics . . . have been originally derived from abroad." With their modest population (compared to larger "nation-states") of a little over six million in both Puerto Rico and the mainland United States, why should people of Puerto Rican heritage be expected to restrict themselves to "island" culture and identity?[1]

Moreover, the issue of Cuban musical culture itself can be seen as a similar contradiction. The forms that have historically constituted Cuban national styles have in fact migrated, diffused from, and been adapted to a number of geographic and national origins, including Nigeria, Ghana, and the Ivory Coast, among numerous other West and Central African locations (as well as Spain and other European contexts). In the literature, Afro-Cuban *bata* drums are not often considered a nationalistic contradiction, when in fact they derived directly from the Nigerian bata drums of the Yoruba culture and their associated religious context; nor are they, through time, referred to as specifically "Nigerian" drums. The diffusion of musical expression and religious ideology has not represented a contradiction in Cuba concerning the emergent nationalist character of Afro-Cuban music as "Cuban"; rather, it has produced a quite flexible, although conflictual and diverse, convergence of philosophies.

Another point of discussion can be centered on the issue that a place such as multicultural Nigeria and its Yoruba migratory cultural history can be tied to numerous past intercultural connections and national identities in various sectors within the north and west of Africa. "Borrowed" and shared cultural forms have consistently signified the emergence of nationalist, "indigenous" symbols. In the *nueva canción* movement of Latin America, Andean forms became one of the most vivid features of the musical style and certainly elicited a nationalist association that strongly reinforced the verbal content of the song, yet the singers of the movement were largely not Aymara—or Quechua—speaking peoples. In southeastern Mexico the *son jarocho* developed as a cultural convergence, within a specific time frame, of indigenous, African, and European interests. But the son jarocho did ultimately become identified as Mexican, and it has recently become associated with numerous Chicano artists in the United States, such as Los Lobos, Fermin Herrera, and Francisco Gonzalez (Loza 1992, 1993).

Puerto Rico and Cuba, as Manuel does note, have been linked historically and culturally for centuries, even before Spanish colonization. Furthermore, Latin America must be considered a cultural entity much like that of other continental areas—for example, the United States, Europe, and East Asia—where intercultural expression ultimately signifies various national identities and "characters." The regional variants of various Latin American countries or even regions of these countries frequently take on the character of Latin America as a larger "nation," similar to the United States and its regional state or geographical variants and thus its identities. Since before and after the Civil War, the issue of North and South in the United States has represented not convergence of nationalist identities and styles but rather their divergence.

The Multicultural Matrix of Latin Music

Since the early experiments and innovations of Cuban musicians Arsenio Rodríguez, Machito, and Mario Bauzá during the thirties, Latin music in the United States has developed as a reflection of its intercultural matrix. The exposure to and experience with jazz that Bauzá adapted in his early arrangements with the Machito Orchestra became both the musical and cultural framework on which Latin dance orchestras, Latin jazz, and salsa would emerge. Puerto Ricans, Cubans, and other Latinos began to interact with African American and white jazz musicians more than ever before in either the United States or Latin America. The other key element of this convergence was the multicultural complex and the human, industrial environment of New York City. The audiences that began to form in the Palladium and other dance halls were, like those of jazz, highly integrated, notwithstanding the elements of discrimination and segregation that still existed in a large part of the society.

Thus, Machito and Bauzá did not simply continue to stylize or develop a Cuban music. Yes, their musical concepts did "Cubanize" jazz, but jazz also "jazzified" their music in both its dance hall and concert contexts. Puerto Rican Juan Tizol's work with Duke Ellington, the Machito Orchestra, bebop, Charlie Parker, Dizzy Gillespie, and Chano Pozo (referred to Gillespie by Bauzá) all represented not only a growing and multicultural matrix but also a changing matrix of style, expression, and thought with various ideological sources and factors.

This multicultural and often "transethnic" ambit that characterized the Latin music movement of the 1950s, of course, has not remained a strong social reality, especially since the "salsa explosion" of the 1970s, when the music became heavily identified and socialized as a pan-Latino expression and movement not separated from the political environment of the period.

129

Following the civil unrest and civil rights movement of the 1960s, Latinos throughout the United States pursued causes similar to those that had been initiated by African Americans.

Thus, it was especially during the 1960s and thereafter that the numerous Latino and African American musical genres converged in diverse forms throughout the United States. The boogaloo style was one of the earlier syntheses of Latin music and R&B, epitomized through New York artists such as Joe Cuba, Joe Bataan, and Willie Colón. In California such intercultural compatibility or "resolution" (as opposed to "intercultural conflict") took form through the artistry of Carlos Santana, Azteca, and Malo in San Francisco and Thee Midniters, Li'l Ray Jiménez, El Chicano, and Tierra in Los Angeles.

Such intercultural compatibility among Latinos and African Americans has been noted and rationalized by artists and critics citing a number of theories. Crediting Machito as the cultural mediator who "stood at the juncture of Caribbean and Afro-American musical traditions," Juan Flores (1988) provides some significant analytical insight concerning the interaction of Puerto Ricans and African Americans in musical and aesthetic choices, tracing the contemporary hip-hop of both communities to the 1950s and 1960s.

> These years saw the dawning of the second-generation black and Puerto Rican communities in New York; it was the time when the first offspring of both migrations, many of them born and raised in New York, were settling into their new situation. They comprised, and still today comprise, the two largest nonwhite groups in the city. They came from southern, largely rural backgrounds; they lived in the same or bordering neighborhoods, attended the same schools, and together occupy the most deprived and vulnerable place in the economic and cultural hierarchy; they are the reserve of the reserve.
>
> Small wonder, then, that young blacks and Puerto Ricans started liking the same kinds of music, doing the same dances, playing the same games, and dressing and talking alike. Their common experience of racist exclusion and social distance from their white-ethnic peers drew them even closer. In groping for a new idiom, young blacks and Puerto Ricans discarded rural trappings and nostalgic "down home" references, but retained the African rhythmic base and improvisational, participatory qualities of their inherited cultures. In so doing, black and Caribbean peoples came to recognize the complementarity of what seemed to be diverse origins. (34)

Flores's analysis lends itself to expansion. The intercultural compatibility of African Americans, Cubans, Puerto Ricans, and other Latinos was forged through social and cultural relationships, traditions, and aesthetic forces. Marginal societies became sensitized to what Flores refers to as complementarity. Instead of instantiating the separatist predictions and fears of many contemporary social and political critics, individually identified cultural communities synthesized the art and ideologies on various levels and in various sectors. Multiculturalism tended to unify and in the process provided much fodder for creativity—but such is the historical pattern of art and many marginal communities throughout the world.

The Case of Tito Puente

Earlier I alluded to the multicultural ambit of the Palladium era, which was represented by artists such as the orchestras of Machito, Tito Puente, and Tito Rodríguez, among many others. In addition to benefiting from the interaction of Latinos and African Americans, however, Latin dance music in New York City, especially during the 1950s, attracted large audiences from the "white" public, including dancers and aficionados from Italian, Jewish, Irish, Polish, German, English, and other European heritages. In a 1994 interview, Max Salazar noted that the social context of the Palladium era integrated the races (in Loza 1999). With more specific reference to Tito Puente, Salazar eloquently expressed the same point of analysis in the program notes that he wrote for the "Discovery Day Concert" honoring Puente at Lincoln Center's Avery Fischer Hall in 1977: "For the last twenty-five years, Tito Puente has accomplished more with his music in improving race relations than any scientific study. Since 1949 he has thrilled Anglos with mambos, cha-chas, Latin jazz, *pachangas*, bossa nova, and *guaguancós*. To the non-Latinos the Spanish lyrics seemed unimportant. Puente's music made the point. The almost one thousand tunes in his repertoire firmly established 'TP' as Latin music's most productive and progressive leader" (Salazar 1977).

Attesting to this multicultural ambit are the reflections of songwriter Mort Shuman, who credited much of his creative development to Latin music in New York. "The Puerto Rican influence was very strong in New York. You had terrific bands like Tito Puente, Tito Rodríguez, and [Cuban] Machito. There was a great ballroom, the Palladium at 53rd and Broadway, and every Wednesday night was mambo night. You'd get two or three bands on the same bill. The place was jam-packed with people who worked in factories. Cleaning ladies. It was a great melting pot and the catalytic agent was Latin music. I was there every night it was open" (in Escott 1988).

Perhaps one of the most significant aspects of Puente is that he became enmeshed with various generations—the adults, the children, and the babies of the 1940s through the 1990s. Race and intercultural relations have taken different courses during these years, but Puente has attempted to adapt to each era. It can be said that he has taken more of the multicultural versus nationalistic course, consistently emphasizing the international popularity and charisma of his music and himself. At the same time, however, he has often been active in the artistic and political solidarity of the Latino community in the United States. On some particular political fronts, however, he has expressed no interest; for example, he has not performed in or visited Cuba since before the 1959 revolution.

In assessing Puente's relationship to and perception of these issues of identity, nationalism, and the multicultural ambit, some of the artist's own statements shed light on his philosophy. In 1981 Puente expressed the following thoughts:

> It's very difficult to put a big Latin band on the *Johnny Carson Show*. He doesn't need me. He has a big band of his own there. I can't go on by myself. Buddy Rich goes out there. He does it by himself, but that's jazz; they can go in. Count Basie—I've seen him play by himself [on the show], but you'll never see a Latin artist go by himself. You can't, because they can't play our music, they can't interpret it. They're great musicians, naturally, but you can't play a guaguancó on Johnny Carson because the people that he caters to don't know what guaguancó or a typical Latin tune is, so you have to go with a semicommercial thing. Maybe an "Oye como va" they might understand, or a "Tico Tico," a Brazilian thing, or "Chin Chin Chin"—Cugat type music, and that's not my music, really, so it's a challenging thing. You're in between, and then you don't know what to do. . . . So we're Latins and yet we're not. We still got to play commercial music for the masses [and shows such as] *Johnny Carson*. Then our Latin people put us down for playing that type of music, so we're in the middle of both sequences. And when you cater to masses you never know which way you're heading. You could become lucky or not. You have to know that and it's very difficult.
>
> But I have always had a big, large English-speaking audience, and I always, as we say in Spanish, "Plantao bandera"—wherever I go I represent more or less, the Puerto Rican people. . . . Wherever I go, [wherever] I travel, they ask me, "What are you?" I say "I'm Puerto Rican." Bam, bam, bam, I talk. But I am international, too. I play for all kinds of people, and they dance to my music and I have all kinds of a following; so I don't want to tag myself . . . but when they ask me who I am, I represent Puerto Rico. In festivals . . . like in Venezuela, "La Festival de la Canción," I represent Puerto Rico. . . . The State Department has never sent me to

South America and . . . embassies representing the United States. But yet they send Woody Herman playing for the Latin embassies down there, and I wrote six of the arrangements, and I recorded an album with Woody Herman. They sent Dizzy Gillespie also . . . and Herbie Mann; the State Department for the Latins down there. They haven't sent one Latin band down there . . .

I've been in Mexico with my orchestra, played right there, and I've gone to see the State Department concert to see Sarah Vaughn singing there! In Mexico. And everybody's Mexican, Spanish. And she was jazz, beautiful, and she gives me recognition 'cause she's my friend, but yet this is the Latin State Department Centuries Band. There hasn't been no Latin band that's been able to do that yet. The American bands are doing that. So we have all these problems, really, and there's a lot to talk about there. And our representation is not being done the right way. So therefore, to play in the White House like I've done [shows that] there are new doors that are opening up. I think it's going to be easing up in the decade. It'll take another decade to do it. I hope I'm around to finish it up, but I'm starting it and I have a feeling it's going to be there. It's going to make it. (Puente 1981)

Certainly Puente's words must be considered somewhat prophetic. Since these words, recorded in 1981, Tito Puente has continued to perform for every US president and to receive major national and international honors and recognition. During the same 1981 interview Puente also commented considerably on the state of the Latin music industry as a business.

We have a major problem [in] that we don't have Latin executives in our business—people that are well studied. In other words, you'll always find the owners of Latin companies are other races than Latin. The people that are making money in Latin music are not Latin people. They're other people, other nationalities. The people involved in television—we don't have no big Latin producer or big Latin director. We don't have great Latin arrangers. I mean we have a few South American arrangers, but in this country we don't have the Quincy Jones or people of that category— or Henry Mancini. Sure we have Lalo Schifrin, but he came through Dizzy Gillespie and had a connection in Argentina. He's out there.

What we need is executive-type people in our public relations, executives in our recording companies, executives in magazines, and exposure to the media, radio, and airplays. We need executives, Latin executives, that know of our music and culture, that could be able to go out and present something. I'm on the board of governors for the Grammy Awards, and why do they have me there? They have me there because I represent the Latin category, let's say, and they could send me to Nashville, Tennessee, where I'll meet people there, where[as] if they send another Latin person down there to talk or categorize our music . . .

They'll listen to me because I'm Tito Puente. I'm a known bandleader, an artist. But if you send somebody else that maybe knows more about how to present their music, they won't accept them at this point. So therefore, that's why we need our young people to go to school, continue their education, don't quit school, don't be disappointed. Don't feel bad, disillusioned, 'cause I know times are bad and the music business is a very rough business. I'm asked by some people, "Would you do it again if you had to?" Yes, I would do it again because God put me into this world to do this and this is what I have to do, and he made me creative. I don't come from a musical family, so any talents I have I would say he gave them to me mostly. It was his wish, and I thank him for it very much. There may be a lot of young people here of our people that are very talented also, but it has to be developed. They have to go to school, learn how to use the tools, the books, and go to the conservatories and learn how to play the instruments. And then when you get out there, because everybody graduates at the same time, and everybody has the same books . . . doctors, dentists, everybody has the same education. Then they spread out, they go into their own field and they develop a following and a business or their professions. Same thing in the music field. Then you develop, you become creative, you become arrangers, you become executives. You go into marketing or whatever. The music business is a very, very, very big multi–million dollar business. You go into recordings and you go into media and you go into video, because you'll be coming up in our future videotaping and video recording, digital recording. And producers, we need good Latin people that can evolve into producing good digital records, good videotapes, putting shows together, and choreographers. This goes for dancers, too. Ballets, singers, opera singers, all involved with music.

So our young people should study, and in the future you'll always find that all of a sudden the recognition is there. Like a José Ferrer—he's there, a Puerto Rican. He's one of our top great artists. How many José Ferrers do we have? We have a lot of young people coming up, but it takes time. A lot of people, like Miriam Colón, will develop . . .

We have a lot of Hispanic people in this country, and all we need is the people and the forefront. What they're doing in the political scene—a lot of Hispanics—there's congressmen all over the country. They're all over in California, in Sacramento. We have a lot of Mexican people out there that are into big politics, recognition. We had one person that was running for mayor in New York not many years ago, so we have a lot of big, big people in that field. So why not in the music field? And the big thing—so that we can put our music to be recognized throughout the world. That's what my object is—to get recognition for our Latin American music throughout the whole world, where throughout, when people talk about one kind of music in Europe, they can compare it with Latin music. When they talk about it in Japan, Latin music is right at their level. Whatever kind of music they discuss, Latin music could be at their level. And to get that we need the education and the experience and the creativeness of our young people coming up today to do their will in this decade now. If not, we're going to lose everything we have. (Puente 1981)

Since this interview, many of Puente's concerns have resolved themselves in creative, productive fashion; others have remained problematic. One of the issues Puente raised was that of the lack of Latino record executives. In 1981 Jerry Masucci, an Italian American, had achieved a high level of success in recording and marketing the Latin music style salsa under his Fania label. Martin Cohen not only was the chief executive of Latin Percussion, Inc., but also initiated and managed Puente's Latin Jazz Ensemble, which became the bandleader's principal and highly successful musical project through the 1980s and 1990s. Puente's recording outlet for this Latin jazz period was Concord Records, owned by Carl Jefferson.

By the 1990s, however, Puente was also recording on two other labels, RMM and Tropijazz, both owned and managed by Ralph Mercado, Puente's longtime business manager, and distributed through Sony Records (formerly Columbia Records), one of the leading international record companies, with corporate ownership based in Japan. The emergence of Mercado's record companies by the mid-1990s represented a new and significant shift in the Latin music industry, especially that segment associated with salsa and Latin jazz artists. By this period Sergio George, who had been the predominant arranger and producer for many of Mercado's productions (including work on Puente's one-hundredth album), had also initiated a production and recording company, thus also emerging as a competitive actor in the newly changing market. Simultaneously, the Latin divisions of Sony and EMI Records continued to expand internationally, primarily in the area of "pop," which by this time was incorporating major influence from the new "salsa erotica" artists such as Luis Enrique, Eddie Santiago, Tito Nieves, and La India.

As commercialization of Latin music spread, the music was adapted and changed markedly. Another issue emerged, one echoed in Puente's 1981 transcript: many of the Latin music aficionados complained of what they perceived as major artistic compromise and a decaying musical quality. Puente's response to the situation of change has been outspoken yet moderate. He actually promoted and produced one of the younger artists, Millie P., who performed with his ensembles for several years during the late 1980s. He has also been critical of much of the new salsa, however, noting its lack of spontaneity, improvisation, dynamics, and traditional structure. At the same time, Puente has seemed to appreciate and applaud the growing emergence of Latin executives and producers, for he has worked with many of them in the production of both recordings and performances.

Puente's emphasis on the importance of formal education is readily apparent in the 1981 interview with Patricia Wilson Cryer. It was actually during this same period that I met and started working on projects with Puente. At the time I was a doctoral student in music at UCLA, and I always felt that Tito paid particular attention and respect to that aspect of my work. It is certainly one of his more passionate premises, for he envisions formal education as the primary issue related to the future of Latin culture within US society.

From this vantage point, it might also be significant to cite Puente's apparent interest in the pan-Latino movement since the end of the 1960s. With his references to the growing solidarity of Latino politicians, artists, and other professionals throughout the United States, Puente has emerged as one of the leading advocates for Latino unity in the country. Although not as lyrically direct as artists such as Rubén Blades, Puente has managed to focus on political issues at various critical points and places. His role in educational projects is possibly his principal activism in this area; examples include his scholarship foundation, his honorary doctorates, and his many seminars and workshops at various schools and universities throughout the world.

Certainly one of Puente's priorities, as elicited in the 1981 interview, is that of the recognition and development of Latin music as a major world art form. By taking Latin music into countries previously unexposed to the art, Puente has facilitated its world transmission. As a performer of Latin music (as conceived in this book), he has traveled to more parts of the world than any other artist to date and has become an international institution.[2] The goals he expressed in 1981 have been achieved to a greater extent than even he might have imagined.

It is also significant to reflect on Puente's comments concerning the lack of Latinos in the media, especially television. This is an area that has remained extremely problematic. A national study published in 1996 revealed that whereas 3 percent of personalities appearing on television during the 1950s were of Latino heritage, the figure had decreased to 1 percent by the mid-1990s (Center for Media and Public Affairs 1996, 6). These statistics became a highly controversial and disturbing issue for the Latino community in the United States, estimated to constitute in 1997 about 11 percent of the national population (Ybarra-Frausto and Gutierrez

1997). As of 1996 the issue continued to foment much controversy and political action in the arts industry in general. *People Weekly*'s cover story for its March 18, 1996, issue was based on the fact that only one African American had been nominated for the 1995 Academy Awards (out of 166 nominations). *People* referred to the situation as a "Hollywood Blackout" and a "national disgrace." The Reverend Jesse Jackson proceeded to mobilize minority groups nationally in protest of the state of the film industry, especially citing the lack of African Americans and other minorities in executive positions. The *Los Angeles Times* published the following excerpt as part of its front-page story the day following the internationally televised Academy Awards show staged at the Music Center of Los Angeles County: "The protests were being billed as a launching pad in a campaign spearheaded by Jackson and his Rainbow Coalition to fight what he called 'race exclusion and cultural violence' within the motion picture industry. He said Hollywood continues to resist employing people of color in influential decision-making positions and that it hides behind the terms of 'creativity and artistic license' to resist diversity" (Welkos 1996).

One vivid example of some of the Motion Picture Academy's inflexibility was expressed by Pam Lambert, author of the *People Weekly* article, who cited the elimination of a Los Lobos film-track song as a nominee for an Oscar:

> The absence of adequate Hispanic representation probably accounted for its most notorious recent blooper.
> What happened was that "Canción del Mariachi," Los Lobos's guitar-driven ballad in last year's *Desperado*, was nearly declared ineligible for consideration as Best Original Song because its Spanish lyrics were deemed "not intelligible" by the Academy's music branch. (The Academy later blamed a "clerical mistake" for the ruling.) Frank Lieberman, the Academy's spokesman, says that data on its racial demographics "is not information that we keep," but that there is "no voting [by] color in the Academy." (Lambert 1996)

Much of this reflects the critical perspective of Tito Puente in his previously cited thoughts on the music industry and the difficulty Latin musicians have experienced in their attempts to "mainstream" and market their product. Mirroring Puente's stance on the problem of the Grammy Awards was a recent statement made by Latin artist Willie Colón via e-mail:

> Winning the Grammy has nothing to do with talent. . . . It doesn't even have anything to do with sales or airplay. It's about money and name recognition. It's about record companies buying hundreds of general

memberships and voting in a block for a slate of their artists. . . . There are artists out there who have made their fame and fortune as minor league pop stars and have found the secret of getting a guaranteed Grammy for their mantle. Record a "Tropical" album! That way they can use their pop name recognition on the General voting members of the Academy and "steal" a Grammy. . . . Today, all "Latino Musics," from Julio Iglesias to Milton Nascimento to Lil' Joe to Tito Puente to Gloria Estefan, must compete for three (3) slots. Gospel music has eight (8). I [have] continued to press for more categories or a separate Latino Grammy, to which a NARAS (National Academy of Recording Arts and Sciences) official snorted before the membership one night, "Everyone in Latin America is in bed with somebody. We need to know where everybody is when the lights are out." Hello! Is this the old pot calling the kettle black? . . . I . . . was subsequently voted out of my seat on the Board [of Governors of the New York chapter of NARAS]. I was one of the very few people who was not being paid to sit on that board. The others worked for different companies and trade associations and would come to the meetings on company time. These are the people who make the decisions.

I really can't be happy for Linda Ronstadt, Gloria Estefan, David Byrne, or Paul Simon when they are nominated in our category because it almost always means that some artist like myself, the Gran Combo or Celia Cruz, who has lived for this music, will be overlooked and possibly miss a once in a lifetime opportunity because of someone's little musical excursion. . . . It's too late for many to get their due but the word has to be spread so that it will be more difficult and eventually impossible for NARAS to continue this arrogant fraud. We deserve better. (Colón 1996)

The issue of the arts industry and its integration with Latin culture in the United States is one that merits much more discussion, analysis, and critical assessment. As George Lipsitz has eloquently noted, we learn both of place and of displacement through music, in effect constituting a "poetics of place" (Lipsitz 1994, 4). The views of Tito Puente, among many other artists of various cultural perspectives, attest to the issue as a pervasive one in contemporary society, especially in the light of the aesthetic cultural questions that I have raised in this essay.[3]

There are, of course, contrasting perspectives on the issue. Some will point to the fact that some artists have included leading Latin music artists on their albums, in effect promoting and giving deserved recognition to these great artists. One example is Estefan, whose Grammy-winning tropical albums include performances by Tito Puente, Cachao, and numerous others. Likewise, Ronstadt made use of leading Latin musicians and arranger Ray Santos on her Grammy Award–winning album *Frenesi*. In addition to finally adding a Latin jazz category to the Grammy Awards in 1996, NARAS has also initiated a major plan for a specific Latin American Grammy Awards. Colón's arguments, however, represent the sentiments of many Latin music artists, producers, critics, and aficionados.

The multicultural challenges posited by the constant global diversifica- tion of the music industry and market demand serious critical assessment of the needs of individual "cultures" versus those of the larger, predominant society. Jacques Maquet (1979) has suggested that culture is based on society, although one can argue the opposite. But Maquet observes a basic flaw in much contemporary thought and analysis: the "multicultural inter- pretation" is often focused on the issues of diversity and difference rather than on the condition of human interaction in society, for example, in the music industry. Maquet makes no claims as to the egalitarianism of society; he speaks only to its inevitable, manipulative, and expanding dominance in the world at large.

The Aesthetic Locus of Latin Music

In his treatment of art from an anthropological perspective, Maquet defines an "aesthetic locus" as follows: "It does not seem that a society maintains an equally intense aesthetic interest in all the things made within its borders. There are certain privileged fields where awareness and performance are higher, where expectations and efforts converge. The class or classes of objects that are localized in these areas of heightened aesthetic conscious- ness constitute the aesthetic locus of a culture" (Maquet 1979, 30).

It is through conceptual frameworks such as those of Maquet that we can attempt to understand, perhaps on a more meaningful basis, the art and aesthetic locus of Tito Puente and his place in Latin music and its world community. From his earliest days as a professional artist, Puente has created and worked within a matrix of constant dialectics: the tension between his own work and style and the external forces at work—namely, the public and the music industry. Puente manipulated this dialectic in a number of ways.

One can also interpret the other side of this equation, one in which the public and the industry manipulated him. But Puente's verve has driven the equation. Although he was consistently aware of the wants and needs of the public and the techniques and strategies of the industry, Puente was able to integrate the elements of another of Maquet's constructs, that of a societal, productive, and ideational triad. From the societal ambits of the Palladium and the international effects of his music to the productive contradiction of recording industry issues such as the Grammy Awards and the lack of Latino representation to the ideational incorporation of Afro-Cuban religious themes and music on albums such as *Cuban Carnival* and *Top Percussion*, Puente has manipulated this interactive matrix in a most creative way.

Another mode of thought conducive to such an analysis is that of Johannes Wilbert, who suggests that life as expressed through culture can be examined on three specific levels: the cosmic, the cultural, and the telluric. Through the physical, material form of cultural expression, the concepts of cosmic form (those of spiritual or religious philosophy) and telluric form (which encompasses the environment, flora, seasons, and lifecycle) converge into a fuller concept of meaning, purpose, and the interrelationships of so-called life categories, including expression, culture, and the cosmos.

As with Maquet's triadic concept, Wilbert's three-part model can illuminate the case of Tito Puente, who has negotiated Wilbert's three levels through his cultural production. Predominantly working within an urban industrial context and his telluric and, in part, cultural environment, Puente has utilized the physical cultural forms of music, dance, and lyrics to negotiate various goals, including aesthetic fulfillment, financial sustenance, economic production, spiritual motivation, and the embrace of his own social and moral standards.

A number of scholars, such as Duane Champagne (1989) and Maria Williams (1996), have been critical of a dominant trend in the social sciences and humanities to "compartmentalize" the factors and functions of a culture. To Champagne, Williams, and others, culture and its collective expression are composed of interactive, inseparable meanings and functions wherein the spirit is not separated from the body or the universe. I might also allude to the tendency by many in the so-called positivist or materialist school of thought to separate the intellectual from the intuitive. Puente's art personifies the union of these various areas of meaning, action, and purpose. His musical manifestations cannot be compartmentalized in terms of societal, ideological, or productive factors, although I do not negate the usefulness of various approaches to assess his work on such bases of analysis. But we cannot permit the analysis to become the meaning. As Albert Murray eloquently assessed in *The Hero and the Blues*, it is the "artist, not the social or political engineer or even the philosopher, who first comes to realize when the time is out of joint. It is he who determines the extent and gravity of the current human predicament, who in effect discovers and describes the hidden elements of destruction, sounds the alarm, and even . . . designates the targets" (Murray 1973, 11).

In the final analysis, the aesthetic locus of Tito Puente is large—indeed, worldwide—and it represents an integrated, interactive matrix of ideation, society, and production. It is a cross section of the cosmic, the cultural, and the telluric. By crossing cultures, Puente was able to access not only the "universal language" of music but also a universal art and ideology and, ultimately, a universal soul.

And the soul thus leads us back to the union of the intuitive and the intellectual, conducive to Benedetto Croce's idea of the "supremely real" domain of the metaphysical. In addition to Croce, numerous twentieth-century philosophers and artists, including José Vasconcelos, Pierre Teilhard de Chardin, Deepak Chopra, John Coltrane, and Carlos Santana, have ultimately detected the connection between art, the universe, and a unity of all life in a metaphysical, mystical body. The interactive, organic cells of Puente's music reflect and express this higher unified form.

The Reclamation of Culture

In previous studies I have applied the concept of aesthetic and cultural "reclamation" through a conceptual, cyclical model revolving as an interacting wheel of tradition, reinterpretation, and innovation (Loza 1992, 1993, 1994). The innovation of Tito Puente and his music can certainly be understood as a product of his involvement with tradition and his reinterpretation of it. But innovation is not necessarily the result of any artist's reinterpretations of tradition. Whereas Puente experimented extensively while still being able to feed a traditional appetite, others maintained unchanging recipes. The notable aspect of Puente has been his ability to maintain the flow and integration of tradition, reinterpretation, and innovation.

As a specific example of this process, we may first look at Puente's use of Cuban musical forms. As noted previously in this chapter, Manuel's conceptualization of much Puerto Rican music (in New York and Puerto Rico) as representing a "creative appropriation" of Cuban music partly implies that nationalist motives inspired Puerto Rican musical identity.

Tito Puente's early years of enculturation in Spanish Harlem were contoured less by an exclusive Puerto Rican identity than by a bilingual, multicultural ambit: he was exposed to many cultural concepts and values. Although Puente, in a number of his statements, has expressed his interest in asserting his Puerto Rican heritage, he has simultaneously personified through his musical expression and enterprise the issues of a pan-Latino and international aesthetic. He did not co-opt Cuban music because of a nationalist motive or because of its religious correspondences with, particularly, *santería*. Puente has openly and consistently stated throughout his career that he "plays Cuban music," and he has grappled with the evolved term *salsa* as well as with concepts such as "crossover," for he has realized the historical inevitability of such fusion and cultural interchange. In addition to working with Cuban and Puerto Rican musical forms, Puente has gravitated strongly toward jazz, European classical music, and Mexican and South American forms, among many others. Furthermore, supporting my previous reference to the African origins of Cuban music, Puente has consistently referred to "Mother Africa" as the primary source of his music, a perspective that far outdistances provincial nationalist theories. Puente might well agree with an interesting comment made by a Cuban composer who has resided in the United States since the late 1950s, Aurelio de la Vega.

> For me, true musical nationalism is the one of Vivaldi, of Beethoven, of Debussy, of Crumb, for example—composers who, without citing folklore melodies or waving flags, have attracted the attention, the admiration and the respect of the world for the countries (shall I better say "human communities") where their powerful art developed. . . . All of them created incredibly personal masterpieces, expanding beyond national frontiers, expressed ideas and sounds with their own vocabularies, delivering their works without preconceived ideas about political or geographical boundaries. (in Erin 1984, 3)

There is another dimension to the aesthetic and cultural reclamation that Puente has advanced: that of his constantly evolving musical style, which is powered by the cycle of tradition, reinterpretation, and innovation. Puente has made a practice of recycling past concepts and restyling them, revitalizing them, and giving them new meaning while reaffirming their original meanings. A list of examples would include his treatment of tradition through musical arrangements such as "Picadillo," his original "mish-mash" composition recorded in 1949, which he later reinterpreted in more modern compositions and arrangements, notably on the LP *Un poco loco* (1987), where he disguises the tune, retitled "Chang," in a progressive, innovative mode. On his Grammy Award–winning *Goza mi timbal*, Puente directly reinterpreted his classic arrangement, renaming it "Picadillo a lo Puente."

But Puente's reinterpretation of his own and others' music was not simply a career afterthought during the 1980s and 1990s. It was in the 1950s that Puente first experimented with traditional Afro-Cuban drumming as the exclusive content of his early LPs *Puente in Percussion* (1956) and *Top Percussion* (1958). Other examples of converging religious and popular tradition include arrangements and compositions such as "Elegua Changó" on his *Cuban Carnival* LP of 1956, a remarkably innovative experiment that nonetheless achieved success on the dance floor. It was on his highly acclaimed *Dance Mania* album that Puente first incorporated the marimba, an African-derived instrument with origins in Central America and southern Mexico, where he acquired the one he brought back to New York. On this album, as on his "Hong Kong Mambo," he adapted the role of the marimba using a theme that he associated with the Far East (he would reinterpret this basic theme in a 1992 composition titled "Japan Mambo"). From his early days to his recent ones, Puente's multicultural experiments continued to invigorate and renovate the energy and imagination of dancers, musicians, and record executives.

On his important LP *Tito Puente and His Concert Orchestra* (1973), Puente reaffirms the role of his rumba-driven timbal virtuosity while juxtaposing it with an assortment of orchestration concepts and instrumental experimentation. The album *The Legend* (1977) literally paid homage to the tradition and innovations of Puente through Rubén Blades's text and music. Another vehicle on that album that attests to Puente's consistent innovation was his "Fiesta a la King," a composition that surprised many traditionalists of Latin music yet reinvigorated many others.

Puente's reinterpretations of classic pieces from jazz to Latin and their combinations constitute another notable product of his innovative, interpretive arrangement skills and conceptualization. His composition "Machito Forever," dedicated to his mentor, represents his utilization of traditional Latin musical frameworks constructed with numerous new and progressive harmonic, melodic, and rhythmic elements. Such experiments, although new and different, emulated the experimental spirit of Machito as much as they did the use of traditional Latin rhythms and structure. In his contemporary tribute "Ode to Cachao," Puente invokes the traditional *charanga* texture and cha-cha-cha format with musical echoes of both Cachao's "Chanchullo" and his own "Oye como va," two compositions related historically and musically. Again, the arrangement is traditional yet modern—or what some may today refer to as postmodern, for it incorporates not only a mosaic of the past and the present but also, more important, the mutual contradictions and relationships of both. In Puente's rerenderings of his classics "Oye como va" and "Pa' los rumberos," he incorporates readaptations of Santana's experiments with the compositions. On one of his most recent albums, *Jazzin'*, Puente, with vocalist La India, reinterprets classic Latin American and jazz standards including María Grever's "Cuando vuelva

143

a tu lado" ("What a Difference a Day Makes"), Antônio Carlos Jobim's "Wave," and Cole Porter's "Love for Sale." On another scale of innovation have been Puente's consistently creative adaptations of the giants of the jazz repertory, including the music of Fats Waller, Charlie Parker, Dizzy Gillespie, Thelonious Monk, Miles Davis, and John Coltrane. Metamorphosing, for example, Coltrane's "Equinox" into an Afro-Cuban 6/8 interpretation or his "Giant Steps" into an accelerated *clave* pace signifies Puente's unprecedented approach and ability to innovate on the innovative.

The list of examples could go on and on. Throughout his over fifty years in music, Tito Puente has consistently allowed his passion for innovation and tradition to mold an art form that continues to change while retaining its integrity as an intercultural vehicle for human expression. Puente has discovered a multitude of modes for his reinterpretations of an art form and its many meanings—meanings that have also remained the same.

The Limits of the Word

Throughout this essay it has been my aim to address the issues of identity, nationalism, and aesthetics and their relevance to the art of Tito Puente. Such analysis, based on historical data and creative artifact, can claim to arrive at only a fraction of understanding and must be acknowledged as taking account of only selected criteria; even this judgment may result in a multiplicity of meanings. In the final analysis, words are not sufficient to represent the infinity of realities, physical and metaphysical, that can be arbitrarily attributed to human expression—in this case, the art of music and the question of its meaning. In this both Maestro Puente and I, after substantial discussion, are in agreement. Words have their limits. However, we do not negate the challenge of these words as part of our art and the learning of it. We offer the following words of Michel Foucault, from his *Archaeology of Knowledge*, who has, we believe, made a valuable point.

> This rarity of statements, the incomplete, fragmented form of the enuncia-tive field, the fact that few things, in all, can be said, explain that statements are not, like the air we breathe, an infinite transparency; but things that are transmitted and preserved, that have value, and which one tries to appropriate; that are repeated, reproduced, and transformed; to which pre-established networks are adapted, and to which a status is given in the institution; things that are duplicated not only by copy or translation, but by exegesis, commentary, and the internal proliferation of meaning. Because statements are rare, they are collected in unifying totalities, and the meanings to be found in them are multiplied. (Foucault 1993, 119–20)

Notes

An earlier version of this essay appeared in *Tito Puente and the Making of Latin Music*, by Steven Loza. Champaign: University of Illinois Press, 1999. Reprinted by permission.

   1. The Puerto Rican population in the United States is reported as 2,727,754 in the US Census of 1990. The population of Puerto Rico is reported as 3,522,037 in the *World Almanac and Book of Facts* (1995), 670.

   2. See Loza 1999b.

   3. In a separate study (Loza 1998), I pursue the dynamic of Latin music's popularity and adaptation in Asia and Europe, where it enjoys a far more prolific level of engagement than has been developed by non-Latino US musicians and industry. Why is this so? Is there a possible hypothesis that could be linked to linguistic aesthetics, abilities, or intercultural conflict and prejudices?

Works Cited

Aparicio, Frances R. 1998. *Listening to Salsa: Gender, Latin Popular Music, and Puerto Rican Cultures*. Hanover, NH: Wesleyan University Press.

Center for Media and Public Affairs. 1996. *Don't Blink: Hispanics in Television Entertainment*. Prepared by S. Robert Lichter and Daniel R. Amundson. Washington, DC: Center for Media and Public Affairs.

Champagne, Duane. 1989. *American Indian Societies: Strategies and Conditions of Political and Cultural Survival*. Cultural Survival Report no. 32. Cambridge, MA: Cultural Survival.

Colón, William Anthony. 1996. "The Grammy Deception." Statement emailed to author, February 29.

Erin, Ronald. 1984. "Cuban Elements in the Music of Aurelio de la Vega." *Latin American Music Review* 5, no. 1: 1–32.

Escott, Colin. 1988. Liner notes to *The Drifters 1959–1965: All-Time Greatest Hits and More*. Atlantic 81931-2.

Flores, Juan. 1988. "Rappin', Writin', and Breakin'." *Centro de Estudios Puertorriqueños Bulletin* 2, no. 3: 34–41.

Foucault, Michel. 1993. *The Archaeology of Knowledge and the Discourse on Language*. Translated by A. M. Sheridan Smith. New York: Barnes and Noble.

Lambert, Pamela. 1996. "What's Wrong with This Picture?" *People Weekly*, March 19. http://people.com/archive/cover-story-whats-wrong-with-this-picture-vol-45-no-11/

Lipsitz, George. 1994. *Dangerous Crossroads: Popular Music, Postmodernism, and the Poetics of Place*. London and New York: Verso.

Loza, Steven. 1992. "From Veracruz to Los Angeles: The Reinterpretation of the Son Jarocho." *Latin American Music Review/Revista de música latinoamericana* 13, no. 2: 179–94.

———. 1993. *Barrio Rhythm: Mexican American Music in Los Angeles*. Champaign: University of Illinois Press.

———. 1994. "Identity, Nationalism, and Aesthetics among Chicano/Mexicano Musicians in Los Angeles." In *Musical Aesthetics and Multiculturalism in Los Angeles*, edited by Steven J. Loza, 51–58. Selected Reports in Ethnomusicology, no. 10. Los Angeles: UCLA Department of Ethnomusicology and Systematic Musicology.

———. 1998. "Latin American Popular Music in Japan and the Issue of International Aesthetics." *Popular Music: International Interpretations*, edited by Toru Mitsui, 391–97. Kanazawa, Japan: Kanazawa University Graduate Program in Music. Proceedings of the Ninth International Meeting of the International Association for the Study of Popular Music, Kanazawa, August 1998.

———. 1999. "The Salazar Perspective." In *Tito Puente and the Making of Latin Music*, chapter 3. Champaign: University of Illinois Press.

Manuel, Peter. 1994. "Puerto Rican Music and Cultural Identity: Creative Appropriation of Cuban Sources from Danza to Salsa." *Ethnomusicology* 38, no. 2: 249–80.

Maquet, Jacques. 1979. *Introduction to Aesthetic Anthropology*. Malibu, CA: Undena Publications.

Murray, Albert. 1973. *The Hero and the Blues*. New York: Vintage.

Puente, Tito. 1981. Recorded interview with Patricia L. Wilson Cryer for the Latin Music Museum of the Boys Harbor School of Performing Arts, New York, January 28.

Salazar, Max. 1977. Program notes for Discovery Day concert honoring Tito Puente, Avery Fisher Hall, November 13.

Welkos, Robert W. 1996. "Braveheart Is Top Film." *Los Angeles Times*, March 26, 1.

Williams, Maria del Pilar. 1996. "Alaska Native Music and Dance: The Spirit of Survival." PhD diss., University of California, Los Angeles.

Ybarra-Frausto, Tomás, and Ana Sol Gutiérrez. 1997. *Towards a Shared Vision: US Latinos and the Smithsonian Institution*. Final report of the Latino Oversight Committee. Washington, DC: The Smithsonian Institution.

CHAPTER 8

Poncho Sánchez, Latin Jazz, and the Cuban *Son*

A Stylistic and Social Analysis

Within the past twenty years, Poncho Sánchez has emerged as one of the major stylists and leaders in the cross-genre known as Latin jazz. Since the innovations of Machito, Mario Bauzá, Dizzy Gillespie, and Chano Pozo in the 1940s, this style has blended, in dynamic fashion, essential elements of Afro-Cuban music and jazz. Sánchez, a Mexican American from Los Angeles, California, has maintained this progressive, stylistic blend while at the same time continuing with a traditional Cuban base of interpretation and performance practice. Previous to performing and recording with his own ensemble, he spent more than seven years as the *conguero* for Cal Tjader (till the latter's death in 1982), one of the major constituents of Latin jazz. After various nominations, he was awarded a Grammy Award for his 1999 CD *Latin Soul*.

In this article I will present a general account of the historical and stylistic aspects of the Cuban *son*, followed by stylistic (i.e., musical, poetic, and other structural) analyses of two examples from the recorded repertoire of Sánchez incorporating the form. The analysis presented is based on primary, original fieldwork that I conducted, including professional work with Poncho Sánchez. In addition to examining the traditional format of Sánchez's use of son in Latin jazz, I conclude with some deliberation of the converse use of the jazz idiom in Latin jazz.

One of my principal goals in this study is to reiterate the importance of what has been referred to as the "juncture" of musical and social analysis.[1] Through the musical analyses presented here, we can detect some of the elements of change in the compositions and arrangement of Poncho Sánchez, which are based on the traditional Cuban son and incorporate various elements of the jazz tradition. Such change, or innovation, becomes an essential feature of Sánchez's recognized style, asserting him as an individual identity among the public, the music industry, and the musicians' community. It also reflects the artist's and the public's perceived need for innovative yet qualitative change within the context of tradition.

Analysis based on the musical-social matrix should be considered interactive and interdependent. Although many studies in ethnomusicology have focused on these analytical interrelationships, various shifts in such practices have emerged, and many studies borrow more from social science paradigms than stylistic analyses. Thus, in many studies, the "juncture" of the musical and social remains elusive. In noting the significance of this issue, James Porter and Hershel Gower posit that analyses of music

> encompass more than simply a concern for structural organization. Structural analysis of music may answer such questions as these: how does a particular style or piece work? how is it structurally successful? . . . Analysis of traditional repertoires, for instance, as one strategy in scrutinizing whole bodies of music or song, can uncover the concepts, preferences, and ordering systems that musicians or singers bring to their overall style, as well as changes they make under certain circumstances. (1995, 278–79)

Porter and Gower also posit that "transformativity of form and content in songs is bound up with their arrangement by the singer [or other musician]. Such form and content are verbal and musical" (278). They define transformativity as "the capacity to stimulate change" and state that it is "best understood as an artistic process. In sure hands, it is a powerful tool for influencing perception of the world" (276). Porter and Gower thus conceptualize transformativity as a form of creation that can help change the world—improve it—if the art is truly creative and positive. "Transformativity connotes the active, transitive capacity of a skilled performer (a singer, say) to bring about qualitative change" (277). Adapting such concepts to the study of Poncho Sánchez's role in Latin jazz and the Cuban son, we can learn how tradition, structure, and innovation vary from one artist or performance to another. We may thus shed light on the direct interrelationships between the musical and the social.

The two models presented for analysis are "Este son," from Sánchez's *Sonando* album, and "Bien sabroso," the title track of his 1985 Grammy-nominated album. Both examples represent adaptations of the Afro-Cuban son form, which became an integral part of the formulation of various salsa styles in New York City and Puerto Rico and elsewhere. The concept of son implies more than a particular rhythm or dance. In Cuba, it is a word that describes a particular sound, structure, and instrumentation, characterized by a certain rhythmic and stylistic complex. It originally emerged from the population of African heritage in the rural districts of Cuba as a vehicle for entertainment at informal gatherings. In the early 1900s it migrated to the urban sector, eventually molding the entire landscape of Cuban popular music.

Sánchez's interest in Afro-Cuban music is illustrated by the two examples selected here in addition to the majority of material on his twenty recorded solo albums, which also include the Afro-Cuban genres of mambo, cha-cha-cha, *son montuno*, rumba, bolero, *guaguancó*, guaracha, and danzón. Brazilian rhythms such as bossa nova and samba are also interpreted by Sánchez's ensemble.

Musical Structure of the Cuban Son

The traditional son form is composed of two major sections. The first part, or verse, is a solo melody sung by the lead singer, usually comprising a maximum of eight measures. The second part, called a *montuno* or *estribillo*, demonstrates a denser rhythmic character and a more sharply defined melody than the first part. The montuno, or estribillo, normally does not encompass more than four measures per phrase. The term *montuno* is also commonly used for the piano rhythmic-harmonic pattern constructing this section. The meter of the son is most frequently in cut time, or, as in the case of Sánchez's "Este son," 4/4.

One of the son's more outstanding rhythmical characteristics is its use of a highly anticipated bass pattern of unique character (fig. 1). Carlos Borbolla (1975) notes that this compositional formula, representative of son, is unique among popular music and dance. Although other musical forms may demonstrate elements of anticipation, they are not as calculated or of such definite character as in son. Borbolla defines this characteristic in terms of musical structure. As illustrated in the sample above, the dominant accent of the son rhythmic patterns falls on the upbeat of the second count. Both this anticipated bass pattern and also the pattern performed on the congas are commonly referred to as *tumbao*.

Figure 1. Anticipated bass pattern in Cuban son.

The son has retained its strong tradition and vigor since its emergence in Cuba in the early part of this century. It has been a vehicle for a constantly evolving landscape of Cuban musical forms including the bolero, the conga (dance), the rumba, and the guaracha, among others, as exemplified through the efforts of Arsenio Rodríguez in the late 1930s. Since its inception in Cuba, the innovative quality of the son has been its unique use of anticipation. For this reason it has not dissipated as a tradition; it has constantly conformed to the offbeat rhythms common to the wide array of Afro-Cuban genres and has proved to be a Cuban expression of musical, poetic, and social innovation. Its influence has penetrated musical culture throughout the Americas, Africa, Europe, and Asia. Poncho Sánchez dynamically symbolizes that influence within the Chicano musical culture of Los Angeles and the US Southwest.

"Este son"

"Este son" was composed by Poncho Sánchez and the frequent *sonero* (vocalist) of his early group, José "Perico" Hernández, who is of Cuban birth. The arrangement of the composition is a modern interpretation of son structure, basically conforming to a guaracha-son form. Guaracha, a popular traditional Cuban dance and musical genre, has become a frequently adapted form in modern salsa arrangements. Like *son montuno*, a guaracha-son employs the rhythmic base of reverse, or 2-3, *clave* (fig. 2). The introduction consists of eight bars of an ensemble riff based on the basic verse melody, which is subsequently the main verse of the vocal part. An upbeat rim shot on the timbal (called an *abanico*) anticipates the ensemble's entrance on the first beat of the melodic phrase at measure 1. Measures 7 and 8 are an ensemble rhythmic break. The timbal player (*timbalero*) inserts a roll on the fourth beat of measure 8, anticipating the vocal entrance on the main verse at measure 9.

Figure 2. Reverse (2-3) clave.

The verse structure of the piece adheres to the following scheme: ABCD/EFGH IJKL/ABCD (stanza 4 is a replica of stanza 1). The poetic stanza type of the text to "Este son" is that of the *copla* (couplet), consisting of a paired rhyme scheme (ABCB). Such structure is quite typical of the Cuban son as previously outlined. Loosely structured in four octosyllabic lines, the texts of the four stanzas are as follows:

Oye china, este son	Hey pretty girl, this son
Ven y báilalo y verás	Come and dance to it, and you will see
Que gozarás tú conmigo	That you'll have a good time with me
Hasta por la madruga[da].	Dancing until dawn.
Mira que se pone buena	Look how good it's getting
Ven y arrimate pa'cá	Come, get closer here
Si no te apuras, mi china	If you don't hurry, girl of mine
Este son se acabará.	This son is going to end.
Cuando tú bailas mi ritmo	When you dance my rhythm
En seguida aprenderás	You will then learn
Que tu cuerpo se menea	That your body shakes
Como el son y cha cha chá	Like the son and the cha-cha-cha
Oye china, este son	Hey pretty girl, this son
Vey y báilalo y verás	Come and dance to it, and you will see
Que gozarás tu conmigo	That you'll have a good time with me
Hasta por la madruga[da].	Dancing until dawn.

Generically, the major requisite of the copla, the major assonance of the second and fourth lines, is generally adhered to in this son verse. As in the Mexican son, the number of syllables in each line may be less than eight; likewise, as in the latter, an extended syllable or pause in the text delivery adapts the rhythmic form to the length of the musical phrase.

The basic strophic melody of the verse structure based on the AABA form is notated in the transcription (measures 9–40). Stanzas 1, 2, and 4 conform to a common melody and harmonic progression. The text of stanza 3 is melodically and harmonically set to a different structure, although still in the copla poetic form, and can be considered as a "bridge." The overall nuclear harmonic pattern of the verse section of "Este son" conforms to the schematic in figure 3. This harmonic sequence can be perceived as ii-V7-i in B minor (or the iii of G major) followed by V7/ii-ii V7-I in the tonic. The full progression is also built on a cycle of fifths (C#-F#-B-E-A-D-G). Such a cycle of fifths structure in the song bridge is somewhat unique for the son. It is, however, typical to jazz practice, especially bebop. As this son composition merges with jazz, it gains this harmonic feature.

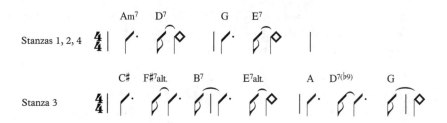

Figure 3. *Harmonic structure of "Este son."*

Instrumentation of the piece includes congas, bongos, timbales, electric bass, acoustic piano, trumpet, alto saxophone, and trombone. Miscellaneous percussion utilized are claves and the cowbell (*cencerro*). As demonstrated in the previous analysis of son structure, the bass adheres to the rhythmic concept of anticipation so essential to the Afro-Cuban form. One of the typical bass patterns throughout the piece can be notated as in figure 4.

Figure 4. *Typical bass pattern in "Este son."*

One of the most important and distinguishing factors is the typical rhythmic structure of the piano patterns, which construct an organic framework of both the clave base and the syncopated tumbao of the bass and conga (as illustrated above in the typical anticipated quality of the bass contrasted with the clave). The rhythmic chordal structure of the piano part, referred to as *guajeo* or montuno, is thus syncopated through the utilization of broken, interlocking fingering patterns that can be played according to the scheme in figure 5, shown with two variations.

Following the vocal section of "Este son," the piano and bass engage in a solo version of the composition's basic harmonic progression. This is accomplished through the use of a series of breaks contrasted with an interpolated conga solo (measures 41–44). The juxtaposition of a structured piano-bass framework against the conga solo dynamically demonstrates the extensive diversity of rhythmic variation that can be executed by the conguero (in this case, Poncho Sánchez) within a very typical style.

Next in the arrangement is a horn ensemble section juxtaposed with the same piano-bass series of breaks (measures 41–58). Arriving at this point,

Figure 5. Piano guajeo *(or* montuno*) and variations in "Este son."*

which has become a climactic juncture, is the *coro* (chorus) statement and response section, traditionally called the estribillo, typically featuring a coro section of vocalists singing rhymed, responsorial phrases. Between the coros the sonero sings in improvisatory fashion a series of *inspiraciones*, thematically expressing the content of the son's text while creatively displaying rhythmic and melodic variation. The *bongosero* switches from playing bongos to the cowbell. The intersecting context of the estribillo manifests a constant, repetitive background of vocal and instrumental structure, thus highlighting the solo inspiraciones in a very driving, dance-oriented section. This is frequently the portion of a salsa- or son-structured arrangement in which the singer, other musicians, and dancers at large extensively embellish their music or dance movements in a free, expressive style. The estribillo section also refers to the traditional African practice of call and response.

It is also quite typical during coro sections for the instrumentalists to solo between the coros, usually in four- or eight-bar phrases. In the case of "Este son," an additional instrumental section follows the coro section (measures 62–70) through a chordal progression that deviates somewhat from the basic

153

nuclear harmonic pattern of the piece. Instead of the ii7-V7-iii7-V7/ii progression, the ensemble section alters the chord progression by flatting the iii7 and the V7/ii and then alternating it twice with the original chords B minor (iii7) and E major 7 (V7/ii). Immediately following the interlude, the montuno section arrives, layered with piano and trumpet solos. Such improvisation is characteristic of the montuno section. During the piano solo the bongosero, in order to relax the rhythmic intensity of the montuno section, returns to the bongos. The piano solo culminates in sixteen bars of horn figures (measures 75–81) that lead to a climactic entry of the trumpet solo, structured on the repeated progression beginning at measure 71. The horn figures again signal the last sixteen bars of the solo, and the conjunto returns to the coro, interspersed again with inspiraciones by the sonero. The piece ends with a recapitulation of the introductory ensemble section (measures 1–8).

"Bien sabroso"

"Bien sabroso" is a progressive interpretation of the son montuno rhythmic form. In deference to the use of a montuno section in other Afro-Cuban son forms such as the guaracha-son type analyzed above, son montuno as a compositional form entails the adaptation of its rhythmic pattern throughout the context of a complete piece. Superimposed on the motivic base of the son montuno are the elements of instrumental sections, coros, and inspiraciones in a variety of applications. Rhythmically, reverse clave is employed as is standard in son montuno. The essential component, however, is the employment of a son montuno pattern; in the case of "Bien sabroso," the piano pattern is notated in figure 6.

Figure 6. Piano pattern in "Bien sabroso."

Progressive instrumental sections, as compared with more *típico* (typical) arrangements of son montuno such as those of early son innovator Arsenio Rodríguez, are illustrated by the ensemble orchestration in measures 1–8, which comprise the basic head of the composition. A unison instrumental break occurs at measures 32–36, and the use of extended chords is prevalent at measures 39–55. Also, melodic configurations are reminiscent of jazz phrasing and intervallic structures and relationships. Such stylized composition is common in the adaptation of Afro-Cuban rhythms to those of groups that are basically instrumental, similar to the octet on the recording being analyzed.

The verse structure of "Bien sabroso" consists of a simple unison vocal passage sung over the son montuno riff (fig. 7). Poetically, the verse structure adheres to the scheme of ABCD/ABCE. The text is as follows:

Para tí	For you
Mi son montuno está	My son montuno is
Bien sabroso	Really nice
Para bailar.	For dancing.
Para tí	For you
Mi son montuno está	My son montuno is
Bien sabroso	Really nice
Para gozar.	For enjoying.

In contrast to "Este son," coplas are not employed, though the rhyme of the coro-styled verse occurs on the second and fourth lines of each stanza (albeit in an extended sense, adopting the rhyme of *está* and *bailar*). In more exact rhyme are the final words of the two stanzas, *bailar* and *gozar*.

Pa-ra tí   mi son mon-tu-no es - tá   bien sa - bro - so   pa - ra bai-lar___   pa-ra

Figure 7. Vocal line in the chorus of "Bien sabroso."

The Role of Jazz

The predominant influence of jazz in Latin jazz, as documented in the practice of Poncho Sánchez, lies not in the rhythmic or structural form but rather in phrasing and improvisation, specifically in terms of the piano and horns. The percussion section and bass usually conform to the traditional tumbao. Piano and horns vacillate from tumbao, clave, and "Latin" phrasing to instrumental "swing" or jazz riffs, especially when adapting a jazz standard feel to the Latin rhythm and arrangement. Improvised solos are especially the spaces in which instrumentalists venture into the incorporation of significant bop, cool, swing, and progressive jazz concepts that are influenced by performers from Charlie Parker to Woody Shaw.

The issue of phrasing is an essential link in conceptualizing the relationship of jazz and Afro-Cuban son. During the 1920s, the trumpet became one of the instruments of the early son ensemble in Cuba, and musicologists such as Olavo Alén have speculated that it was the influence of early New Orleans jazz that produced this innovation in the son.[2] On the other hand, early jazz artists such as W. C. Handy and Louis Armstrong were also being exposed to the Cuban son instrumental and improvisatory style. In "Este son," the montuno section solos by pianist Charlie Otwell and trumpeter Steve Huffsteter characterize a bebop influence that can be traced to the melodic and rhythmic syncopation of both the jazz and Afro-Cuban traditions. Thus the influence in solo phrasing has been a mutual one and can be traced in jazz and son through the work of instrumentalists such as Jelly Roll Morton and Thelonius Monk to Chucho Valdés, and from Louis Armstrong and Dizzy Gillespie to Chocolate Armenteros and Arturo Sandoval.

Interestingly, vocal style, which maintains an Afro-Cuban improvisatory element in the inspiraciones, has rarely (or at least not dominantly) adapted jazz phrasing (although Sánchez has adapted two rhythm and blues standards of James Brown to the Latin format). It should also be pointed out that Sánchez's group, unlike most Latin jazz groups, incorporates a good amount of solo vocals and inspiración. Additionally, the ensemble will at times interpret a typical salsa arrangement for dancing contexts or in club or concert settings.

Also of merit is the question of the Latin element in jazz, which can be traced back to the early creations of Scott Joplin, W. C. Handy, Louis Armstrong, and Duke Ellington's teaming with Juan Tizol. The "Cubop" experiments and success of Dizzy Gillespie and Chano Pozo consolidated the Afro-Cuban impact on jazz in a period and style development that intersected with the inversion of the equation—that of jazz-influenced Afro-Cuban music as personified through contemporary artists of the same era such as Mario Bauzá, Machito, Tito Puente, and Tito Rodríguez. In sum, Afro-Cuban music has "Latinized" jazz, but jazz also "jazzified" Cuban dance music.

In examining the role of Poncho Sánchez in this equation, it is interesting to note some of his own perspective in his own words.

> I play it the way I think it should be done. I'm a purist as far as the Latin jazz music goes, and I don't allow certain things in my band or certain sounds. I don't like loud guitars, rock drummers playing a back beat to a Latin groove; I don't go for that at all. That's like having a rock drummer

playing with a Latin band. That doesn't do a thing for me. I like a *tim-balero*, a conga player, a bongo player, and that's it. I think it should be left alone that way. You always do your own thing, although I definitely follow the lines and the patterns and the roads that Cal Tjader, Mongo Santamaría, Tito Rodríguez, Tito Puente and guys like that have left for us, or have set for us. (Loza 1993, 201)

Although claiming the purist philosophy, it is of interest that Sánchez has also accomplished some major innovations—for example, his adaptation of James Brown's R&B, soul/funk music to his Latin jazz format, interpreting with his ensemble and singing lead vocals to tunes such as "Cold Sweat" and "Funky Broadway" (see *A Night at Kimball's East*). Also, unlike many Latin jazz artists, Sánchez also sings both the typical Cuban son style and the traditional bolero, the slow-tempo romantic ballad style also of Cuban origin but highly popular and reinterpreted throughout Latin America. Another feature of Sánchez's style is his phrasing, an essential element to the Latin jazz concept since the innovations of the Machito Orchestra and the Gillespie-Pozo interchange. Sánchez's conga style is as informed by jazz and R&B phrasing as it is by typical Cuban rhythms. In its subtle presence and hybrid energy and form, Sánchez's Latin jazz–R&B equation is a grossly overlooked dimension of his performance style, interpretation, and ensemble.

Jazz and the Neoclassic Style

Within the past twenty years, a particular jazz movement or trend has occurred that has been referred to as "neoclassicism." The figure largely associated with spearheading this style has been trumpeter and bandleader Wynton Marsalis. An interesting critique of this movement is included in Eric Nisenson's *Blue: The Murder of Jazz* (1997). As have a number of contemporary critics, Nisenson cites the music and attitude of Marsalis and the neoclassicists as one characterizing the gradual death of the spontaneous and culturally expressive nature of the jazz tradition. Marsalis, also an interpreter of Western classical music, has emerged as a symbol of both conformity and defiance. His historical place in music is a certainty; his place in jazz, to some, including this writer, is not so certain.

Does Poncho Sánchez represent for Latin jazz what Wynton Marsalis represents (to some) for jazz? I believe the comparison is incompatible. So why do I ask the question? Let me return to the "purist" philosophy of Sánchez that I previously referred to. In many ways it is not so different from Marsalis's musical philosophy of using only acoustic instruments in his ensemble (i.e., piano, string bass) and of reinterpreting a number of jazz standards from the past in addition to presenting his own compositions. Sánchez likewise refuses to use nontraditional instruments on his recordings and consistently reinterprets both Latin and jazz standards. Both have received major recognition from the mainstream recording industry, although Marsalis's business enterprise is undoubtedly much more lucrative.

But there are also many contrasts—contrasts that are perhaps much more meaningful. Marsalis is based in New York City (although born and raised in New Orleans), the recognized hub of jazz culture. Sánchez, ten years senior to Marsalis, is based in Los Angeles, a cultural hub of a number of Latin American musics (i.e., mariachi, banda), but unlike New York, not the "recognized" hub of "Latin music" (i.e., salsa and Latin jazz). Although both reinterpret jazz standards, Sánchez goes a step further and reinterprets R&B. Marsalis is classically trained; Sánchez only in recent years learned to read music. Marsalis writes his own compositions and arrangements; Sánchez composes tunes in his mind and orally and musically conveys them to his musical pianist-directors (who have included Clare Fischer, Charlie Otwell, and currently David Torres), who then orchestrate the arrangement. Marsalis was raised and trained in a musical family, his father being a renowned jazz pianist. He studied for a period at the Julliard School of Music. Sánchez was raised in a working-class environment in which his immigrant parents listened and danced to Mexican music and his sisters listened and danced to mambo. He learned guitar, vocals, and the conga drums by ear. His formal education never included studies beyond high school.

Can we draw relationships between one's musical and social enculturation and the development of style? It is a hard question, but it is still a good question, for most creative musicians will tell us that music reflects the life and times of the artist making the music. In making comparisons of the musical and social enculturation of Wynton Marsalis and of Poncho Sánchez, I am not attempting to post a "Lomaxian" grid or formula for social-musical relationships, but I am searching for relationships that possibly affect individuals in different ways for different reasons and in different contexts—and that in part can be informed and inspired by one's cultural, social, and psychological environment.[3] Returning to Porter and Gower's concept of transformativity and to the jazz critique written by Nisenson (1997), it might be insightful to reflect on the latter's thoughts as related to Porter and Gower's association of transformativity with qualitative change.

If I think about what jazz has done for my own life, the one thing I would say is that, besides simply making living more enjoyable, it has given me courage. If the most profound representation of modern European culture is that of waiting hopelessly, and endlessly, for Godot, in this country I know that my life was made meaningful by waiting for Miles Davis's next album. Jazz gave those of us who loved it something to believe in—as a pointer toward community, understanding of self, the nature of compassion, ecstatic awareness and our deepest humanity. Jazz could even, as John Coltrane showed us, help us find the road toward God through looking within. (245)

The Global and the Local

From the Latin quarters of Los Angeles, where in his earlier days Sánchez performed in clubs and for Mexican weddings (I remember hiring him and his cousins Ramón and Tony Banda to play with my group) to his present international acclaim in Africa, the Americas, Asia, Australia, and Europe, Sánchez represents both the local and the global. He is locally identified as a Chicano and is recognized by Latinos and Angelinos in general as a virtuoso artist and a source of pride. But for many years, he has been and continues to be an individual with a global view. His readiness and ability to transform tradition into newness and freshness lie at the heart of his musicianship and style. His charisma and leadership skills place him in that special breed of musical transformers, of innovators that still manage to understand and respect tradition. It is for these reasons and others that his mentors such as Mongo Santamaría, Cal Tjader, and Tito Puente have looked to him as one of the major links to the present and future of their art form and as a keeper of the flame.

Part of the global complex, of course, is that of the music industry, international marketing, and the industrial or public sphere of recognition. This includes not only record sales but also the formal recognition of the industry, such as the Grammy Awards presented by the National Academy of Recording Arts and Sciences (NARAS). Critics have noted that the Grammy Awards, like the Oscars for film, are highly related to commercialism and the market. Nevertheless, such awards have had a profound effect on both artists' issues of integrity and public perception. With the growing global popularity of Latin jazz, the question as to which category this style generically belongs in the recording industry has been a difficult one. For the past ten years, as a member of the Grammy Award National Screening Committee, I have continually witnessed debate in the Latin categories panel. This centers on the question of which category to assign artists such as Poncho Sánchez, Tito Puente, Eddie Palmieri, Pete Escovedo, Mongo Santamaría, and Jerry González, among many others. As panelists, we even requested that an additional category, "Latin Jazz," be added to the Grammy Awards competition. To the final satisfaction of many in the music industry, such a category was finally approved by NARAS for the 1994 Grammy Award competition, and Arturo Sandoval was the first recipient in the new category (included in the general category of jazz).

Regardless of the question involving the formal recognition of Latin jazz, there can be no question as to the major impact that the style has generated among audiences and musicians in the domains of both jazz and Latin music throughout the world in the last five decades. Poncho Sánchez plays a vital role in the progressive integration and remarkable compatibility of these two rich traditions. He symbolizes both the local and the global dimensions of Latin jazz, the Cuban son, and the stylistic, social possibilities that these traditions of regenerative innovation represent.

Notes

An earlier version of this essay appeared as chapter 9 in *Situating Salsa: Global Markets and Local Meanings in Latin Popular Music*, edited by Kuse Waxer. New York: Routledge, 2002. Reprinted by permission.

I extend my utmost gratitude to Daniel Castro for his complete critique of the article and his highly useful suggestion for the analysis and musical transcriptions. I also thank my research assistants, Jay Keister and Sarah Lee Peterson, for their editorial assistance and graphic formatting.

1. Both Charles Seeger (1997) and Kwabena Nketia (1979) used the term *juncture* in their critiques on the field of ethnomusicology and its relationship to the musical, the social, or the field of musicology in general.

2. Alén offered this explanation in a public lecture he presented at California State University, Los Angeles, on March 3, 2001.

3. I refer to Alan Lomax's theory and method of his "cantometrics" project. See Lomax 1968.

Works Cited

Borbolla, Carlos. 1975. "El son, exclusividad de Cuba." *Anuario interamericano de investigación musical* 11: 152–56.

Lomax, Alan. 1968. *Folk Song Style and Culture*. New Brunswick, NJ: Transaction.

Loza, Steven. 1993. *Barrio Rhythm: Mexican American Music in Los Angeles*. Champaign: University of Illinois Press.

Nisenson, Eric. 1997. *Blue: The Murder of Jazz*. New York: St. Martin's Press.

Nketia, Kwabena. 1979. "The Juncture of the Social and the Musical: The Methodology of Cultural Analysis." *World of Music* 23, no. 2: 22–35.

Porter, James, and Hershel Gower. 1995. *Jeannie Robertson: Emergent Singer, Transformative Voice*. Knoxville: University of Tennessee Press.

Seeger, Charles. 1977. "The Musicological Juncture: 1976." *Ethnomusicology* 11, no. 2: 179–88.

Discography

Sánchez, Poncho. 1983. *Sonando*. Concord/Picante CJP-201.

———. 1984. *Bien sabroso*. Concord/Picante CJP-239.

———. 1991. *A Night at Kimball's East*. Concord/Picante CJP-472C.

———. 1999. *Latin Soul*. Concord/Picante CCD 4863-2.

CHAPTER 9

Assimilation, Reclamation, and Rejection of the Nation-State by Chicano Musicians

> Those who cannot remember the past are condemned to repeat it.
> —George Santayana, *The Life of Reason*

Chicano musicians, since about the early 1960s, have undergone divergent stylistic periods and movements that have generally followed a chronological pattern of *assimilation*, *reclamation*, and *rejection* of their own role as citizens of the United States. As part of my argumentation I will define the way I use these three terms and I will also, at the outset, admit that the historical pattern I conceptualize here does not necessarily pertain to *all* Chicano musical experience, but that it may indeed characterize a number of historically united and related episodes within the past forty to fifty years.

Phase 1: Assimilation

By the early 1960s, if not earlier, Chicano musicians throughout the Southwest were assimilating various musical styles fermented in the United States. These included blues, R&B, rock, and jazz, among other styles such as mambo, cha-cha-cha, and Latin jazz. Here, I focus on the former group, the styles that were being performed by African Americans and whites (*white* is a problematic term in that it includes not only Anglo Americans but also those of Italian, Jewish, and other European heritages). Examples of young Chicano artists of the 1960s who re-created such styles included Cannibal and the Headhunters, Sunny and the Sunglows, Li'l Ray Jiménez, Thee Midniters, and Vikki Carr. Cannibal and the Headhunters, a vocal quartet from East Los Angeles, released its recording of "Land of a Thousand Dances" in 1965. The song was highly successful and achieved rating in the national Top 40 record list. The same song had been recorded by Thee Midniters in 1964. Cannibal and the Headhunters toured with the Beatles soon after their hit had reached the national radio stations. The Columbia Records subsidiary Date Records secured a contract with the group, but another hit record never materialized. Sunny Ozuna, from San Antonio and lead singer of Sunny and the Sunglows, recorded along with his group a national hit titled "Talk to Me" in 1962 and appeared on the nationally syndicated Dick Clark's *American Bandstand* television show. Although never achieving a national hit, Li'l Ray (Jiménez) and the eight-piece group Thee Midniters (featuring lead vocalist Willie Garcia) became highly popular recording artists and performers in the local pop music network of East Los Angeles. Their respective major local hits were "I Who Have Nothing" and "Sad Girl." All of the examples cited thus far can be categorized as songs related to the African American R&B style popularized during the late 1950s through the 1960s and personified by artists such as James Brown, The Drifters, The Miracles, The Temptations, Martha and the Vandellas, Stevie Wonder, The Supremes, and Little Richard.

One of the essential factors to note in the above examples, beyond the assimilation of African American rock-and-roll styles, was the preponderant use of the English language in the pop music of Chicanos, usually with an African American inflection and sound. Following World War II, many Mexican Americans strove to assimilate the "American" lifestyle of the 1950s and 1960s. It was also the period in which the "greaser," the "wetback," and the Mexican in general was socially derided and marginalized. Many middle-class Mexican Americans, many of them veterans of World War II, made decisive attempts to raise their children as "Americans." It was from this baby boom generation of young Chicanos that emerged the "would be" rock and roll stars of the 1960s. At least such was the dream woven from the threads of attempting to socially and culturally assimilate.

However, most Chicano aspirants of this musical generation did not achieve the national recognition that some undoubtedly deserved. Why? Ironically, Chicanos were attempting to fit into a national culture represented almost exclusively by white and black artists. The few Chicano artists that had attained national success included a few that had changed their Spanish surnames: for example, Andy Russell (Andrés Rabágo), Ritchie Valens (Richard Valenzuela), and Vikki Carr (Victoria Cardona).

Even Sunny Ozuna was able to evade his surname by being fronted as Sunny and the Sunglows.

One note that might be reserved here for the moment is that assimilation is not acculturation. In spite of many Chicanos' attempts to assimilate, they were in fact acculturating to the dominant Anglo social order. A Chicano subculture was indeed developing, as it had been doing since the forced, legal or "illegal," break with Mexico as a result of the Mexican-American War, in which Mexican land and cultural capital was stolen by the United States through its initiation of a bloody war.

Some Retrothought

In 1930, Max S. Handman wrote the following in his article "Economic Reasons for the Coming of the Mexican Immigrant": "American community . . . has no social technique for handling partly colored races. We have a place for the Negro and a place for the white man: the Mexican is not a Negro, and the white man refuses him an equal status" (609–10). Similar sentiments of the early twentieth century are echoed in statements by businessmen and politicians, some of the more inflammatory by none other than President Theodore Roosevelt, whose name still enshrines places such as the Chicano-populated Roosevelt High School in the Eastside of Los Angeles, one of the sites of the 1970 high school "blowouts" (student strikes). Néstor García Canclini (1999) poses a question related to Handman's statement, although his response is much more recent and symbolic, when he asks why there is no word in English for *mestizo*, the Spanish word used in Latin America for those castes of mixed race and culture. He reminds us that the word does indeed exist in both Portuguese (*mestiço*) and French (*métis*).

The displacement factor for Chicanos in US society has been a given for many artists since the early twentieth century, a period during which many US-born Mexicans began to realize that the reclamation of their country, Mexico, would probably never happen in materialist terms—at least not in the twentieth century (and of course, it did not occur). Many Chicano artists have referred to themselves as the "invisible people." Luis Valdez conceived the idea of *Hollywood Olvidado*, eventually produced as a musical revue created and directed by Miguel Delgado, which was dedicated to the forgotten Latino images and artists of Hollywood film. Manuel Peña (1999), who has dedicated a great portion of his scholarship to a class/ethnic analysis of Chicano music in the Southwest, has made some lucid arguments relative to the late nineteenth to early twentieth-century predicament of Mexicans in the United States and their struggle to sustain their own culture within the dominant Anglo hegemony.

> The net effect of the new economy was not only to disfranchise the Hispanic communities, but to force upon them an alien system and its social relations and cultural practices. This system, capitalism, coupled with the harsh discrimination against Mexicans which it fostered, imposed great hardships upon the new Mexican Americans, hardships they only gradually overcame. (19)

Tapping into the ideas of both Raymond Williams and Charles Briggs, Peña (1999) notes that "in the clash of cultural economies and their changing course, several musical forms have been enlisted" (19) and gives as an example the corrido, in which "the Anglo is seen as 'the enemy' who is valiantly confronted by a Mexican hero" (20). Consistently relying on the insightful theories of Américo Paredes, Peña makes more specific remarks concerning the role of the corrido ballad form.

As Américo Paredes (1995) has demonstrated convincingly, this narrative ballad functions historically as an expression of stark cultural contrasts in the conflict surrounding Anglo-Mexican relations in Texas. It flourished at a time when that conflict was intense and not yet mediated by the gestures of intercultural accommodation that emerged much later. The corrido of intercultural conflict is a product of an early historical era that Paredes has labeled the "open hostility" stage in Mexican folklore in its encounter with the Anglo (20). This was a time, roughly from the second half of the nineteenth century until the early twentieth century, when the Mexicans of the Southwest still entertained hopes—however those hopes may have diminished with time—that they might yet reclaim the sovereignty they had enjoyed before the territory was annexed by the United States.

So that what remains, in terms of a national or cultural identity, takes place in large part by means of what Williams conceives as a "residual culture" or, in Gramscian terms, a "war of maneuver."[1] In this manner, Mexicans throughout the Southwest have in various ways and points of time expressively struggled and waged this "war of maneuver" from within their subordinate position in their new, post-Mexico social order, "in which they openly defended their sovereignty against the Anglo invaders" (Peña 1999, 16). Clarifying the power of expressive culture, Peña reminds us that "more important, verbal warfare, in the form of folklore such as the corrido, emerged as a potent expression of resistance, even if in time the goal of political emancipation became increasingly unrealistic" (21).

Phase II: Reclamation

In a previous study, I conceptualized the idea of the "formulation of a collectively resistant aesthetic system" that had developed as a result of and by Chicano artists dissatisfied with "Anglo-American cultural and social institutions." I stated that "the stronger sense of identity, social power, and cultural legitimacy achieved in the wake of the Chicano movement among Mexican Americans was accomplished in large part through a collective process of musical appropriation and reinterpretation" (Loza 1992, 192). I thus suggested that a "reclamation" of culture was occurring among groups such as Los Lobos through the interpretation of genres such as the Mexican *son jarocho*, which became a "dominant cognitive metaphor . . . referencing the Mexican nation and nationalist sentiment, a nostalgic yearning for rurality, a particular sense of Chicano 'tradition,' and a united Chicano resistance in Los Angeles to the cultural hegemony of the United States all at once" (190).

Such reclamation of culture can be observed during the period following that of assimilation of the 1950s and 1960s that I outlined above. Among the many artists involved in what can be interpreted as this movement of reclamation are Carlos Santana, El Chicano, Little Joe y La Familia, Tierra, and Los Lobos. In 1969 Mexican-born and San Francisco–based Santana recorded an album with his blues-, rock- and Latin-oriented ensemble that included the international hit track "Evil Ways," which became the watershed for what from then on would be labeled by the music industry as "Latin rock." In 1971 the virtuoso and highly innovative guitarist and son of a mariachi musician proceeded to fuse Tito Puente's cha-cha-cha "Oyé como va" with a rock-blues feel and achieved yet another international hit. Santana's formula, in which he mixes Latin forms, largely Caribbean, such as cha-cha-cha and mambo, with rock, blues, and jazz, has functioned to the present date.

In 1970, the year of the high school blowouts in East Los Angeles and during what might be called the apex of the Chicano movement, El Chicano emerged as one of the most notable Eastside groups, releasing a rendition of jazz composer Gerald Wilson's "Viva Tirado," dedicated to Mexican bullfighter José Ramón Tirado. (Wilson, an African American composer and director of a jazz orchestra, had migrated to Los Angeles during the 1940s and married a Chicana from there. He became an avid aficionado of bullfighting and composed much music inspired by it.) "Viva Tirado," an instrumental piece based on a cha-cha-cha vamp and a unique, harmonically extended blues-riffed bridge, became a major hit on Los Angeles radio in addition to other radio markets in Baltimore, New York, the South, and the Midwest. The tune represented the reclamation I describe above on a number of fronts. First, it incorporated a Latin rhythm fused with some rock and R&B accents; second, it turned away from the previously more popular pattern of Chicano musicians re-creating styles from the US mainstream of popular music; third, the group name and thus its social and political identity was literally fused with and interpreted by the emergence of the "Chicano" as a new member of that same old dominant social order and with the Chicano movement itself, of which the tune "Viva Tirado" has become one of a number of anthems, including one ("Las nubes") that has been interpreted by another of the artists that I examine here.

In 1971 El Chicano released another LP titled *Revolución*, an artistic effort that "reclaimed" Mexican symbols on various levels, characterizing the ambience and ideology of the Chicano movement. Included on the LP was the classic bolero "Sabor a mí" by Mexican composer Alvaro Carrillo, which had become a uniquely popular bolero in Latin America. The song had attained a particular and special affinity among Chicanos and Latinos in the United States. (Eydie Gormé [Edith Gormezano] had recorded the song with Mexican Trío Los Panchos.) El Chicano's version featured the group's recently added lead female vocalist, Ersi Arvizu, and the recording emerged as a local favorite. Tracks on the LP included tunes sung in both Spanish and English.

Another East LA group to follow suit in terms of musical transformation after the 1960s assimilation trends was Tierra. Featuring the Salas brothers, Rudy and Steve (the latter the group's trademark vocalist), the horn-embellished ensemble recorded a string of LPs beginning during the early 1970s that included a remake of the bolero "Gema," popularized internationally by Mexican vocalist Javier Solís, in addition to a Latin-influenced repertory that included the salsa-infused "La feria" and that dealt with socially relevant themes, as indicated by the title *Barrio Suite*. In 1980, Tierra attained an international profile with the platinum hit "Together." The success of "Together" resonates with a number of social and musical issues. The original version of the romantic ballad was released in 1967 by the Intruders, an African American vocal quartet formed in 1960. Rudy Salas discussed the issue of Tierra's black R&B sound by citing instances where African American audiences, who followed the group's music in cities such as Washington, DC, and Atlanta, assumed the group was African American, often being surprised once the group appeared on stage. Again, because Chicanos are not a nationally dominant group, Salas joked that many US audiences outside of the Southwest would think that the members of Tierra were "Hawaiian or something."[2]

The hit "Together" can represent the first two of the three phases I present in this essay. On the level of assimilation, Tierra certainly assimilated a black R&B musical style, to the point where even African Americans themselves could not detect a nonblack style. Key here, however, is that the assimilation process is oriented toward African American culture, not that of the white hegemony. As I have pointed out in previous studies (1993a, 1993b), there has developed through the past fifty years various significant relationships, identities, and synergies between African Americans and the Chicano/Latino communities in the United States. Music is one of many areas where this has occurred, and it is perhaps one of the most dynamic. In terms of the phase of reclamation, Tierra, which chose to name itself with the Spanish word for "land," also achieves specific loyalties to Chicano-Mexican culture by: 1) fitting into the style of the "oldie" love ballads so popular among Chicanos, which are in a sense a musical transformation of the Mexican bolero (originally Cuban) style by means of R&B romantic ballads; and 2) recording a second version of the song in Spanish and attaining some modest success in the market within Mexico and other parts of Latin America. I believe that the two perspectives presented above suggest that the movement of reclamation as exhibited by Tierra, although not geared toward a return to Mexican folk music (as in the case, for example, of Los Lobos), still appears to represent a rejection of the musical styles of the white hegemony (the group certainly did not imitate Elvis Presley, even though his style was certainly based on that of African American music). This stream of musical formation appears to fit into the phase between assimilation and rejection, which I refer to here as reclamation (of culture).

Two Tejano artists and their respective ensembles also represent this passing from assimilation to rejection and the resulting cultural reclamation. (To some extent, this reclamation is still personified by many contemporary Chicano groups.) Sunny Ozuna (Idelfonso Ozuna), who was described above as an example of assimilation with his gold hit "Talk to Me," eventually returned by the mid-1960s to the music he grew up with: rancheras, polkas, boleros, and *cumbias*. His own testimony speaks for his decision:

> I'm not saying that I wouldn't like to have another "Talk to Me," and make the money that comes off it, but it's a jungle. You have friends and money only while you're there. The minute that song dies, "Sunny who?" Now, La Onda, what is nice is that if you're cold for a while,

they still come out to see you. The white market is not that way. Chicanos hold on to their roots, and hold on more to their stars.[3] (in Peña 1999, 158)

Little Joe Hernández, born in Temple, Texas, and raised in a black neighborhood, represents a similar chronology of the reclamation experience. Although Hernández, like Sunny Ozuna, had originally begun his recording career with a rock tune titled "Safari" with a group called the Latinaires, his major breakthrough did not occur with Top 40 music. According to Peña (1999), "Safari" may have been the first rock-and-roll recording by a Tejano group. "Like many young Mexican American musicians, the Latinaires hoped to crack the rock-and-roll market" (153). However, unlike Ozuna, Little Joe's group was also performing the music of Beto Villa, Balde González, and other Tejano musicians. "Unable to compete in the Top 40 field, the Latinaires turned to the traditional tejano market" (154). In 1964, however, Little Joe and the Latinaires recorded the LP *Por un amor*, and the title track, a highly popular Mexican ranchera composed by the prolific Mexican songwriter-singer Gilberto Parra Paz, became a major regional hit. Peña comments that the recording "did launch the Latinaires in their drive toward the pinnacle of tejano music" (154). Little Joe y La Familia continued to reinterpret many Mexican rancheras in the Tejano, or Tex-Mex, style characterized by R&B inflections, rock-influenced rhythm sections, horn sections combining ranchera voicings, jazz-rock phrasing and arrangements, and innovative string sections. Instrumental in this innovation were members of the Familia band, such as trumpeter Tony "Ham" Guerrero (aka Martínez) and trombonist-arranger Joe Gallardo. Mexican rancheras and other genres adapted by the band included highly innovative arrangements of "Palabra del hombre," "El corrido de Juan Charrasqueado," "Prieta linda," among many others, and notably "Las nubes," a traditional Mexican ranchera that became another Chicano anthem throughout the Southwest, but especially in Texas during the farmworkers' movement there. Also interpreted by both Little Joe's Familia and Sunny Ozuna were boleros, cumbias, mambos, and pop ballads, some of the latter in English. In 1991 Little Joe was awarded a Grammy Award in the Mexican American category for the album *16 de septiembre*. Another Tejano model of bicultural complexity, although of a more recent generation and not critiqued here, is that of Selena Quintanilla Pérez, a rising star and Grammy Award recipient (in the Mexican American category) who was slain in 1995, at the age of twenty-three.[4]

Los Lobos offers a unique yet classic profile in the group's role as cultural *reclamators*. Its emergence on a major record label in 1983 was preceded by ten years of performing Mexican folk music locally in Los Angeles at weddings, religious celebrations, restaurants, and other events, many for organizations with links to the Chicano community and involved in the Chicano movement of the early to mid-1970s. In 1983 the group felt it was a ripe moment to experiment in the mainstream music market, as no one style seemed to be a prerequisite for entry into the industry. David Hidalgo, one of the group's members, described the transition as follows:

> There was all this new music thing happening on the other side of town, over in Hollywood; well, all over the world, really. It was like punk, everything was going on, just breaking down barriers where everything was all jacked up. You couldn't get anywhere. All of a sudden people were ready for something new, so we felt what we were doing—we were starting to incorporate the electric instruments into our old music. We felt we had a place in there too. So we started pursuing it and that's how we ended up on that side of town [the west side]. We're just adventurous. It just happened. (in Loza 1993a, 240)

A norteño, conjunto-styled ranchera ("Anselma") was voted a Grammy Award in the Mexican American category for the Los Lobos' initial LP for Slash Records, a Warner Bros. affiliate. Subsequently a series of LPs was recorded, and with this unique history, the group gained a unique entry into the mainstream market. Although the group's audiences, especially outside the Southwest, were mostly white aficionados, it was Los Lobos' Mexican folk music that was awarded another Grammy, for *La pistola y el corazón* (1989), again in the Mexican American category. Much of this was related to the fact that the majority of voters in the National Academy of Recording Arts and Sciences (NARAS) were white and active producers, writers, and musicians involved in the mainstream recording industry. Los Lobos was receiving more votes for interpretations of Mexican music than were the major Mexican artists such as Vicente Fernández and Juan Gabriel (this was also before the formation of the Latin Grammys). Los Lobos' double platinum remake of the Ritchie Valens hit "La bamba," for the 1987 film by Luis Valdez, was also certainly a factor. This is not to say that the group was not deserving of international awards for its very high quality Mexican music nor that its very high quality rock and roll in English was not also receiving recognition and being nominated for Grammys and other awards. In fact, it was the rock and roll that became the group's principal visa into the white establishment, while its Mexican musical hybridities enhanced its attractive uniqueness. Another point to be made regarding the Grammy being awarded for *La pistola y el corazón* in the Mexican American category was that it was recorded after the *La Bamba* film and recording. Los Lobos could have opted for what group member Louis Pérez felt would have been an artistic compromise, a "La bamba II." Instead, they recorded what they felt was important for them and their original base—a Mexican folk album. One can justifiably say that the Grammy was thus also an award in poetic justice.

But Los Lobos was a classic group across its bicultural terrain. Absorbing genres such as country rock into its compositions, it delivered major commercial successes with original songs such as "Will the Wolf Survive?," which lyrically portrays the lonely wolf trying to support his family while at the same time satirizing the issue of Mexican immigration in the video version of the song. (Country music star Waylon Jennings quickly recorded the song and attained an even bigger radio hit.) In the blues track "Más y más" (*Colossal Head*, 1996), Los Lobos performs the African American–genre song in both English and Spanish, dedicating it to the legendary Chicano song writer-musician Lalo Guerrero for being the first to compose and promote such bilingual blues forms in the 1940s. In the haunting "Kiko and the Lavender Moon" (*Kiko*, 1992) the group organizes a mosaic of multicultural sounds and video images, making impressive use of the blues form, norteño accordion, North Indian sitar, and a mystical text. Rafael Pérez-Torres (2000) offers a rich description of the group's socio-sonic power, telling us that they "invite their auditors into a space where the terms of mestizaje are re-examined on a political and (most potently) cultural level. . . . Their songs engage on a sonic and discursive level with what mestizaje—what meaning itself—means" (224).

At the same time that Los Lobos was experiencing its own musical and cultural transformations, other mosaics emerged and faded, stabilized, or exploded at the local and international level. Such were the experiences of groups as diverse as the punk–new wave, bilingual, and immigration-themed Los Illegals, the mariachi movement throughout the Southwest, the Mexican banda explosion of the mid-1990s, and internationally acclaimed Mexican groups residing in the United States such as Los Tigres del Norte.[5] From Little Joe and Selena to Tierra and Los Lobos, whether the style interpreted was Mexican or not, the commonality of Mexican heritage was still a major element in these artists' identities.

The persistence of Mexican repertoire and/or metaphor as vehicles of Chicano expression in the Southwest thus continued as one of the major features of Chicano music, both stylistically and ideologically. The persistence to *reclamate* songs of the past, of parents and grandparents, and of the original country, Mexico, to which the Southwest, the so-called Aztlán, belonged, becomes an undeniable referent and expression. The ideal of being both a US and Mexican "American" was often the goal, at various levels of cognition, of all this "sonic power" and cultural consolidation. The question persists, however, as to whether this goal was ever realized at a national, "American" level in terms of the music industry and the recognition of and opportunities afforded Chicano musicians during the period of the 1970s through 1990s.

Phase III: Rejection

With the advent of the third millennium, radical turns and changes emerged in the musical aesthetics and choices of not only young but also older Chicano artists. The attempts to assimilate and *reclamate* cultural concepts in assorted ways achieved highly limited commercial, and thus socially impacting, success. Rejection set in through a variety of musical mediums. Mariachi and banda music, representing a return to full-out Mexican cultural expression and tradition, flourished in numerous innovative manners. Soon after Linda Ronstadt recorded her highly significant *Canciones de mi padre* LP in 1988, a newer mariachi renaissance ensued throughout the Southwest and especially among young female adolescents, who began to reclaim the mariachi tradition as performers in unprecedented numbers. Such reclamation of culture certainly signified an attempt to integrate into the social ambiance and networks of the music industry, but it also signified resistance to a system that had thwarted such integration. Ronstadt's marketing agents had warned her that mariachi music would not sell, but her two sequential LPs, *Canciones de mi padre* and *Más canciones*, both became gold records, selling well over a million units in one year, and both received Grammy Awards in the mainstream music industry. Even more telling of Ronstadt's subversive savvy was her statement on the nationally syndicated *Tonight Show*, hosted by Jay Leno (on which she performed mariachi music), that the United States "nabbed" the Southwest from Mexico. She was also critical of Howard Stern's radio belittlements of Mexican music. Although Ronstadt can claim only partial Mexican heritage in her blood, by way of her father, her pride in and loyalty to Mexican culture was a factor in her success, which exceeded most previous attempts to bring Mexican music into the US mainstream.

Samuel P. Huntington, whose recent book *Who Are We? The Challenges to America's National Identity* (2004) has received blistering, if not violent, rhetorical response to its Mexiphobic ideology, at one point almost seems sympathetic to the cause for a valid Mexican identity within the United States:

> No other immigrant group in American history has asserted or has been able to assert a historical claim to American territory. Mexicans and Mexican-Americans can and do make that claim. Almost all of Texas, New Mexico, Arizona, California, Nevada, and Utah was part of Mexico until Mexico lost them as a result of the Texan War of Independence in 1835–1836 and the Mexican-American War of 1846–1848. Mexico is the only country that the United States has invaded, occupied its capital, placing the marines in the "halls of Montezuma," and then annexed half its territory. Mexicans do not forget these events. Quite understandably, they feel that they have special rights in these territories. (229–30)

Huntington also refers to Peter Skerry, who notes that Mexican Americans "enjoy a sense of being on their own turf that is not shared by other immigrants" (Skerry 1993, 289). Yet the precise problem with Huntington's book is that it analyzes the Mexican and American Mexican sector in the United States precisely as a problem, and as a negative one that is responsible for deconstructing and thus threatening the naive concept of a continuing assimilation model—that is, the melting pot theory of US culture and society. In explicating why "Mexican assimilation lags," Huntington categorically writes that "the criteria that can be used to gauge assimilation of an individual, a group, or a generation include language, education, occupation and income, citizenship, intermarriage, and identity. With respect to almost all of these indices, Mexican assimilation lags behind that of contemporary non-Mexican immigrants and that of immigrants in the previous waves" (230–31). Huntington even goes as far as invoking the "mañana syndrome" (quoting Jorge Castañeda) as one of the characteristics of Mexicans that holds them back. He proceeds to quote various supporters of such theories, all the while not citing critics of such reductive, ethnocentric theories. He further adds:

> While the values of Mexicans are undoubtedly evolving, helped by the spread of evangelical Protestantism, that revolution is unlikely to be completed soon or quickly. In the meantime, the high level of immigration from Mexico sustains and reinforces among Mexican-Americans the Mexican values which are the primary source of their lagging educational and economic progress and slow assimilation into American society. (254)

Finally, in response to Lionel Sosa's concept presented in his book *The Americano Dream*, Huntington provokes our disrespect yet again with his disdain for values other than his own: "There is no Americano dream. There is only the American dream created by an Anglo-Protestant society. Mexican-Americans will share in that dream and in that society only if they dream in English" (256).

This is the rhetoric of an internationally acclaimed Harvard professor of political science, and it pleasantly reminds me of the words of another white Anglo American professor of anthropology, who recently served as provost at the University of New Mexico. Brian Foster has constantly reminded his fellow academics that one of the major contemporary problems of the university system in which we currently work was devised some two hundred years ago in the northeast of the country for a limited number of privileged white males. Huntington's rhetoric certainly enhances the empirical data supporting the notions and causes of resistance and rejection that I present here.

This rejection can be observed through both the art and testimony of numerous musicians and songwriters representing contemporary Chicano musical expression. Many of us have written analyses that can be put into the postmodernist trap of idealizing, even romanticizing, the notion that Chicanos have successfully assembled a polyglot mosaic of ethnic values and resistance aesthetics based on the contradictions of the past, making such conflicts work today through art.[6] Manuel Peña recently stated that postmodernism, unlike Marxism, does not account for the alienation that occurs within a society—that it offers no solutions.[7] One might defend the postmodernist on the basis that the music being studied is largely resistant, anticolonialist music, which is valid; however, a question remains as to how our analyses are part of a solution and if they are not indeed only descriptive theories and intellectual eulogies.

The names and songs of current Chicano groups certainly reflect these issues of resistance and rejection: Rage Against the Machine, Aztlán Underground, Delinquent Habits, Funky Aztecs, The Filthy Immigrants, Quetzal, Ozomatli, Akwid, Mexiclan, among a great many others. Musical and textual themes range from Aztec images such as "People of the Sun" (Rage Against the Machine) and group names such as Quetzal and Ozomatli to the latter two groups' repertoire, which fuses Mexican son, Cuban son, R&B, hip-hop, and cumbia genres into both contemporary hybrids and purebreds. Aztlán Underground's group name references the mythical Aztec/Chicano homeland, configured since the Chicano movement as the Southwest. The group's album *Sub-Verses* highlights both the contradictions and the assonance of Chicano daily life while molding indigenous instrumentation, rap rhythms, and images ("This is a lyrical drive-by,/so hit the ground, / don't make a sound / and watch the truth fly./I got the rage,/I got the rage/to pump the twelve gauge"), statements recorded by EZLN's Subcomandante Marcos ("ser Zapatista es buscar una nueva forma de vida y una nueva forma de relacionarse") [to be Zapatista is to look for a new way of living and relating], and Nahuatl incantations ("Intonan/Intontah/Tlatecuhtli/Tonatiuh") [For our mother/our father/the earth/and the sun]. The numerous political and musical references suggest a movement across national, transnational, and international concerns (Pérez-Torres 2000, 224).

These cultural expressions and their direction in space and time, in addition to their independent, bilingual diffusion networks, undoubtedly will disturb Huntington as he stands by his neat and sterile WASP model so essential to his conceptualization of a healthy and assimilated America. The very issues that Huntington claims are tearing America's fabric apart are holding together the musical expression of the contemporary bicultural Chicano musician. These include the following:

1. The fluidity of the Mexican border and immigration, creating a constantly regenerating Chicano-Mexican encounter and unified experience, contrary to the goal of US assimilation and to the older model of Atlantic immigration and ethnic groups separated by an ocean and increasing time. In 1998, Guillermo Gómez-Peña assessed that "*la mexicanidad* and the Latino/Chicano experience" were becoming "completely superimposed. The two hundred thousand Mexicans who cross the border every month bring us fresh and constant reminders of our past (for Mexican-Americans, the continual migratory flow functions as a sort of collective memory)" (136).

2. Retention of the Spanish language in addition to attempts to reference various Mexican indigenous languages and art forms.

3. The growing enterprise of regional Spanish language and bilingual media that caters exclusively to Mexican/Chicano households and youth audiences. Related to this is the formation of the Latin Grammys, due to the huge market prospects for the US music industry.

4. Awareness and loyalty among Chicanos to *mexicanismo*, again very different from the largely lost relationships of historical non-English, European immigrant groups to the East Coast including Italians, Irish, Germans, Jews, Poles, among many others. Assimilation and reclamation thus becomes almost a passé issue among many young Chicanas and Chicanos.

5. Throughout Greater Mexico (Mexico and the US Southwest), there persists among Mexicans and Chicanos a constant retention of Mexican and other Latin American musical repertoire alongside US-based music. This is not the norm with the general US pop music audiences.

6. The US dependence on the Mexican labor force, without which the national economy would fail. Illegal immigration continues due to this equation, and as a Mexican "illegal" worker once told me, "I have the right to go anywhere in this world—it is God who owns the land, not any nation."

What Huntington and contemporary Chicano musicians in effect represent is a dichotomy of experience and thought. The East Coast perspectives of elite, conservative scholars such as Huntington in addition to journalist-broadcasters such as New York–based Lou Dobbs of CNN—whose nightly news segment "Broken Borders" is ongoing now for a full year—signify an intellectual bias and are indicators of a poverty of knowledge about the Mexican immigrant experience in the Southwest. Chicano musicians have lived the issues they compose about, and their ideologies are thus represented in their lyrics and musical forms. Huntington and Dobbs never get to this essential and prerequisite point for analysis. As they have not experienced the conflicts they critique, I doubt they can dance to the jarabe or even the mambo, the latter of which immigrated to their northeast habitat many years ago.

Even Los Lobos has perhaps given up somewhat on cultural reclamation, asking in the 1996 LP *Colossal Head* the question, "Where did it go?/ Can't say that I know/Those times of revolution . . . But was it late for revolution/Too tired, too tired sister/To hold my fist so high/Now that it's gone." In an interview that I conducted with Los Lobos in 1984, César Rosas stated, "We didn't carry the flag, we just carried the guitars" (Loza 1993a, 238). Regarding the current phase that I have referred to here as rejection, I must wonder if any of the contemporary set of Chicano musicians that I include as part of this phase can indeed relate to the US national flag, or to the Texas "Lone-Star-Republic"–symbolized flag, or to the "California-Republic"–emblazoned flag with its image of the bear representing the "Bear Flag Republic" (a declaration of independence from Mexican rule by a small group of eventual gold-whiffing US citizens which was quickly subsumed in the US effort to steal yet another lucrative piece of land—a huge and rich piece). Perhaps there is some truth to Jorge Castañeda's reference to the cliché that "Mexicans are obsessed with history, Americans with the future," cited by Huntington in order to support his WASP superiority hypothesis (Huntington 2004, 254). It is perhaps both ironic and funny that I actually understand the obsession with history and do not see it as part of a problem—or to be more precise, Huntington's obsession with Mexicans and their spawned Mexican Americans and their inferiority due to their unwillingness to conform to his cultural values and bias. In observing the extreme views of Huntington, could one expect that a culture of resistance and rejection to the nation-state would *not* currently thrive among Chicano musicians and thus Chicanos in general? It was Albert Murray (1973) who so eloquently perceived that it is the artist who first knows when the joint is out of sync. Antonio Gramsci's "wars of maneuver" idea comes to mind as I ponder on whether or not the Greater Mexico of Américo Paredes is necessarily such an impossibility.

Notes

An earlier version of this essay appeared in *Postnational Musical Identities: Cultural Production, Distribution, and Consumption in a Globalized Society*, edited by Ignacio Corona and Alejandro L. Madrid. Lanham, MD: Lexington Books, 2008. Reprinted by permission.

1. Peña applies Gramsci's concept in addition to others and offers a sharp theoretical and analytical critique of the context and history of Tejano music. See Peña (1999), 14–24.

2. Interview conducted by the author with Rudy Salas in 1993.

3. The term *la onda* refers to a particular movement in Tejano music characterized by groups such as Little Joe y La Familia and Sunny Ozuna, among many others that considered themselves part of the Chicano movement.

4. For a concise and insightful analysis of Selena's role in the development of Tejano music, see Peña (1992), 203–6.

5. For Los Illegals, see Loza (1993a); for the mariachi movement, see Sheehy (1999); for banda, see Simonett (2001, 2008).

6. See Lipsitz (1986), Loza (1993b), and Perez-Torres (2000).

7. Peña expressed this observation at a conference held at UCLA in April 2004 titled "Issues in Chicano Music and Musicology" and sponsored by the UCLA Chicano Studies Research Center and the UCLA Department of Ethnomusicology.

Works Cited

García Canclini, Néstor. 1999. *La globalización imaginada*. Buenos Aires: Paidós.

Gómez-Peña, Guillermo. 1998. "1995—*Terreno peligroso*/Danger Zone: Cultural Relations between Chicanos and Mexicans at the End of the Century." In *Borderless Borders: U.S. Latinos, Latin Americans, and the Paradox of Interdependence*, edited by Frank Bonilla, Edwin Meléndez, Rebecca Morales, and María de los Angeles Torres, 131–138. Philadelphia: Temple University Press.

Handman, Max S. 1930. "Economic Reasons for the Coming of the Mexican Immigrant." *American Journal of Sociology* 35, no. 4: 609–10.

Huntington, Samuel P. 2004. *Who Are We? The Challenges to America's National Identity*. New York: Simon and Schuster.

Lipsitz, George. 1986. "Cruising Around the Historical Bloc: Postmodernism and Popular Music in East Los Angeles." *Cultural Critique* 5: 157–77. Reprinted in *Time Passages: Collective Memory and American Popular Culture*, edited by Stanley Aronowitz with Sandra M. Gilbert and George Lipsitz, 133–62. Minneapolis: University of Minnesota Press, 1990.

Loza, Steven. 1992. "From Veracruz to Los Angeles: The Reinterpretation of the *Son Jarocho*." *Latin American Music Review/Revista de música latinoamericana* 13, no. 2: 179–94.

———. 1993a. *Barrio Rhythm: Mexican American Music in Los Angeles*. Champaign: University of Illinois Press, 1993.

———. 1993b. "Marginality, Ideology, and the Transformative Expression of a Chicano Musician: Lalo Guerrero." *NARAS Journal* 4, no. 1: 79–100.

Murray, Albert. 1973. *The Hero and the Blues*. New York: Vintage.

Paredes, Américo. 1995. *A Texas-Mexican Cancionero: Folksongs of the Lower Border*. Austin: University of Texas Press. First published 1976.

Peña, Manuel. 1999. *Música Tejana: The Cultural Economy of Cultural Transformation*. College Station: Texas A&M University Press.

Pérez-Torres, Rafael. 2000. "Mestizaje in the Mix: Chicano Identity, Cultural Politics, and Postmodern Music." In *Music and the Racial Imagination*, edited by Ronald Radano and Philip V. Bohlman, 206–30. Chicago: University of Chicago Press.

Sheehy, Daniel. 1999. "Popular Mexican Musical Traditions: The Mariachi of West Mexico and the Conjunto Jarocho of Veracruz." In *Music in Latin American Culture: Regional Traditions*, edited by John M. Schechter, 34–79. New York: Schirmer Books.

Simonett, Helena. 2001. *Banda: Mexican Musical Life across Borders*. Middletown, CT: Wesleyan University Press.

———. 2008. "Quest for the Local: Building Musical Ties between Mexico and the United States." In *Postnational Musical Identities: Cultural Production, Distribution, and Consumption in a Globalized Society*, edited by Ignacio Corona and Alejandro L. Madrid, 119–36. Lanham, MD: Lexington Books.

Skerry, Peter. 1993. *Mexican Americans: The Ambivalent Minority*. Cambridge, MA: Harvard University Press.

CHAPTER 10

Cultural, Economic, and Political Implications of the Globalizing Latin Music Industry

A dance club named "Latin Palace: Chango," which I noticed in the streets of Frankfurt; a day later being greeted at my Bielefeld hotel with the unmistakable sound of Carlos Santana on the lobby sound system—these serve as anecdotal evidence of the global presence of Latin music. With this essay I intend to explore the globalization factors of Latin American musical culture and its related industry through the following themes:

1. Mestizaje, the mixing of race and culture, as related to art and to development theory.

2. The social, political, and industrial dimensions of the Latin American artistic experience and intercultural conflict as related to economics.

3. The apparent propensity of the Latin American musical culture, by means of what can be termed as an aesthetically, ideologically, almost military-driven equation, to grasp so many individuals and cultural spheres and even nations throughout the contemporary world.

Why do so many people throughout the world want to sing and dance and to not only imitate this musical culture but also live it so intensely? And how has the globalization of Latin American culture been accessed and pushed, and how has it also been deflected and blocked?

Mestizaje

In understanding the Latin American concept of mestizaje, the mixing of race and culture, we need to consider how globalization in Latin America began five hundred years ago. Serge Gruzinski, in his book *The Mestizo Mind*, places this well into perspective:

> If we knew the sixteenth century better—the century of Iberian expansion, not just of French religious strife and Loire-style *chateaux*—we would no longer discuss globalization as though it were a new, recent situation. Nor are the phenomena of hybridization and rejection that we now see on a worldwide scale the novelty they are often claimed to be. Right from the Renaissance, Western expansion has continuously spawned hybrids all over the globe, along with reactions of rejection (the most spectacular of which was the closing of Japan in the early seventeenth century). Planetwide mestizo phenomena thus seem closely linked to the harbingers of economic globalization that began in the second half of the sixteenth century, a century which, whether viewed from Europe, America, or Asia, was the Iberian century *par excellence*, just as our own has become the American century. . . .
>
> . . . Finally, if a mestizo way of thinking does indeed exist, how does it express itself? (2002, 3–4)

Through the multiple identities of Native America, Iberia, and Africa, cultural intersections of daily experience in Latin America exist at the multiple levels of religion, technology, economy, aesthetics, identity, thought, and the products of these various, intersecting forms of behavior (fig. 1). As far back as sixteenth-century Latin America, there has been a system of classification of the products of mestizaje, that of the *castas*. Various sets of paintings, an aesthetic product, imaged mixed race matrimonies, encouraged by the Catholic Church, and their resultant children, referred to as *mestizo, mulato, castizo, lobo, coyote, chino-cambujo*, among another forty or so different classifications, some of them interchangeable.

Figure 1. *Multiple identies and cultural intersections.*

The images of the castas allow us to reflect on the intercultural and transcultural process at work in the biological and social mixing of race and culture as well as the area of the aesthetic, including that of the arts, and at various levels of the popular, ecclesiastic, and elitist contexts. As examples we can study the sixteenth-century musical works of Hernando Franco, a highly respected composer (now speculated to have been of indigenous origin), who combined the Nahuatl language with European choral polyphony with text based on the Virgin Mary and her convergence with the Aztec mother earth spirit Tonantzin.

We may also listen to the examples of the *cumbees* and *zarambeques* composed by Santiago de Murcia (1673–1739), who developed scored settings of African-derived vocal and dance traditions. We can also trace the origins of the song "La bamba" to eighteenth-century Veracruz and observe in its musical structure and choreography an amalgam of African, Spanish, and indigenous elements combined through space and time into both a past and contemporary form that has continued to evolve—for example, the rural folk version of the song as related to Chicano Ritchie Valens's (Richard Valenzuela) 1958 rock-and-roll version. In this case we can observe not only the time factor of consistent innovation and change but also the placement of Chicano culture in the context of the mestizo experience, again being highly influenced by African elements by way of the African American context of rhythm and blues and rock, to which Valens adapted the traditional *son jarocho* form of "La bamba." Thus, the call and response verses and improvised text of jarocho musical culture in Veracruz, Mexico, represents the ongoing continental trilogy of mestizaje as well as consistent reinterpretive fourth and fifth elements in the Chicano Southwest (previously Mexico): the US African American and the US European American.

I have observed that within the context of the educational hegemony at US universities, the major scholars of mestizaje remain unknown to US scholars and their students. I specifically refer here to José Martí (1999), José Vasconcelos (1925), Gonzalo Aguirre Beltrán (1972), Oswald de Andrade (1928), Mário de Andrade (1972), Roberto Fernández Retamar (1989), among other numerous Latin American, US Latino, and some non-Latin American scholars who have written extensively on the hybridities and intercultural exegesis of the mestizo experience—for example, Américo Paredes (1958, 1995), Manuel Peña (1999), José Limón (1992, 1994), Guillermo Gómez-Peña (1998), Antonio Benítez Rojo (1989), José Antonio Robles Cahero (2003), Serge Gruzinski (2002), and Pierre

Teilhard de Chardin (1959). Néstor García Canclini, one of the few Latin American thinkers in this area to be translated into English, has asked a very pertinent question in his *La globolización imaginada*: "Por qué en inglés no existe la palabra *mestizo*? . . . Mientras en francés, español y portugués las palabras *métis*, *mestizo* y *mestiço* tienen un uso extendido, en inglés no existe un término equivalente" (2000, 109). Yet, in the same book García Canclini poses another fact for reflection, and one contradicting the previous observation, when he notes that there are more PhD degrees conferred in the United States in areas related to Latin American topics than there are PhD degrees conferred in Latin America on any subject or discipline in general. The issue of socio-cultural hegemony as related to its economic equivalent persists in our present analysis of the larger, overarching problems of manipulation and global control.

Economics, Society, "Development," Conflict, and Resistance

Since World War II, specific terms have emerged among various nations of the West to designate "poorer" nations—for example, *underdeveloped world, underdeveloped countries, developing nations, third world, developing world*. Such terms are unacceptable for a number of reasons, as there is "another side" to the concept of "development." This "other side" is not based on economics, technology, or political hegemonies, but rather on other cultural standards of "development"—for example, the arts, literature, religious expression and structure, and even mestizaje—in the manner that Vasconcelos (1925) and Teilhard de Chardin (1959) envisioned racial-cultural mix as a positive form of progress.[1]

A clear, although not widely disseminated example of the above theory is that of African American (here I include Afro-Latin) music, which Christopher Small (1994) has identified as the one musical form that has been essentially globalized throughout the commodified world. This global spread represents a retro-global expansion whereby the colonized, invaded, occupied, or enslaved in effect "send out" and "send back" their evolved, strengthened cultural forms and artifacts of survival and resistance, with much or all of this occurring through one process or another of mestizaje. This colonization-mestizaje paradigm can be conceptualized through what John Blacking referred to as "aesthetic energy" and "creative cognition"—in this case, products of a radical mix and intuitively ideological returning or spreading of this mix.[2]

The above analysis certainly presents a number of intellectual problems and challenges to what I would describe as a contemporary set of standardizing, in-vogue Euroamericentric theories, largely based on social and cultural critical studies, and particularly on a set of academic writers representing so-called postcolonial theory. My own problem with this school is that it emanates largely from the "post-"colonization of colonies that Britain controlled up to the mid-twentieth century—for example, various African nations, India, Pakistan, Hong Kong, Canada, and various Caribbean nations. We must keep in mind that these colonies or areas of civil control, although legally decolonized and civilly liberated, have not necessarily suddenly become culturally or psychologically liberated after many decades of colonial, and thus various levels of socio-cultural, rule.

In America, and I refer here to the Americas, North and South, European colonization was technically eliminated generally during the late eighteenth and early nineteenth century, with the exceptions of Canada, Cuba, and Puerto Rico. US expansion in effect became a colonizing agent with both the 1848 Mexican-American and 1898 Spanish-American Wars. My point is that "postcoloniality" does not fit the historical, political, or cultural paradigms of Latin America or the Chicano-Latino United States. Related to the recent focus of postcolonialist theory is that of postmodernism, another highly problematic conceptual vogue that cannot be randomly applied to any part of the globe or culture with universal validity.[3] Benítez Rojo takes a particularly hard and valid stance on the issue in his *La isla que se repite* (1989). In her critique of the book, Silvia Spitta makes the following notes on this issue:

> Benítez Rojo's analysis, with its emphasis on chaos, discontinuities, fragmentation, counterpoint, and diversity, can be understood as a postmodern reading of Ortiz and the Caribbean. Benítez Rojo, however, is adamant in disclaiming any continuity with postmodernism because it has excluded Latin American/Caribbean forms of knowledge and therefore has to be seen as embodying specifically North American and European sensibilities. For Benítez Rojo, there is a postmodernism implicit in Ortiz and in all Caribbean ways of life that is very different from, and unrelated to, Eurocentric theories of postmodernism. (1997, 169)

Manuel Peña, representing a Chicano/Latino and at times Marxist perspective, has also commented on his difficulty with postmodernist theory, for it "offers no solutions" to the alienation inherent in marginalized societies.[4] This perspective follows similar lines of thought focusing on intercultural conflict as articulated by Peña's mentor, Américo Paredes, author of "*With His Pistol in His Hand*" (1958) and *A Texas-Mexican Can-cionero* (1995), and José Limón (1992, 1994), also a student of Paredes. In a recent study (Loza 2008), I specifically apply the analytical lines of both Paredes and Peña in assessing the issues of cultural assimilation, rec-lamation, and rejection of the US nation-state by contemporary Chicano musicians, citing especially Peña's critique of the US form of capitalism imposed on Mexicans of the Southwest.

At the base of this type of analysis are the issues of marginalization, discrimination, and general "displacement." The displacement factor of Chicanos in US society has been a given for many artists since the early twentieth century, a period during which many US-born Mexicans began to realize that the reclamation of their country, Mexico, would probably never happen in materialist terms—at least not in the twentieth century (and of course, it did not occur). Many Chicano artists have referred to themselves as the "invisible people." Luis Valdez conceived the idea of *Hollywood Olvidado*, which was eventually produced as a musical that was dedicated to the forgotten Latino images and artists of Hollywood film. Peña, dedicating a great portion of his scholarship to a class/ethnic analysis of Chicano music in the Southwest, has made some lucid arguments relative to the predicament of Mexicans in the United States in the late nineteenth and early twentieth centuries and their struggle to sustain their own culture within the dominant, Anglo hegemony:

> The net effect of the new economy was not only to disfranchise the Hispanic communities, but to force upon them an alien system and its social relations and cultural practices. This system, capitalism, coupled with the harsh discrimination against Mexicans which it fostered, imposed great hardships upon the new Mexican Americans, hardships they only gradually overcame. . . .
>
> . . . As Americo Paredes has demonstrated convincingly . . . this nar-rative ballad [the corrido] functions historically as an expression of stark cultural contrasts in the conflict surrounding Anglo-Mexican relations in Texas. It flourished at a time when that conflict was intense and not yet mediated by the gestures of intercultural accommodation that emerged much later. The corrido of intercultural conflict is a product of an early historical era Paredes has labeled the "open hostility" stage in Mexican folklore in its encounter with the Anglo. This was a time, roughly from the second half of the nineteenth century until the early twentieth, when the Mexicans of the Southwest still entertained hopes—however those hopes may have diminished with time—that they might yet reclaim the sovereignty they had enjoyed before the territory was annexed by the United States. (1999, 19, 20)

So that what remains, in terms of a national or cultural identity, takes place in large part by means of what Williams conceptualizes as a "residual culture," or what is in Gramscian terms a "war of maneuver."[5] In this manner, Mexicans throughout the Southwest have in various ways and at various points of time expressively struggled and waged this "war of maneuver" from within their subordinate position in their new, post-Mexico social order, "in which they openly defended their sovereignty against the Anglo invader" (Peña 1999, 16–17).

The intercultural conflict position, if isolated as an overarching analysis, can certainly be challenged, but it has not been intended as an all-encompassing theory and has been conceived as part of a much larger whole. One can focus on, for example, the international artistic success of an artist such as Carlos Santana, who has consistently topped the global popular music industry. Another area that must be assessed is that area within the Latino population of the United States, which comprises 14 percent of the nation and within which context Mexican regional music accounts for two-thirds of the total "Latino music" sales in the US record market. Examples of this musical sector include genres and ensembles such as norteño (performed by, for example, Los Tigres del Norte), ranchera, son, and other styles that include mariachi (Vicente Fernández, Juan Gabriel), banda (Banda Recodo), and *grupero*. The issues of conflict, resistance, and marginalization of the latter differ from, while closely resembling, the contexts examined by Paredes, Peña, and Limón.

The Market: A US Hegemony Based on a Capitalist Pop Music Industry

I present here a contemporary set of questions and observations concerning the US versus Latin American industries and some specific related issues of contradiction and imparity. Why is it that Britney Spears, the internationally popular pop music star from the United States, is able to appear at a sold-out arena concert in Mexico City or most any other major Latin American city, while Luís Miguel, an international pop music star from Mexico, and of mixed Latino heritage, is unable to appear to a sold-out arena concert in comparable major US cities such as Detroit, Indianapolis, Philadelphia, or Seattle? He undoubtedly could fill an arena in Los Angeles, where over 50 percent of the populace is Latino, but he cannot do so in a predominantly Anglo city, whereas Britney Spears can do so in a predominantly Latino or Latin American city. Why do Latin

Americans gravitate toward a Britney Spears or others like her while Euro Americans, and even African Americans, do not gravitate in such mass to Luís Miguel or those many other Latin American artists very much similar to him in musical and cultural style?

I believe the answer is both simple and complex, and that there are various factors, including the following:

1. Unlike much of Europe, Asia, Africa, and Latin America, in the United States most of the populace is generally monolingual and undisciplined in the acquisition of "foreign languages." Additionally, what can be generally described as "anti-intellectual" environment and sentiments pervade many sectors of the country, especially those of the conservative populace.

2. Paradoxically, there is also a white, ethnocentric US market control of the music industry—for example, by Sony Records, which holds huge assets and market domination of many artists in both the United States and Latin America (the latter by way of both Sony Records and Sony Latino). Here, one question that arises is based on optimal profit strategies and whether a Latin American product is not maximally promoted in the United States due to the factors presented in point 1 above and point 3 below.

3. *Hispanophobia*: This is a term that has been presented in the past (see, for example, R. Paredes 1977; A. Paredes 1995; and others) on the central issue of intercultural conflict—mainly, that of prejudice against Mexicans and Latinos by the dominant Anglo class in the United States. Supporting this thesis is the abundance of border studies currently in process, in addition to the many areas of present conflict and its related metaphors—for example, the recent patrolling of the Arizona-Mexico border by the privately organized and racist "Minutemen."

Point 3 above is currently reappearing, as it did especially up to the 1960s, even in the academic literature. Samuel P. Huntington, a Harvard professor of history, recently wrote *Who Are We? The Challenges to America's National Identity* (2004). In this unfortunate, reactionary work, the author consistently expresses an uninhibited, racist, anti-Mexican/Latino immigrant paranoia. He posits WASP (White Anglo Saxon Protestant) values as the sole basis for being American. The following is one of the various irresponsible points of his "analysis":

While the values of Mexicans are undoubtedly evolving, helped by the spread of evangelical Protestantism, that revolution is unlikely to be completed soon or quickly. In the meantime, the high level of immigration from Mexico sustains and reinforces among Mexican-Americans the Mexican values which are the primary source of their lagging educational and economic progress and slow assimilation into American society. (254)

Three levels of capitalism drive the critical equation I am calculating in this paper: those of 1) the industrial, 2) the cultural, and 3) the intellectual. The passage by of Huntington represents one side of what we can refer to as "intellectual capitalism." This type of capitalism also exists in much of the art-based academic literature—for example, in a recent textbook on "American popular music" which affords approximately six pages out of four hundred to the US Latino population.[6]

Taking the various factors cited here in terms of ethnocentricities as related to the capitalist US music industry, we can conclude that the economic and political ramifications of this working complex bear both positive (although compromising) and negative gains for the Latin American musical artist and industry. Selected Latino artists and their agents may do well in the United States, but the trade-off with their US artistic and industrial compadres is far from any form of decent, artistic integrity on the part of the dominant base of control. A very related and similar moral paradox is that of the film industry, where it has been estimated that 92 percent of the films screened in Mexican movie theaters are products of Hollywood—yet another contemporary cultural US hegemony.[7]

Transnational Identities

There is another example that I will offer here in order to contemplate on a different regional and stylistic area that I believe reinforces some of the observations and conclusions I have thus far offered, especially as related to transnationalism, mestizaje, intercultural conflict, and in this case, the occasional unpredictability of the market.

In my book on Tito Puente (Loza 1999), I explore the various aspects of Puente's "Latin music" and what I refer to as its "multicultural ambit." I even compare his celebratory, intercultural musical matrices of performance and musical style to Augustine's noble and unified, intra-religious city—the City of God. Here we can again reflect on the positive elements and possibilities associated with mestizaje, the transnational, and the intercultural.

As a case in point, I offer the example of Orquesta de la Luz, a Japanese salsa group that attained international acclaim during the early 1990s, even being nominated for a Grammy Award in 1995 and performing in concert at Madison Square Garden in New York City. The musicians of the group developed their salsa style in Japan, listening to the recordings of Tito Puente, Rubén Blades, Willie Colón, and other salsa artists before venturing to New York City to develop further, eventually being guided by Latino salsa producer Sergio George. The group's music was heartily accepted by the international Latino salsa community and entered the market with impressive record sales and concert tours.

I found this episode in Latin music history to be a unique study, as it represented an optional form of mestizaje—one minus the racial, time-space (regional), or directly contextual intercultural factors. Orquesta de la Luz learned a cultural form of expression largely by means of technology, that of recordings, in addition to the transmission of knowledge by older Japanese musicians who had learned the music. The juxtaposition of Japanese and Latino cultures did not exist within the musicians' enculturative context in Japan.

Patria Román-Velázquez (1998) sees a similar process at work in England, where she identifies the embodiment and co-optation of Latino musical culture by British musicians. Identity—a Latino one—becomes almost a standard-bearer among these artists. I witnessed a similar context in Japan.[8] In an article that I wrote on the subject, I concluded that what emerges from this long-distance type of acculturation are various patterns and behaviors that we can tentatively refer to, with multiple variants and negotiation, as an "international aesthetic."

During my fieldwork for the above study, I became interested in the fact that Orquesta de la Luz was nominated for a Grammy Award in the Tropical Music (salsa) category, yet no US, non-Latino salsa band, which would have much more contextual access to Latino and salsa culture, has ever attained such a feat. I posed the issue to Nora, the lead vocalist of the group; the following is an excerpt from the resultant published article:

> It was also of great interest to me to ask Nora for her views on one of the main issues I raise in this paper—that of Japanese musicians developing salsa in a much more critical mode than non-Latin Americans in the United States. Her immediate response was that there are "many reasons," including: 1) the pronunciation of Spanish (often more difficult for non-Latin Americans in the United States than for Japanese); and 2) the "image" of Latinos in the United States, where she speculates that

culture and society is "not really mixed [but] separate" in terms of African Americans, Latinos, and others. She referred to these as "different blocs" that are "separate" and that basically "protect their own culture." She noted that the United States is not one race or one nationalism. Thus, Nora feels that the image of salsa, the music of Latinos, has been influenced by these sets of circumstances, prejudices, and conflicts. (1998, 392)

It was, of course, fascinating to me to hear Nora's keen interpretation of the issues related to ethnic conflict in the United States and its relationship to the multicultural yet separate "blocks" of intercultural conflict. Shuhei Hosokawa, who has written extensively on the subject, extends the analysis even further with some impressive, lucid thoughts:

> For Latinos, an all-*gringo* band, if any, would be less surprising but more threatening and scandalous than Orquesta de la Luz. This is because such a band may annihilate in a rather invading manner the assumption about ethnic hierarchy inside which Latinos and gringos have been living for centuries. It may intimidate and subvert the Latino identity which is formed not only by their own biological and familial heritage but also by their constant confrontation with and astute repression by the Anglo-American society. (n.d., 29–30)

Also of significance to the Orquesta de la Luz episode, however, is that the group eventually dispersed in the mid-1990s, and no major Japanese salsa orchestra has followed its international path, although vocalist Nora did continue to record with limited success in the market. Salsa, however, continues to thrive among Japanese musicians in Japan in addition to musicians in Asia, Europe, and Africa.

Conclusions

As Vasconcelos (1925) prophesizes an aesthetic, creative era resulting from the global mixing of races and cultures, perhaps we can conceptualize the beginning of similar patterns in contemporary societies and an emerging global culture. Does the synthesis of cultural ideas enhance our understanding of the world and thus lead to more lofty questions? Is there an aesthetic hunger that is fed by the returning, abstract products of colonization and a multicultural diaspora? Can this possibly metamorphose into the appeasement of a spiritual hunger in different parts of the world?

We might, at this point, make a primal, overarching observation: all of this description, analysis, and theorizing must eventually go way beyond the notions of economics, politics, and materialism. Benedetto

Croce (1965) made it very clear in his aesthetic conceptualizations that the intuitive is superior to the intellectual, and that the most direct bridge to the metaphysical, or the spiritual, is "art," which he defined purely and simply as "intuition." To extend this into another mode of thought that might be useful, we can conceptualize three processes occurring at every level of human behavior and its expressions: those of the 1) materialist/capitalist, 2) intellectual/rational, and 3) aesthetic/intuitive, with the latter as the prime, spiritual motive. A metaphor representing this human way of being and acting might be figured as a rotating windmill in which all three processes are perpetually intersecting and interacting as one (fig. 2).

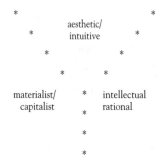

Figure 2. *Rotating windmill of human behavior and its expressions.*

As characterized by the music of Bach and Beethoven, or of Native American chants/dances to West African rituals transversed to the Americas, or spiritual/blues/jazz/rock, or popular musical/cultural forms of the "Americas" retracing and remapping the globe, we can perceive a persistent strain of spiritual ideology and religious context as the birthplaces and cradles of such musical cultures. Upon developing many more historical and cultural questions and hypotheses, perhaps these will be some of the questions that we ultimately will decide to ask, and, with the aid of our spiritual and aesthetic intuition, to even answer.

Notes

An earlier version of this essay appeared in *E Pluribus Unum? National and Transnational Identities in the Americas/Identidades nacionales y transnacionales en las Américas*, edited by Sebastian Thies and Josef Raab. Berlin: LIT Verlag; Tempe: Bilingual Press/Editorial Bilingüe, 2009. Reprinted by permission.

1. It should be pointed out that the idea of progress here was not intended as part of a racist theory, as it assessed the issues of a mixture of race and therefore culture.

2. I cite Blacking's ideas here from a lecture he delivered at UCLA in the 1980s.

3. Related to this discussion is Paulo Freire's (1985) conceptualization of the intellectual, academic formalized system of research and theory as a "banking" system of what I would refer to as a capitalistic, academic form of investment, which supports a power base of "intellectual bank notes"—for example, publications based on a network of hegemonic theories and unidimensional, and oftentimes biased, historical and cultural perspectives.

4. I quote from a lecture delivered by Peña at the UCLA conference on Chicano Music and Musicology in April 2004.

5. Peña cites both Williams (1977) and Gramsci (1971) and incorporates their views into his analysis.

6. I refer here to a textbook titled *American Popular Music* (Starr and Waterman 2003).

7. This estimate was cited to me by Carlos Monsiváis in a personal communication, August 2005. Monsiváis is a leading critic on Mexican popular culture and politics.

8. I base this perspective on a year (1995-96) that I spent in Japan teaching at Kanda University of International Studies, during which time I undertook research and fieldwork based on the topic of Latin American musical culture among the Japanese. I presented the findings of my study at the international conference of the International Society for the Study of Popular Music, held at Kanazawa, Japan in 1998; see Loza (1998).

Works Cited

Aguirre Beltrán, Gonzalo. 1972. *La población negra de Mexico: Estudio etnohistórico.* Mexico City: Fondo de Cultura Económica. First published in 1946.

Andrade, Mário de. *Ensaio sobre a música brasileira.* 3rd ed. São Paulo: Vila Rica; Brasília: INL.

Andrade, Oswald de. 1928. "O manifesto antropofago." *Revista de antropofagia*, no. 1 (May): 3, 7.

Benítez Rojo, Antonio. 1989. *La isla que se repite: El Caribe y la perspectiva posmoderna.* Hanover, NH: Ediciones del Norte.

Croce, Benedetto. 1979. *Guide to Aesthetics.* Translated by Patrick Romanell. South Bend, IN: Regnery/Gateway, Inc. First published as *Breviario di estetica: Quatro lezioni.* Bari: Laterza, 1913.

Fernández Retamar, Roberto. 1989. *Caliban and Other Essays.* Translated by Edward Baker. Minneapolis: University of Minnesota Press.

Freire, Paulo. 1985. *Pedagogy of the Oppressed*. Translated by Myra Bergman Ramos. New York: Continuum. First published as *Pedagogia do oprimido*. Rio de Janeiro: Paz e Terra, 1970.

García Canclini, Néstor. 2000. *La globalización imaginada*. 2nd edition. Buenos Aires: Editorial Paidós.

Gómez-Peña, Guillermo. 1998. "1995—*Terreno peligroso*/Danger Zone: Cultural Relations between Chicanos and Mexicans at the End of the Century." In *Borderless Borders: U.S. Latinos, Latin Americans, and the Paradox of Interdependence*, edited by Frank Bonilla, Edwin Meléndez, Rebecca Morales, and María de los Angeles Torres, 131–38. Philadelphia: Temple University Press.

Gramsci, Antonio. 1971. *Selections from the Prison Notebooks*. Translated by Quintin Hoare and Geoffrey Nowell Smith. New York: International Publishers.

Gruzinski, Serge. 2002. *The Mestizo Mind: The Intellectual Dynamics of Colonization and Globalization*. Translated by Deke Dusinberre. New York: Routledge. First published as *La pensée métisse*. Paris: Fayard, 1999.

Hosokawa, Shuhei. n.d. "Salsa no tiene frontera: Orquesta de la Luz; or the Globalization and Japanization of Afro-Caribbean Music." Unpublished manuscript.

Huntington, Samuel P. 2004. *Who Are We? The Challenges to America's National Identity*. New York: Simon and Schuster.

Limón, José. 1992. *Mexican Ballads, Chicano Poems: History and Influence in Mexican-American Social Poetry*. Berkeley: University of California Press.

———. 1994. *Dancing with the Devil: Society and Cultural Poetics in Mexican-American South Texas*. Madison: University of Wisconsin Press.

Loza, Steven. 1998. "Latin American Popular Music in Japan and the Issue of International Aesthetics." In *Popular Music: International Interpretations*, edited by Toru Mitsui, 391–97. Kanazawa, Japan: Kanazawa University Graduate Program in Music. Proceedings of the Ninth International Meeting of the International Association for the Study of Popular Music, Kanazawa, August 1998.

———. 1999. *Tito Puente and the Making of Latin Music*. Champaign: University of Illinois Press.

———. 2008. "Assimilation, Reclamation, and Rejection of the Nation-State by Chicano Musicians." In *Postnational Musical Identities: Cultural Production, Distribution, and Consumption in a Globalized Scenario*, edited by Ignacio Corana and Alejandro L. Madrid, 137–50. Lanham, MD: Lexington Books.

Martí, José. "Our America." In *José Martí Reader: Writings on the Americas*. Edited by Deborah Shnookal and Mirta Muniz, 118–27. Melbourne, NY: Ocean Press. First published as "Nuestra América," *La revista ilustrada de Nueva York*, January 10, 1891.

Paredes, América. 1958. *"With His Pistol in His Hand": A Border Ballad and Its Hero*. Austin: University of Texas Press.

———. 1995. *A Texas-Mexican Cancionero: Folksongs of the Lower Border*. First published in 1976.

Paredes, Raymond. 1977. "The Origins of Anti-Mexican Sentiment in the United States." *New Scholar* 6: 139–65.

Peña, Manuel. 1999. *Música Tejana: The Cultural Economy of Artistic Transformation.* College Station: Texas A&M University Press.

Robles Cahero, José Antonio. 2003. "Occidentalización, mestizaje y 'guerra de los sonidos': Hacia una historia de las músicas mestizas de México." In *Musical Cultures of Latin America: Global Effects, Past and Present,* edited by Steven Loza, 57–78. Los Angeles: UCLA Department of Ethnomusicology and Systematic Musicology. Proceedings of the conference, University of California, Los Angeles, May 28-30, 1998.

———. 2005. "Cantar, bailar y tañer: Nuevas aproximaciones a la música y el baile populares de la Nueva España." *Boletín del Archivo General de Ia Nación* 6, no. 8: 42–76.

Román-Velázquez, Patria. 1998. "Salsa Musicians and the Performance of a Latin Style and Identity." In *Popular Music: International Interpretations,* edited by Toru Mitsui, 383–90. Kanazawa: Kanazawa University Graduate Program in Music. Proceedings of the Ninth International Meeting of the International Association for the Study of Popular Music, Kanazawa, Japan, August 1998.

Small, Christopher. 1994. *Music of the Common Tongue: Survival and Celebration in African American Music.* New York: Riverrun Press.

Spitta, Sylvia. 1997. "Transculturation, the Caribbean, and the Cuban-American Imaginary." In *Tropicalizations: Transcultural Representations of Latinidad,* edited by Frances Aparicio and Susana Chavez-Silverman. Hanover, NH, and London: University Press of New England.

Starr, Larry, and Christopher Alan Waterman. 2003. *American Popular Music: From Minstrelsy to MTV.* New York: Oxford University Press.

Teilhard de Chardin, Pierre. 1959. *The Phenomenon of Man.* New York: Harper. First published as *Le phénomène humain.* Paris: Éditions du Seuil, 1955.

Vasconcelos, José. 1925. *La raza cósmica: Misión de la raza iberoamericana: Notas de viajes a la América del Sur.* Madrid: Agencia Mundial de Librería. Published in English as *The Cosmic Race.* Translated and introduced by Didier T. Jaen. Afterword by Joseba Gabilondo. Baltimore: Johns Hopkins University Press, 1997.

Williams, Raymond. 1977. *Marxism and Literature.* New York: Oxford University Press.

CHAPTER 11

From Veracruz to San Francisco
The African Diaspora through Greater Mexico

The African presence in the musical culture of Mexico can be considered a trilogy of trilogies: *migration*, moving from Spain, Africa, and within Native America; *mestizaje*, the mixing of race and culture among, principally, Native Americans, Africans, and Spaniards; and the *music* itself, a byproduct of the migrating mestizo experience linked to the blood and aesthetics of the African, Spaniard, and Amerindian.

My aim here is to focus on the story of the African in Mexican musical culture while constructing a schematic of the various patterns, regions, and musical forms that played roles in the trilogy proposed above. There has arisen a rich abundance of data related to the African population and its influence in Mexico since the sixteenth century, enabling me, for this essay, to fuse historical data with musical analysis to explore the following contexts: the Mexican *son* and other folk traditional forms in their different regional hybrids; the use of Mexican Afro-mestizo forms in ecclesiastic, chamber, and symphonic music since the seventeenth century; the dissemination of Afro-Cuban musical genres throughout Mexico; and the impact of African American musical culture on the Chicano people of the US Southwest (Aztlán) and in Mexico.

Some points of clarification might be in order at the outset. The term *Greater Mexico*, as used by the eminent scholar of Chicano music, Américo Paredes, among others, refers to the geographical boundaries and cultures of contemporary Mexico in addition to its pre-1948 territory and cultures, the US Southwest, known in various contexts to the Mexican American, or Chicano, population as Aztlán, the mythical homeland of the Aztecs. The use of the metaphor of Aztlán became popular during the political movement of Chicanos during the 1960s and 1970s, and it is still in wide use among them, especially in much of their contemporary musical expression.

Another semantic point to be made concerns the use of the term *Afro-mestizo*, which is the common and widely accepted term used by Mexican scholars studying the African context of Mexican culture in general. The reason for this, as opposed to using, for example, the terms *Afro-Mexican* or *Afro-American*, is both complex and perhaps ideological. Unlike the experience of race relations in the United States, racial and cultural mixture, or mestizaje, began to occur in Mexico by the early sixteenth century. Enhancing this context was the historical pattern of north African culture that existed among the Spanish colonists, especially those from southern Spain (Andalucía) who went to Mexico (or New Spain, as they titled it). Mestizaje was, in effect, already a common practice in Spain, not only in terms of the African element but also with the Islamic Arabic and the Jewish Sephardic cultures, among other provincial cultures that have also evolved and exist to this day. As early as the seventeenth century in "New Spain," church clergy blessed marriages that involved a vast number of interracial couples. In spite of the massive mistreatment being inflicted upon them, Indians and Africans were recognized as human beings with spiritual souls, and marriage was considered by church officials as the moral form of conduct for couples and thus encouraged. The offspring of those representing the trilogy of continental cultural origin, *españoles*, *negros*, and *indios*, were also given classificatory names (*castas*) to describe their racial mix, including mestizo (*indio* and *español*), *mulato* (*negro* and *español*), *castizo* (*español* and mestizo), *chino-cambujo* (*negro* and *indio*), *lobo* (*chino-cambujo* and *indio*), *coyote* (*indio* and mestizo), among another forty-seven various classifications (some of these being interchangeable). The castas were represented in different sets of eighteenth-century paintings depicting the mixed-race marriage couples along with their mestizo daughters or sons—for example, the paintings by Miguel Cabrera (1763) (figs. 1, 2).

Returning to the issue of the use of the term *Afro-mestizo*, and in light of the complex classifications based on complex racial and cultural mixing that was occurring in New Spain, it becomes apparent that the African element in Mexico cannot be separated from the experience of mestizaje, so that a highly intercultural context of race and culture became what we can call the Mexican cultural experience, recognized or not at various historical points of time. Anthropologist Gonzalo Aguirre Beltrán, after years of compiling data on Africans in Mexico and writing numerous ethnographies on the subject, specifically noted the problem of ignorance and prejudice complicating the research of African culture in Mexico (it might be noted that the same had occurred with indigenous culture, especially up to the turn of the twentieth century):

Figure 1. Miguel Cabrera, De español e india, nace mestiza, *1763. Oil on canvas, 147 × 117 cm. Private collection. Reproduced by permission.*

I published *La población negra de Mexico* in 1946. The first reprint of the book appeared in 1972, some twenty years after. That fact conveys the significant lack of interest among Mexican intellectuals in the study of the black population. Besides, there had always existed a certain aversion to the blacks, a kind of embodied racism expressed against the black population. In Mexico, not only in the coastal regions such as Veracruz and Guerrero do we find traces of our black heritage, but in the entire

Figure 2. Miguel Cabrera, De español y negra, mulata, *1763. Oil on canvas, 148 x 117.5 cm. Private collection. Reproduced by permission.*

country as well. There were blacks in every city. There were black slaves in the factories. . . . There were black workers in the haciendas, known as *Jarochos*. They are descendants of crossing between Indians and blacks. (interview in *La raza olvidada* 2001, my translation)

Aguirre Beltrán made specific observations concerning the effect of African culture within the evolution of Mexican musical forms, noting that en realidad durante el siglo XVII hubo una estira y afloja de prohibiciones y licencia, entre cantos y bailes permitidos y condenados, entre operaciones españolas deliberadas y negra espontanea, es decir, se produjo una interacción que vino finalmente a originar el baile y el canto mestizo, pero mestizo principalmente de español y negro. (1972, 3–5)

(In reality, during the seventeenth century there was both give and take of prohibitions and license among songs and dances permitted and condemned, and among deliberated Spanish behavior and black spontaneity; in other words, an interaction eventually developed that originated mestizo dance and song, but mestizo principally based on the Spanish and African.) (my translation)

Although estimates have been conjured as to how much of the present Mexican population is of African origin, it becomes an impossible issue of speculation, owing to the complex and massive quantity of interracial mixing through the past five centuries. The concept of "multiple identities" is one that contributes to an understanding of how Mexicans have perhaps conceptualized their multiethnic identities. José Antonio Robles Cahero, who has written extensively on the interplay of musical sounds as they relate to the interaction of identities, made the following comments to me on the issue:

There emerged a new identity, and all of these cultures gave to the American culture a variety of multiple identities, so we cannot talk about only one, or a Mexican or American identity, but of multiple identities of different elements. For instance, elements from Africa, from the Indians, from different European societies such as Spain, Italy, and others came into the New World. And this is what we Latin Americans inherited in the nineteenth century when our countries became independent. (2005b)

Attesting to the major penetration of Africans into mid-seventeenth-century Mexico are the recorded statistics of the period, citing more Africans (app. 20,000) than Spaniards (8000) in the vicinity (*obispado*—archdiocese) of Mexico City during that period. We must keep in mind, of course, that of the remaining population in the area, about 600,000 were of indigenous cultures, with castas counted as Euro-mestizos (app. 95,000), Afro-mestizos (app. 43,000), and Indo-mestizos (app. 43,000) (see Aguirre Beltrán 1972, 211–19). In assessing these seventeenth-century census numbers, we can reflect on the cycles of mestizaje and the manner in which the multiple identities as conceived by Robles Cahero have come to characterize contemporary Mexican culture.

Specific Historical Musical Development

Perhaps the most dominant, if not the most recognized musical genre to emerge from the mestizo trilogy exhibiting major African participation is that of the Mexican son, which has developed and evolved since the seventeenth century in various major regions of Mexico: the south of the state of Jalisco, the two areas referred to as "Tierra Caliente" in the states of Michoacán and Guerrero, the Pacific coastal area known as the "Costa Chica" in the states of Guerrero and Oaxaca, the Gulf of Mexico regions in the states of Veracruz and Tabasco, the Huastec area including the state of Tamaulipas, and the north of the state of Puebla. Recent research has been conducted in these areas by scholars working in Mexico, including the Cuban Rolando Pérez Fernández (1990) and Mexicans Alvaro Ochoa Serrano (1994, 1998), Antonio Corona Alcalde (2005), and the above-cited Robles Cahero (2003, 2005a), among numerous others. I will focus here on two examples of the son tradition, those of Veracruz and Jalisco.

A specific example of the son tradition in Veracruz from the colonial period to contemporary times is a son dating from the eighteenth century, "Chuchumbé." Although its original musical format is unknown, except that it was a *son jarocho* from Veracruz, the text, due to its official condemnation by church officials, was recorded and has served as a vivid document of the textual style of the Afro-mestizo culture of the period, as has its choreography, as descriptions of the dances were also recorded. The sones combined elements of social criticism and religious satire with erotic metaphors. The son "Chuchumbé" and its choreography was condemned by church officials in official documents no less than eight times between 1766 and 1784 (Robles Cahero 2005a), and numerous other son and dance practices considered to be lewd and indecent were likewise prohibited—an example of differences in moral philosophy and artistic expression within this highly intense intercultural context of intersecting values. Recently, a number of contemporary jarocho ensembles called Chuchumbé, Mono Blanco, and Son de Madera have performed and recorded versions of the historical "Chuchumbé," creating new music that is within the orally transmitted tradition that has survived through the past three centuries but is based on the original text.

El Chuchumbé fue penado	The Chuchumbé was punished
Por la Santa Inquisición	By the Holy Inquisition
Pero ellos olvidaron	But they forgot
Que es un ritmo sabrosón.	That it is a very rich rhythm.

199

Que te vaya bien	May things go well,
Que te vaya mal	May things go bad,
Que el Chuchumbé	The Chuchumbé
Me has de agarrar.	Will finally get me
El Chuchumbé fue penado	The Chuchumbé was punished
Siempre anduvo pene y pene	It always went around grieving and grieving
Y por fin ha regresado	And it has finally returned,
Cierren las puertas que ahi viene.	Close the doors, it is coming over there.
Que te pongas bien	May you get well,
Que te pongas mal	May you get bad,
Que el Chuchumbé	The Chuchumbé
Me has de agarrar.	Will finally get me.

To clarify the "erotic" interpretation of these verses, it should be noted that the word *pene* in the second stanza has a double meaning in this text. The verb *penar* translates as "to suffer" or "to feel pain." The word *pene*, however, in a different formal usage, also translates as "penis." The play on words here is thus evident, and the church's stand on the text becomes clear, although it is necessary to recognize a diversity of moral standards among the different social classes and ethnic castes of the period.

Although only the text and not the actual music of "Chuchumbé" was recorded in writing in the eighteenth century, the contemporary groups that have reconstructed different versions of the son have adapted in these arrangements the traditional son jarocho musical form. These include the groups Chuchumbé (based in Mexico) and the collaboration of Mono Blanco (based in Mexico) and Stone Lips (based in the United States). The latter was recorded in San Francisco under the coordination of Chicano baroque guitarist Eugene Rodríguez. A son jarocho movement currently thrives both in Mexico and the US southwest, especially in California.

I switch now to another example of son and its associated dance and textual referents, that of "Son de la negra" (The *Son* of the Black Woman), a *son jalisciense* from the state of Jalisco and most likely composed sometime during the nineteenth century. As in the son jarocho—for example, "Chuchumbé"—the combined elements of musical structure, choreography, and text derive from an assortment of the Mexican trilogy of Spanish, indigenous, and African input; but the latter, the African, holds an especially keen relationship to this piece. "La negra" has become the "anthem" of mariachi (the ensemble that evolved with the son jalisciense or *son de mariachi*) culture and its standard sonic emblem. The African referents of this national symbol provide much of the basis for the arguments made by Ochoa Serrano (1994, 1998) as to the African presence in the western regions of Mexico not only in music but also in the general cultural development of the region—for example, in the emergence of charro (cowboy) culture and its relationship to the Afro-mestizos of the colonial period in the western states of Jalisco, Michoacán, and Nayarít, among others.

The other factor reinforcing the African presence in the son de mariachi is the musical structure based on an interaction of Andalusian hemiola and *sesquiáltera* (superimposed rhythmic patterns) and African polyrhythm, syncopated rhythmic patterns, and unison chorus sections. Pérez Fernández (1990) offers a detailed musical analysis of "Son de la negra."

Segment of "La negra" text:

Negrita de mis pesares	Black girl of my heartaches
Ojos de papel volando.	With eyes like floating paper.
A todos diles que sí	Tell them all yes,
Pero no les digas cuando.	But don't tell them when.
Así me dijiste a mí,	That's how you told me
Por eso sigo penando.	And for that I'm still aching.

It can be noted here that the term *la negra* can generally refer to a woman of dark complexion, which could be that of African, Indian, or Spanish racial heritage, or any combination of these. However, it can also be noted that the term *negra/o*, in its strict sense as related to the casta configuration, refers specifically to a person of African race. Thus, there is ample room and flexibility here in terms of deciphering or speculating on what racial heritage the "negra" referred to in this son may originally and presently represent.

Sacred, Chamber, and Symphonic Music

Although a movement that has been referred to as "nationalism" emerged in Mexico and throughout Latin America during the first half of the twentieth century, mestizo traditional forms have been adapted to chamber music in Mexico since the sixteenth century—for example, the choral pieces accompanied by pipe organ composed by Hernando Franco in the Nahuatl language and dedicated to the Virgin Mary by way of the Aztec earth mother Tonantzin. Within the same century, various pieces based on African-derived folklore and Afro-mestizo forms being practiced by the Mexican populace began to appear—for example, the multiracially themed

201

poetry in the form of religious villancicos written by sixteenth-century Sor Juana Inés de la Cruz, which were later orchestrated for chamber choirs and ensembles. Other examples of the early colonial period included *negrillos*, *guineas*, guarachas, and *cumbees*, forms based on Afro-mestizo song and/or dance traditions and applied by composers to both ecclesiastic music for church use or for public concert orchestrations.

Of interest here are the theories of Akin Euba (2003) that are based on his concepts of intercultural composition and creative ethnomusicology. The examples I have cited and that I cite below interestingly fit into both of Euba's categories, and to cite again an observation made by Robles Cahero (2005a), some of the baroque traditional forms in Mexico in effect served as ethnomusicological study, as dances were described in song and forms were being adapted to chamber music in diverse contexts and for diverse reasons.

Twentieth-century symphonic adaptations of traditional musical forms in Mexico have ranged from composer Carlos Chávez's incorporation of indigenous sources in *Sinfonía india* to Silvestre Revueltas's metaphoric use of Nicolás Guillén's Afro-Cuban poetry in *Sensemayá* to the use of the mestizo son in Blas Galindo's *Sones de mariachi* and José Pablo Moncayo's *Huapango*.

A contemporary example of symphonic and chamber works inspired by Afro-mestizo genres is the music of composer Arturo Márquez. Since the 1990s he has gained international recognition, and there have been numerous performances of his series of symphonic interpretations of the Cuban danzón, a strict dance form related to the habanera and *contradanza* (the latter traced through both the French *contredanse* and the English country dance) and the Afro-Cuban son. Márquez's danzón series (the most recorded and performed is the "Danzón #2") are based on the Mexican version of the Cuban danzón, which arrived in Mexico at the port of Veracruz at about the turn of the twentieth century. The dance rapidly became one of the most popular styles in all of Mexico. Aaron Copland's *Salón de México* was actually inspired by the danzones performed and danced at the Salón de México dance hall of 1920s–1930s Mexico City. In an interview that I conducted with Márquez, he made the following comments:

> With music on the [Mexican] coast, with Cuban music, music from Veracruz, from the city, with the son, African rhythms are always in this music. The danzón is a Cuban dance from the nineteenth century, but it came to Mexico in the early twentieth century, and it stayed here. It stayed because so many people danced it. It is alive. I use the form because it is very rich. It is dance music, and I have been working with

dance music for many years. The danzón is the main traditional dance hall music in Veracruz and Mexico City. (2005)

Márquez has also composed works inspired by the Mexican son, including the ballets *Tierra* (1991) and *La Nao* (1992), both composed for the ballet company Mandinga. The company is named after the lake and town just outside the city of Veracruz, which were named after a West African ethnic group, many members of which came to Veracruz from Africa. (The company's director, Irene Martínez, is originally from Veracruz.)

The Chicano Southwest

Thus far I have provided but a very brief sketch of a highly complex, intense, and highly developed historical framework and some of its various equations of intercultural, musical dynamics in Mexico. How then do these African equations survive, or reinterpret themselves, or create themselves anew in the realm of the Mexican American—the Chicano Southwest, a sector of land, culture, and history that was once part of official Mexico? As I have proposed at the outset of this essay, there also exists the contention that the Mexican cultural diaspora does not stop at the US-Mexico border and that the binational, and now even multicultural fluidity of creative work in "Greater Mexico" has never ceased since the end of the Mexican-American War in 1948.

I will present here two examples of contemporary Chicano musical expression that I believe not only continues the African diaspora inherent in Mexican musical culture but also has adopted and adapted to African American culture in the United States. The reasons for this behavior is a complex yet simple equation of two cultures considered more different in the United States than they would be in Latin America, due to the United States' history of compartmentalizing cultural product, behavior, and civil rights. Although Mexicans and African Americans in the US Southwest have been told they are different cultures, the musical expressions created by these two groups have defied such contentions and limited definition.

During the past thirty-five years, Carlos Santana has emerged as a consummate artist, a spiritual guru, and an icon of global pop culture. Yet he fits almost perfectly into the schematic I have thus far sketched out. Born in Jalisco, Mexico, his father was a mariachi musician. He moved with his parents and siblings to Tijuana, Mexico, and finally, as a teenager, he migrated to San Francisco, California, where he rapidly rose as a talented young blues guitarist. By 1969 he had recorded his first of many LPs featuring his signature guitar virtuosity along with his innovative mestizo blend of Latin, blues, and rock, a mixture that would be credited to him as the beginning of Latin rock. He proceeded to work with some of the highest acclaimed blues and jazz musicians of recent times, including Muddy Waters, B. B. King, Wayne Shorter, John McLaughlin, Ndugu Chancellor, and McCoy Tyner. African American music has been his dominant music teacher. He was married to an African American woman for over thirty years. In 1999, after thirty years of international success, Santana received an unprecedented eight Grammy Awards for his youthful album *Supernatural*, yet another progressively changing, yet unchanging, blending of Latin, blues, and rock. After he received the award and was asked for his reaction, he responded by thanking West Africa for its profound musical influence in his music. He did not thank Latin America or the United States or any other region of the world, except West Africa.

Although a number of individuals were confused by his statement, especially some of those familiar with the Afro-Cuban and Afro-Brazilian musical sources in his music, those of us with some historical perspective were not so surprised; in fact, we were gladdened not only by Santana's knowledge but also by his—as he always seems to display—courage in telling things the way they actually are. Carlos Santana, in my way of looking at things, represents the schematic I have constructed here, for he emerged from a mestizo world and came to another one where the word *mestizo* did not even exist, and where mixtures had occurred, as with African American culture, but where there was a strong and dominant fracture between black and white. His constant changes and adaptations in style parallel the process of mestizaje in Mexico and Latin America, where old traditions take on new forms and meanings, but where old meanings do not have to die with such change, and perhaps where the words "West Africa" do not have to imply a wildly distant and idealistic idea, but instead can be relative to everyone.

My other example of the Chicano experience as related to its closeness to African American, and thus African culture, is one representing a whole movement in the Southwest, but especially in the city of Los Angeles—that of Latino hip-hop. I will focus on the Grammy-nominated duo Akwid, which has become highly popular in the United States, Latin America, and Spain (Sauceda 2004). These two hip-hop artist brothers (Sergio and Francisco Gómez) are the sons of Mexican immigrants. They were born in the state of Michoacán and raised in South Central Los Angeles. They rap in Spanish to yet another mestizo blend of African American hip-hop and Mexican regional styles. In their "No hay manera" we can hear the interface of rap, hip-hop groove and stylizations, Chicano and African American actors, and perhaps most unexpectedly, the Mexican banda brass musical style. Banda, from Sinaloa, Mexico, has been popularized over the past ten years, especially in northern Mexico and the US Southwest, and intensely so in the city of Los Angeles. Also of interest is that one of the brothers makes note at the outset of the piece that this performance is similar to the traditional presentation of the Mexican corrido, a song in which a story is told in poetic verse. As evident in the DVD version of the piece, the negative stereotypes are part of a story, of things that actually, fortunately or not, happen in society. They are not necessarily suggestions for how to live life. These issues include images satirizing the iconization of money, sexism, violence, materialism, fashion, and the contemporary racial intermix (especially that of Latinos and African Americans) in urban complexes such as Los Angeles.

Conclusions

In conclusion, we might at this point reflect on these issues as they are conceptualized by Robles Cahero—as multiple identities—and the manner in which we can certainly observe various dimensions of life experiences, expression, and their related identities in the making of a musical culture that has so many diverse historical and personal referents. Robles Cahero makes specific reference to the theories of Serge Gruzinski (2002), who, in developing a model based on Antonio Gramsci's "wars of maneuver" concept between social classes, perceives a historical and cultural process in Mexican iconography and art that he describes as a "war of images." Robles Cahero extends this idea to the Mexican musical context, which he conceptualizes as a "war of sounds." Gruzinski sees both conflict and the cooptation of visual symbols as a battle of cultural ideologies that ensued in colonial, mestizo Mexico, but Robles Cahero sees the same with the interactions, both fluid yet conflictual, of musical development and creativity (as did the previously cited Aguirre Beltrán in his observations of the "give and take" between Spaniard and African in music and dance). Robles Cahero also looks at mestizo expression in the arts as having been to a large extent an elixir to the colonial chaos that disrupted cultural stability among indigenous, African, and European family and social structures. In line with Gruzinski and Robles Cahero, Ochoa Serrano has also developed a historical rationale on how and why mestizos formulated musical expression of the three general cultures at work—indigenous, African, and Spanish—as a mode of resistance against the colonial framework and cultural hegemony and against conformity and inequality.

Upon reflecting on the African-based songs and dances of eighteenth-century Mexico, such as "Chuchumbé," and the censorship surrounding them, we can also reflect on the contemporary hip-hop artists and their very similar predicament concerning censorship and the conflict of values as expressed through art. At present among Chicanos living in California, from San Diego to San Jose and from Los Angeles to San Francisco, there exist thriving musical movements based on the Mexican son, African American hip-hop, and the combination of these and numerous other forms, all sharing elements of the Mexican Afro-mestizo legacy. I recently witnessed a musical show in Santa Ana (a heavily Mexican-populated suburb near Los Angeles), where the Mexican, Veracruz-based jarocho group Chuchumbé was joined on stage by African American and Chicano rappers—in a sense, a triangular cycle. The same three elements that define in part the eighteenth-century Mexican mestizo son still characterize this very contemporary, improvised setting: social criticism, cultural satire, and human metaphor.

The musical mestizaje that has developed in Mexico and the Chicano Southwest, from son to symphony to contemporary formats, is an example of a global aesthetic, even though much of the globe considers musical mestizaje to be a small, local view of the world. But I would reject such a perspective, and even say that mestizo artists and their music have traveled much further than many other past or contemporary citizens of the globe, and without cars, planes, space shuttles, or even cyberspace.

Note

An earlier version of this essay appeared in *Composition in Africa and the Diaspora*, vol. 3, edited by Akin Euba and Cynthia Kimberlin. Proceedings from the conference at Churchill College, Cambridge University, 2005. Port Richmond, CA: MRI Press, 2011. Reprinted by permission.

Works Cited

Aguirre Beltrán, Gonzalo. 1972. *La población negra de Mexico: Estudio etnohistórico.* Mexico City: Fondo de Cultura Económica. First published in 1946.

Corona Alcalde, Antonio. 2005. "El documento y la realidad: Dos fuentes complementarias para reconstruir las prácticas musicales del barroco hispánico." *Boletín del Archivo General de la Nación* 6, no. 8: 77–132.

Euba, Akin. 2003. "Intercultural Music in Africa and Latin America: A Comparative view of Fela Sowande and Carlos Chavez." In *Musical Cultures of Latin America: Global Effects, Past and Present,* edited by Steven Loza. Los Angeles: UCLA Department of Ethnomusicology and Systematic Musicology. Proceedings of the conference, University of California, Los Angeles, May 28-30, 1998.

Gruzinski, Serge. 2002. *The Mestizo Mind: The Intellectual Dynamics of Colonization and Globalization.* Translated by Deke Dusinberre. New York, London: Routledge. First published as *La pensée métisse* Paris: Fayard, 1999.

Márquez, Arturo. 2005. Interview by Steven Loza, July 2005, Mexico City.

Ochoa Serrano, Alvaro. 1994. *Mariachi, fandango, y mitote.* Zamora: Colegio de Michoacán.

———. 1998. *Afrodescendientes sobre Piel Canela.* Zamora: Colegio de Michoacán.

Paredes, Américo. 1976. *"With His Pistol in His Hand": A Border Ballad and Its Hero.* Austin: University of Texas Press. First published in 1958.

Pérez Fernández, Rolando. 1990. *La musica afromestiza-mexicana.* Xalapa: Universidad Veracruzana.

Raza olvidada, La. 2001. Documentary film. Directed by Rafael Rebollar. Mexico City: Producciones Trabuco.

Robles Cahero, José Antonio. 2003. "Occidentalización, mestizaje y 'guerra de los sonidos': Hacia una historia de las músicas mestizas de México." In *Musical Cultures of Latin America: Global Effects, Past and Present,* edited by Steven Loza, 57–78. Los Angeles: UCLA Department of Ethnomusicology and Systematic Musicology. Proceedings of the conference, University of California, Los Angeles, May 28-30, 1998.

———. 2005a. "Cantar, bailar y tañer: Nuevas aproximaciones a la música y el baile populares de la Nueva España." *Boletín del Archivo General de la Nación* 6, no. 8: 42–76.

———. 2005b. Interview by Steven Loza, July 2005, Mexico City.

Sauceda, Isis. 2004. "Del centrosur de LA al mundo." *La opinión,* June 10–16, 2004.

CHAPTER 12

Challenges to the Euroamericentric Ethnomusicological Canon
Alternatives for Graduate Readings, Theory, and Method

Traveling often in other countries as part of my research and for family reasons, I am constantly made aware of the capitalist hegemony at work, one that has existed for some time. Billboards in Mexico announce Camel and Marlboro cigarettes, Whiskers cat food, Paris Hilton's latest publicity, and VISA credit cards. An estimated 92 percent of the films screened at public theaters in Mexico are from Hollywood, and Britney Spears fills arenas with fans.[1] Chryslers, Fords, and Chevys flourish on the streets, and Walmarts are available in the major urban centers, where Colgate, Zest soap, and Listerine also prosper in the market. By contrast, Mexican products do not exist in the United States, save in those cities with high concentrations of Mexican and Latino immigrants. To many, this situation represents a double standard and demonstrates the economic and cultural hegemonies of the so-called developed countries, especially the United States.

This hegemonic scenario is duplicated in the academic world in the guise of an intellectual capitalism. While ideas ranging from those of Bronisław Malinowski to Alan Merriam to Clifford Geertz to numerous current thinkers are translated into Spanish and reach the academic world in Mexico and Latin America, much if not most of the intellectual work there does not reach the United States in the same fashion, save a few exceptions, as in the case of a small portion of the writings of Nestor García Canclini, among some others. In his book *La globalización imaginada*, García Canclini (1999) makes the observation that, on an annual basis, there are more PhD degrees granted in the United States on Latin American topics than there are doctoral degrees granted in all of Latin America on any topic.

The major thrust of my presentation thus focuses on the problem that arises out of this academic hegemony, this chauvinism of intellectual dominance, especially in the way that it affects graduate students in US universities who are studying ethnomusicology. In the Society of Ethnomusicology's 2004 President's Roundtable, Professor Jacqueline Djedje of UCLA initiated the discussion by noting the problem that exists in the reading lists that our graduate students are being given to study. There is a shortage of native voices in these largely Eurocentric, or what I here term as *Euroamericentric*, works (that is, of authors from both Europe and United States), and one must ponder how it is for the underrepresented to be reading lists devoid of representatives of their own cultures. During my twenty years of teaching graduate seminars on the history, method, and theories of ethnomusicology, I have been given and I have seen reading lists employed that consist entirely of essays and books written by scholars of ethnomusicology, anthropology, and other disciplines exclusively from the United States, Western Europe, and Canada. Last year, a text on the history of anthropology was suggested to me for use in my graduate seminar on the history of ethnomusicology. I quote from the introduction to that book: "I have limited myself to anthropologists from the United States, Great Britain, and France and emphasize Anglo-American anthropology, which I assume is of most interest to my audience" (Moore 2004, xiv). At least half of the graduate students in the seminar that I taught were students whose backgrounds were neither Anglo-American nor Euroamerican nor European. The author's point was not well taken, and I will not use the book again.

In addition to the problem of the written canon, there is the problem of the cultural, psychological complex of the way that nontraditional students in US universities are conditioned to think in terms of their specific heritages. Part of this complex is that of development theory, which has been a psychological deterrent; the negative economic rhetoric of the terms *developing nations*, *Third World*, and *underdeveloped nations* creeps into the consciousness of scholars at every level, and the net effect becomes problematic. One can easily argue that "developing nations" are more developed than the so-called developed nations in various areas of culture—for example, literature, religious expression, family structure, cuisine, and also, in a number of cases, music and dance.

Chronic Issues

I can cite at least five issues that I feel dominate the problem at hand and its effect on the experience and perceptions of graduate students:

1. The university system is still largely dependent on the Euroamericentric canon, theory, and method. Although a number of scholars represent alternative points of view (e.g., critiques of orientalism and postcolonial studies), there is still not a major diversification of the concept of "theory" (especially, it might be argued, in terms not only of race, ethnicity, and gender but also of class and the psychology of a stratified, racialized society). Solutions that some of us have proposed are not about lowering standards but about enhancing, diversifying, broadening, and thus improving them.

2. To borrow some terms from a model proposed by Timothy Rice (2003) in a recent issue of *Ethnomusicology*, we (minorities) are perceived, at various levels, as very different from the majority in the ascription of the terms *time* (concepts of "order," progress, oral versus written traditions, sometimes even "pace," social behaviors, semantics and linguistic/language styles, religion, aesthetics, among others), *place* (we often live in separate quarters of our cities), and *metaphor*, or what would extend to include the "cognitive"—the way we "know" as cultures. The upshot of this, as I can testify from personal experience, is that it can be very difficult for us to get our work published in *Ethnomusicology* when that work does not correspond to hegemonic ways of knowing.

3. Academic faculty and research personnel are still dominated by academic "majorities," especially in light of the continued abolishment of affirmative action programs. Many of these programs actually made use of minorities in a very often compromising and exploitative way. However, the elimination of the programs has also had highly negative effects in terms of enrollment and representation.

4. Curriculum: As Lester Monts, one of my colleagues on the round-table last year and the chair of this panel, told me quite a few years ago, most music schools are still following the "five-country, one-continent (Europe)" plan of teaching. This situation has perhaps changed somewhat in recent years, but not to a great extent. Related to this dilemma are such scenarios as that of the UCLA College of Letters and Sciences, the only University of California entity still resisting a diversity course requirement.

5. The "Theory" problem: I have often, along with others, referred to this issue as the "theoretical fetish." Many minorities strongly feel that an intellectual hegemony has dominated scholastic culture, and we have felt constant pressure to conform to this form of "intellectual capitalism." If you do not use the fashionable, current body of "theory" (most of it, by the way, borrowed from other areas of the social sciences and humanities), you do not fit in and are criticized for it—and this has happened in the

form of "blind" evaluations of submitted articles. How do we fight this machine of "Do it our way or no way?" Some of us have fought it—and have paid a price.

Alternative and Resistant Perspectives, Approaches, Sources, and Readings

Brazilian scholar Paulo Freire (1985) critiqued much of Western academic culture and education as a "banking" system of notes, and we can also interpret this perspective as one recognizing that intellectual work and research in many ways is commodified as an "investment" and held as an accruing, materialist academic wealth, ultimately serving as a base of power. We should also be able to admit that the same tools do not fit every culture.

Cuban scholar Antonio Benítez Rojo (1996), for example, has expressed his position that postmodernist theories do not fit Latin American cultures and are thus invalid there, and that theories similar to postmodernism (and yet more useful than postmodernism) were conceived by Latin American intellectuals decades before the movement became fashionable. (I would add that the historical and cultural concepts of modernity and premodernity are also problematic Western biases.) But many of these intellectuals are not known among the standard hegemonic intelligentsia. One example is the very one Benítez Rojo cites as a pre-postmodernist, if you will: scholar Fernando Ortiz, whose book *Cuban Counterpoint* (1947) becomes the metaphor for Benítez Rojo's argument in his book *La isla que se repite* (which has been translated into English; see Benítez Rojo 1996). Mexican American Américo Paredes also harshly critiqued the interpretive, analytical divide between Anglo-American and Chicano/Mexican scholars in a classic article titled "Folklore, Lo Mexicano, and Proverbs" (1982). Native American scholar Vine Deloria has been highly critical of the capitalist academic world, citing especially the theories and fieldwork of anthropologists.[2] In his book *Custer Died for Your Sins: An Indian Manifesto* (1988) he makes the following observations: "The massive volume of useless knowledge produced by anthropologists attempting to capture real Indians in a network of theories has contributed substantially to the invisibility of Indian people today. . . . Over the years, anthropologists have succeeded in burying Indian communities so completely beneath the mass of irrelevant information that the total impact of the scholarly community on Indian people has become one of simple authority" (81–82).

Yet another classic example of thought resistant to Eurocentric academic work was that of Nigerian scholar and composer Fela Sowande (1972), who cited many of the major differences between Western and African forms of philosophy, culture, and art. Thus, many of us have asked the question, "Where are 'we' in the history of ethnomusicology?"

Part of the solution, obviously, is to add the names, such as those cited above, in addition to many others, to the reading lists we prepare for our graduate students in ethnomusicology. To illustrate an area that I work in, Mexico, I can provide numerous examples of scholars and composers who by the 1920s had become highly influenced in the type of research that we now refer to as ethnomusicology. These individuals include Manuel Ponce ("El folklore musical mexicano," 1919) and Rubén Campos ("Las fuentes del folklore mexicano," 1919), who edited the journal *Revista Musical de México*. In 1962 Colombian Andrés Pardo Tovar's article "Musicología, etnomusicología y folklore" was published in the *Boletín Interamericano de Música*. In 1976 and 1981 two articles by the Chilean María Ester Grebe that analyze the field of ethnomusicology were published in *Revista Musical Chilena*. In 1993–94 one of my own articles, "Fantasmas enmascarados: Pensamientos sobre nuestra investigación y lo académico en etnomusicología" (in large part a harsh and critical assessment of some of Alan Merriam's ideas), was published in the Mexican journal *Heterofonía*, and in 1993 Luís Merino edited a set of papers on the topic "Relación entre la investigación histórico-musical y la etnomusicología en Latinoamérica" for the Spanish journal *Revista de Musicología*.[3]

Part of the problem here is that so few US scholars become sufficiently adept in the Spanish language to be able to read these works. We might take heed of the economic and political analysts predicting that the three major global languages will soon be English, Mandarin Chinese, and Spanish.

There are also some classic Latin American thinkers to whom I feel our students should be exposed, and I will cite four out of hundreds: José Martí, José Enrique Rodó, José Vasconcelos, and Roberto Fernández Retamar. Social critic, poet, and one of the political activists of Cuba's independence from Spain, José Martí has been equated in importance with Friedrich Nietzsche by Fredric Jameson, yet his name is not well known in the United States.[4] His essay "Our America," published in 1891 in *La Revista Ilustrada de Nueva York* and, in the same year, in the Mexican newspaper *El Partido Liberal*, is considered by many to be his manifesto. It is a critique of the historical and cultural nature of Latin America, especially in terms of native and transplanted aboriginal cultures and of mestizaje, the mixing

of race and culture. He also addresses Latin America's many conflicts with
US and European culture and society. I quote from the piece:

> The European university must yield to the American university. The
> history of America, from the Incas to the present, must be taught letter
> perfect, even if that of the Argonauts of Greece is not taught. Our own
> Greece is preferable to the Greece that is not ours. We have greater need
> of it. National politicians must replace foreign and exotic politicians.
> Graft the world onto our republics, but the trunk must be that of our
> republics. And let the conquered pedant be silent: there is no homeland
> of which the individual can be more proud than our unhappy American
> republics. (Martí 1999, 118)

Contemporary with Martí, but far away in Uruguay, was José Enrique
Rodó, author of the 1900 Latin American classic *Ariel*, a satirical, metaphoric allusion to Shakespeare's *The Tempest*. The dominant theme in the
work is, again, the cultural conflicts between the Americas to the south
and the America to the north. Published in 1925 was *La raza cósmica*, by
the Mexican philosopher, national minister of education, and politician
José Vasconcelos. The importance of this book is the impact it has had on
its theme, that of Latin American mestizaje, and Vasconcelos's envisioning
of it as a process that will eventually become global—the *final*, or *cosmic
race*.[5] Finally, the literary work and analysis of Cuban essayist and poet
Roberto Fernández Retamar is yet another example of classic thought that
should find much wider exposure in US universities and across the spectrum
of the social sciences, the humanities, and the arts. In his most adulated
essay, "Caliban," Fernández Retamar socially critiques the character, and
metaphor, of Caliban, the Caribbean indigenous/native figure adapted by
Shakespeare and reinterpreted by Rodó; but Fernández Retamar's critique
represents a keenly political, historical, and cultural insight and analytical
genius that again focuses on the historical and cultural conflicts between
north and south and between the tropical Americas and Europe. Written
in 1971, seven years before Edward Said's *Orientalism* (1978), "Caliban"
enriches our understanding of another American worldview with which
very few of our ethnomusicology students (or faculty, for that matter) are
familiar. Fernández Retamar (1989) makes a strong point in exposing the
relative ignorance of Martí among scholars of anticolonialist perspective.
Referring to this situation as a painful one, he writes, "We have been so
thoroughly steeped in colonialism that we read with real respect only
those anti-colonialist authors disseminated from the metropolis" (18). He
proceeds with some historical reflection, proclaiming:

> It is only right and fair to ask in what relationship we, the present inhabitants of this America in whose zoological and cultural heritage Europe has played an unquestionable part, have to the primitive inhabitants of this same America—those peoples who constructed or were in the process of constructing admirable cultures and who were exterminated or martyred by Europeans of various nations, about whom neither a white nor black legend can be built, only an infernal truth of blood, that, together with such deeds as the enslavement of Africans, constitutes their eternal dishonor. (19)

Fernández Retamar echoes the perspective of Benítez Rojo, comprehending that there exist very different histories, that there are ways of judging, analyzing, and evaluating such histories and cultural contexts, and that blanket theories or philosophical perspectives cannot be applied everywhere.

In assessing intellectual thought in Latin America, it may be quite appropriate to venture into the areas of creative literature. I recall a graduate student telling me that she considered the novelists and poets of Latin America such as Carlos Fuentes, Mario Vargas Llosa, Octavio Paz, and Gabriel García Márquez to be the actual theorists of Latin American culture. Such writers continue to work in the mode of José Martí, who was as much a creative writer as a social critic. I do not take that student's view lightly, and I have included creative pieces not only of literature but also of film in my graduate seminars, and I plan to increase this method in my teaching.

In the areas of African and African American studies, there has been a great amount of literature that has been ignored in our field and thus in the general readings of our graduate students, especially those who do not specialize in these areas; yet many of these sources are what I would consider to be "general" intellectual works to be placed on the shelf alongside those that have dominated the field.[6] I mentioned Sowande above, and I would add names such as Kwabena Nketia (one of my mentors during my graduate studies), who has been involved in ethnomusicology and recognized for many years, and Akin Euba, whose concept of "creative ethnomusicology" deserves more attention and who is currently developing a Center for Intercultural Musicology at Cambridge University.

There are some other scholars of African studies whose works, I feel, are germane to our field, and those include Marimba Ani, Molefi Kete Asante, and Kofi Agawu. (I should note that I am not supporting the idea of any *one* canon—there are many sources I have not read or seen, as the international volume of literature is overwhelming.)

In her book *Yurugu: An African-Centered Critique of European Cultural Thought and Behavior* (1994), Ani presents some alternative models for the comprehension of cultures, emphasizing that "Europe represents a fraction of the world's ideological and cultural creations" (97). Among her thought-provoking points is the following (which interestingly reverberates with some of the previously cited views of José Martí):

> It is appropriate . . . to make some obvious observations about what African, Amerindian, and Oceanic majority thought-systems have in common to the exclusion of European thought. All of the views mentioned are spiritual in nature, that is, they have spiritual bases and thereby reject rationalism and objectification as valued epistemological modes. Obviously, they do have rationalistic and pragmatic aspects but these do not dominate. These views generate an authentic cosmology, the interrelatedness of all being. (98–99)

Like Ani, Molefi Kete Asante (1998) has also taken much heat for his Afrocentricity from conservative critics who do not grasp his method as an alternative approach for understanding cultures from both a native and a comparative point of view. In his book *The Afrocentric Idea*, Asante makes his position clear when he notes:

> Any criticism of society is, definitionally, a criticism of the ruling ideology of that society. I have the insight that comes from having been born black in the United States. That fact puts me in a critical mood within the intellectual and social milieu I share with the Eurocentricists. As the critic, I am always seeking to create a new world, to find an escape, to liberate those who see only a part of reality. (2)

Directly akin to the field of ethnomusicology is the work of Kofi Agawu, as presented in his 2003 book *Representing African Music: Postcolonial Notes, Queries, Positions*. Agawu's work here proves to be applicable to the study of music in general and should be another basic reading source for a more integrative approach to our field and our relationship with our graduate students. Agawu's candid and sound criticism of a number of factors echoes many of the ideas I have presented here. For example, he notes that many associate African music research with ethnomusicology, but he points out that "the ethnomusicological approach is only one among several" (xii). He is critical of the "noncomparison that has become a permanent temptation for ethnomusicology" (xiii) and cites the problems that characterize *Ethnomusicology*, the SEM journal: "*African Music* . . . mixes anecdotal, informal, and even experimental ways of ordering knowledge with more formal styles of reportage to produce a far more interesting mix than the professional voice that emerges from the pages of *Ethnomusicology*" (xxxi). Agawu further blasts *Ethnomusicology*, "whose African offerings," he notes, are "drenched in institutionally sanctioned methodology [and] leave little room for contestation" (xvii). Agawu, as many of us, also expresses his concern with what may well be the most fundamental issue, that of the offensive nature of the word *ethnomusicology*, citing Klaus Wachsmann's similar sentiment in addition to that of the previously cited Akin Euba, who has characterized the term as "unsuitable for African music studies" and "irrelevant to African culture" (in Agawu 2003, xvii). Echoing these opinions are recent comments made to me by Steven Feld, who sees the term as "colonialist" and prefers use of the phrase "contemporary world music," and the most recent editor of *Ethnomusicology* itself, Peter Manuel, wrote in his inaugural volume as editor that ironically, he prefers to think of himself not as an ethnomusicologist but as a musicologist. Charles Seeger expressed similar sentiments over fifty years ago. These are perspectives upon which we and our graduate students must dialogue with a more serious and activist basis.

Agawu (2003) sees himself as a "postcolonial" scholar and asserts:

> Postcolonial theory encourages a new self-awareness, rewards the eagerness to lay bare the situatedness and precariousness of various frames of knowledge construction, and takes particular pleasure in relativizing and decentering European intellectual hegemony. (xvii)

He also recognizes, however, that postcolonialist theory emanates from the experiences of people whose identities are "inflected by the metropolitan habits exported to Africa through British, French, Belgian, and Portuguese colonialism" (xvii). This is, although similar, also somewhat different from some of the various Latin American intellectual movements against intellectual imperialism.

Concluding Thoughts

This critique could run many more pages, for a new wave of not only postcolonial scholars but also resistance thought and criticism is growing constantly in Latin America, the marginalized and even mainstream sectors of US society and Europe, the Middle East, and other parts of the world. We are living in a disjunctive era and a troublesome one for those of us in academe, for a conservative wave envelops much of the social and cultural contexts in which we must work. We Americans in the United States are presently involved in an unjust war that has made our image and our goals of an integrative approach even more problematic, and certainly in many cases, hypocritical, regardless of our individual ideologies, for we continue to work in a context of economic privilege and access that is higher than that of many other nations. It is in part due to this situation that a standard and a quantity of scholarship are emerging from the United States and Europe that are in many ways not only disproportionate to other sectors of the globe but also intellectually biased and distorted as well.

We owe it to ourselves and to our students to work toward a closer global unity in intellectual thought and ideological action. George Lipsitz, a white historian who has written extensively on contemporary musical currents and their social implications, sets a noble standard in recognizing the disproportions not only in society but also in scholarship and in the privileged status of being the power brokers representing the dominant group. He does this in his recent book *The Progressive Investment in White-ness: How White People Profit from Identity Politics* (1998). This work is in great contrast to another recent work, by another white historian, Samuel P. Huntington, who teaches at Harvard. Huntington (2004) makes the following comment among many others of similar character in his pathetic, racist book *Who Are We? The Challenges to America's National Identity*:

> While the values of Mexicans are undoubtedly evolving, helped by the spread of evangelical Protestantism, that revolution is unlikely to be completed soon or quickly. In the meantime, the high level of immigration from Mexico sustains and reinforces among Mexican-Americans the Mexican values which are the primary source of their lagging educational and economic progress and slow assimilation into American society. . . .
> . . . There is no Americano dream. There is only the American dream created by an Anglo-Protestant society. Mexican-Americans will share in that dream and in that society only if they dream in English. (254, 256)

Play it again, Sam! Remember: English, Mandarin, and *Spanish*!

Again, what is the effect of this type of scholarship not only on those of us with faculty positions, striving for a more integrated world, but also on our graduate students, especially the so-called minorities, who, again, are facing an even more serious conservative onslaught than most of us did in our graduate years? But the prejudiced rhetoric can be countered with the many sources I have cited here, from Martí to Agawu to Lipsitz.

As I expressed earlier in this paper, part of the solution to part of the problem exposed here is to add readings and other sources, such as those cited here, to the reading lists we prepare for our graduate students in ethnomusicology. I have done this for a number of years in my graduate seminar on the history of ethnomusicology. My students—US minorities, foreigners, mainstream, majorities, and others not fitting into these inadequate categories of humanity—have reacted very positively to my expanded lists. I have found that solutions such as these, in the spirit of Paulo Freire, dissipate fear. Perhaps developing a national and international circulating list of sources would help.

Natives and nonnatives in a growingly diverse world must work together toward bold enhancements, expansion of standards, and ways of thinking, knowing, relearning, and unlearning. We should be cautious in not "overdeveloping" the theoretical fetish and the materialist metaphor of the intellectual. I truly believe we can enhance our understanding of music, the arts, and humanity if we can be candid, critical, and creative.

Notes

An earlier version of this essay appeared in *Ethnomusicology* 50, no. 2 (2006). Reprinted by permission.

This paper, originally read at the 2005 SEM annual conference, evolved out of the 2004 SEM President's Roundtable panel, which discussed the issue of diversity. My suggestions for alternative sources, concepts, and readings are enveloped within my general critique and narratives formulating this paper.

1. This estimate was cited to me in personal communication by Carlos Monsiváis in August of 2005. Monsiváis is a leading critic on Mexican popular culture and politics.

2. I am indebted to Maria Williams for introducing me to the writings of Vine Deloria.

3. The papers were published in *Revista de Musicología* in 1993 (vol. 16, no. 3) and reprinted in 1995 in *Actas del 15 congreso de la sociedad internacional de musicología*, vol. 3 (Madrid: Real Conservatorio de Música de Madrid). Participants and their presentations were: Luís Merino (Chile), "Relación entre la investigación histórico-musical y la etnomusicología en Latinoamérica: Una sesión de estudio"; Victoria Eli Rodríguez (Cuba), "La acción musicológica latinoamericana requiere de un nuevo marco"; María Ester Grebe Vicuña (Chile), "Contribuciones de la antropología de la música al desarrollo de la etnomusicología y musicología histórica en Latinoamérica"; Gerardo V. Huseby (Argentina), "Hacia una nueva musicología

latinoamericana"; Steven Loza (United States), "Otra escuela: horizontes sobre nuestra 'praxis' en la musicología latinoamericana"; Irma Ruiz (Argentina), "La integración musicológica y su aplicación a la investigación en las regiones rurales de las antiguas misiones católicas en Sudamérica"; and Leonardo J. Waisman (Argentina), "Una musicología integrada para Latinoamérica." Luís Merino served as moderator for the panel.

    4. Jameson makes this note in his introduction to Fernández Retamar (1989).

    5. For a contemporary study of mestizaje, see Serge Gruzinski (2002).

    6. I have used the texts of Henry Louis Gates (1992) and Cornel West (1993) and have found them to be of great value to my students.

Works Cited

Agawu, Kofi. 2003. *Representing African Music: Postcolonial Notes, Queries, Positions*. New York: Continuum.

Ani, Marimba. 1994. *Yurugu: An African-Centered Critique of European Cultural Thought and Behavior*. Trenton, NJ: African World Press.

Asante, Molefi Kete. 1998. *The Afrocentric Idea*. Philadelphia: Temple University Press.

Benítez Rojo, Antonio. 1996. *The Repeating Island: The Caribbean and the Postmodern Perspective*. Translated by James E. Maraniss. Durham: Duke University Press. First published as *La isla que se repite: El Caribe y la perspectiva posmoderna* (Hanover, NH: Ediciones del Norte, 1989).

Campos, Rubén M. 1919. "Las fuentes del folklore mexicano." *Revista musical de México* 1, no. 1: 19–23.

Deloria, Vine, Jr. 1988. *Custer Died for Your Sins: An Indian Manifesto*. Norman: University of Oklahoma Press. First published 1969.

Fernández Retamar, Roberto. 1989. *Caliban and Other Essays*. Translated by Edward Baker. Minneapolis: University of Minnesota Press.

Freire, Paulo. 1985. *Pedagogy of the Oppressed*. Translated by Myra Bergman Ramos. New York: Continuum. First published as *Pedagogia do oprimido*. Rio de Janeiro: Paz e Terra, 1970.

García Canclini, Néstor. 1999. *La globalización imaginada*. Buenos Aires: Paidós.

Gates, Henry Louis. 1992. *Loose Canons: Notes on the Culture Wars*. New York: Oxford University Press.

Grebe, María Ester. 1976. "Objeto, métodos y técnicas de investigación en etnomusicología: Algunos problemas básicos." *Revista musical chilena* 30, no. 133: 5–27.

———. 1981. "Antropología de la música: Nuevas orientaciones y aportes teóricos en la investigación musical." *Revista musical chilena* 35, nos. 153–55: 52–74.

Gruzinski, Serge. 2002. *The Mestizo Mind: The Intellectual Dynamics of Colonization and Globalization*. Translated by Deke Dusinberre. New York, London: Routledge. First published as *La pensée métisse*. Paris: Fayard, 1999.

Huntington, Samuel P. 2004. *Who Are We? The Challenges to America's National Identity.* New York: Simon and Schuster.

Lipsitz, George. 1998. *The Possessive Investment in Whiteness: How White People Profit from Identity Politics.* Philadelphia: Temple University Press.

Loza, Steven. 1993–94. "Fantasmas enmascarados: Pensamientos sobre nuestra investigación y lo académico en etnomusicología." *Heterofonía* 26–27: 4–16.

Martí, José. 1999. "Our America." In *José Martí Reader: Writings on the Americas.* Edited by Deborah Shnookal and Mirta Muniz, 118–27. Melbourne, NY: Ocean Press. First published as "Nuestra América," *La revista ilustrada de Nueva York,* January 10, 1891.

Moore, Jerry D., ed. 2004. *Visions of Culture: An Introduction to Anthropological Theories and Theorists.* Lanham, MD: AltaMira Press.

Ortiz, Fernando. 1947. *Cuban Counterpoint: Tobacco and Sugar.* Translated by Harriet de Onis. New York: Knopf. First published as *Contrapunteo cubano del tabaco y del azúcar.* Havana: Heraldo Christiano, 1940.

Parades, Américo. 1982. "Folklore, Lo Mexicano, and the Proverb." *Aztlán: A Journal of Chicano Studies* 13, nos. 1–2: 1–11. Reprinted in *The Chicano Studies Reader: An Anthology of Aztlán, 1970–2000.* Edited by Chon Noriega, Karen Mary Davalos, Chela Sandoval, Rafael Pérez-Torres, and Eric R. Avila, 271–80. Los Angeles: UCLA Chicano Studies Research Center Press, 2001.

Pardo Tovar, Andrés. 1962. "Musicología, etnomusicología y folklore." *Boletín interamericano de música* 32: 3–10.

Ponce, Manuel M. 1919. "El folklore musical mexicano: Lo que se ha hecho, lo que puede hacerse." *Revista musical de México* 1, no. 5: 5–9.

Rice, Timothy. 2003. "Time, Place, and Metaphor in Musical Experience and Ethnography." *Ethnomusicology* 47, no. 2: 151–79.

Rodó, José Enrique. 1900. *Ariel.* Montevideo: Dornaleche y Reyes. Published in English as *Ariel,* translated by Margaret Sayers Peden (Austin: University of Texas Press, 1988).

Sowande, Fela. 1972. "The Role of Music in Traditional African Society." In *African Music: Meeting in Yaoundé (Cameroon),* 59–69. Paris: La Revue Musicale. Also published as "Le role de la musique dans la société africaine traditionelle." *La musique africaine: Réunion de Yaoundé (Cameroun),* special issue, *La revue musicale,* nos. 288–89 (1972): 57-68.

Vasconcelos, José. 1925. *La raza cósmica: Misión de la raza iberoamericana: Notas de viajes a la América del Sur.* Madrid: Agencia mundial de libería. Published in English as *The Cosmic Race,* translated by Dider T. Jaen. Baltimore: John Hopkins University Press, 1997.

West, Cornel. 1993. *Race Matters.* Boston: Beacon Press.

Works Consulted

Camara de Lande, Enrique. 2004. *Etnomusicología: Collección múisica hispana: Textos, manuales*. Madrid: Instituto Complutense de Ciencias Musicales.

Delgado, Richard, and Jean Stefanic, eds. 1997. *Critical White Studies: Looking Behind the Mirror*. Philadelphia: Temple University Press.

García Canclini, Néstor. 1995. *Hybrid Cultures: Strategies for Entering and Leaving Modernity*. Translated by Christopher L. Chiappari and Sylvia L. López. Minneapolis: University of Minnesota Press. First published as *Culturas híbridas: Estrategeías para entrar y salir de la modernidad* (Mexico City: Editorial Grijalbo, 1990).

Gómez-Quiñones, Juan. 1977. *On Culture*. Los Angeles: UCLA Chicano Studies Center Publications. First published in *Revista chicana-riquena* 5, no. 2 (1977).

Loza, Steven. 1988. "El estilo musical como concepto." *Heterofonía* 21: 28–33.

———. 2003. "Introduction: Latin America, the Globe, *Mestizaje*, and the Myth of Development." In *Musical Cultures of Latin America: Global Effects, Past and Present*, edited by Steven Loza, 4–16. Selected Reports in Ethnomusicology, no. 11. Los Angeles: UCLA Ethnomusicology Publications.

Paredes, Américo. 1958. *"With His Pistol in His Hand": A Border Ballad and Its Hero*. Austin: University of Texas Press.

Peña, Manuel. 1985. *The Texas-Mexican Conjunto: History of a Working Class Music*. Austin: University of Texas Press.

Valdés, Francisco, Jeane McCristal Culp, and Angela P. Harris, eds. 2002. *Crossroads, Directions, and a New Critical Race Theory*. Philadelphia: Temple University Press.

About the Author

Steven Loza is professor of ethnomusicology at the University of California, Los Angeles (UCLA), where he has taught since 1984. His areas of research include the Chicano/Latino United States, Mexico, and Cuba, and topics such as religion as art and musical *mesitzaje* (the mixing of race and culture). He is the author of books that include *Barrio Rhythm: Mexican American Music in Los Angeles* (1993) and *Tito Puente and the Making of Latin Music* (1999), both published by University of Illinois Press; *The Jazz Pilgrimage of Gerald Wilson* (University of Mississippi Press, 2018), and editor of the anthology *Religion as Art* (University of New Mexico Press, 2019). In addition to his extensive research and publications, he has been active as a performer and composer and as a producer of major concerts and festivals at UCLA and in Mexico City. He has directed ensembles in the Department of Ethnomusicology that focus on Latin American music, world jazz, and intercultural improvisation. *All Is One*, on the Merrimack label, is the most recent of three CDs of his music. In 2008 he composed a tone poem titled *America Tropical*, which was premiered by the Mexico City Philharmonic Orchestra. Loza has recently served as chair of the Department of Ethnomusicology in the UCLA Herb Alpert School of Music. He presently chairs the Global Jazz Studies Interdepartmental Program and directs the UCLA Center for Latino Arts.

Index